Nonviolent Struggle

Nonviolent Struggle

Theories, Strategies, and Dynamics

Sharon Erickson Nepstad

OXFORD
UNIVERSITY PRESS

OXFORD

UNIVERSITY PRESS

Oxford University Press is a department of the University of Oxford.
It furthers the University's objective of excellence in research, scholarship,
and education by publishing worldwide. Oxford is a registered trade mark
of Oxford University Press in the UK and in certain other countries

Published in the United States of America by
Oxford University Press
198 Madison Avenue, New York, NY 10016,
United States of America

Library of Congress Cataloging-in-Publication Data
Nepstad, Sharon Erickson.
Nonviolent struggle : theories, strategies, and dynamics / Sharon Erickson Nepstad.
p. cm.
Includes bibliographical references and index.
ISBN 978-0-19-997599-0 (hardcover : alk. paper) —
ISBN 978-0-19-997604-1 (pbk. : alk. paper) 1. Nonviolence. I. Title.
HM1281.N467 2015
303.6'1—dc23
2015004161

1 3 5 7 9 8 6 4 2

Printed in the United States of America on acid-free paper

For my sisters, Kathryn and Sandra

CONTENTS

LIST OF TABLES AND FIGURES

PREFACE

Nonviolent resistance has been around for a long time. Scriptures depict cases of civil disobedience thousands of years ago, when the Egyptian king ordered Jewish midwives to kill all Hebrew male infants since he feared that one might grow up to challenge his power. Instead of complying, the midwives delivered the children but told Pharaoh that Hebrew women were so strong that they gave birth before they arrived.[1] In the creation of the Roman Republic, the plebs (the free Roman citizens who were not part of the elite ruling class) also used civil resistance. From 495 to 402 BCE, they refused to enlist in the military or pay war levies. They repeatedly engaged in general strikes, physically withdrawing from the city, leaving the elites to run things on their own. These actions eventually enabled the plebs to win greater political leverage and liberties.[2]

Nonviolent action has been used in contemporary times as well, in ways both big and small. There have been large-scale nonviolent movements, such as the U.S. civil rights movement led by Martin Luther King, Jr. and the antiapartheid movement in South Africa that organized boycotts and divestment campaigns, culminating in the election of President Nelson Mandela. Others have used nonviolence in smaller-scale acts of everyday resistance, such as when Prague residents changed the street signs overnight to confuse Soviet troops and obstruct their ability to consolidate control over Czechoslovakia in 1968. Currently, members of Greenpeace use inflatable boats to nonviolently obstruct commercial whaling practices.

As these examples illustrate, the methods of civil resistance are diverse and wide-ranging. Nonviolence scholar Gene Sharp documented 198 distinct tactics, including mass demonstrations, tax resistance, general strikes, work slowdowns, civil disobedience, noncooperation, boycotts, building alternative institutions, sit-ins, and nonviolent intervention, to name just a few.[3] When these tactics are incorporated into a systematic strategy, they can be powerful, bringing about significant social, cultural, and political change.

Despite the historical prevalence and frequent success of nonviolent action, this area of study remained a small and somewhat ghettoized subfield within Peace Studies for many decades. But that has changed. Today, it is thriving and rapidly expanding as dozens of academic books and journal articles have been published on this topic in recent years. It is garnering greater attention from traditional academic disciplines. Political scientists interested in violent conflict and terrorism have begun comparing the relative efficacy of armed and unarmed movements. Social movement researchers are exploring how resisters decide to make tactical shifts and what the long-term consequences of that decision are. Revolutions scholars are noting the differences between traditional guerrilla-style uprisings and civil resistance uprisings. Perhaps spurred by the flurry of recent nonviolent movements—from the "velvet revolutions" in Eastern Europe, to the so-called color revolutions in the former communist regions, to the Arab Spring uprisings—these studies have grown in both number and quality.

As academic studies of nonviolence have increased, so too have their visibility and influence. Some publications have been highly celebrated, receiving international acclaim. For instance, Erica Chenoweth and Maria Stephan's (2011) *Why Civil Resistance Works: The Strategic Logic of Nonviolent Conflict* won the 2012 Woodrow Wilson Award for the best book on government, politics, or international affairs. It also won the 2013 Grawemeyer Award for Ideas Improving World Order. The insights of such books have captivated academics, political analysts, and policymakers alike. In short, there has been a lot of activity and interest, which has brought this small but vibrant field into the scholarly limelight.

HISTORICAL DEVELOPMENT OF THE FIELD

With so much recent scholarship, some may assume that this field of study is new. In reality, the study of nonviolent civil resistance dates back many decades and the field has gone through several major shifts. I will briefly review the evolution of the field.

The Beginnings: Gandhian Studies and Principled Nonviolence (1920s–1950s)

The academic study of civil resistance began when Mohandas Gandhi waged nonviolent campaigns for Indian independence from Great Britain, against caste oppression, and for economic self-sufficiency. Gandhi's campaigns in India, lasting from 1919 to 1948, piqued the interest of many, leading to the publication of several books that explained the philosophy and strategy of Gandhian civil resistance. Early works included Clarence Case's 1923 study[4] that emphasized the sociological dynamics of "nonviolent coercion" and Richard Gregg's 1935 study[5] of the moral and psychological dynamics of suffering within nonviolence campaigns. Krishnalal Shridharani, an Indian nationalist, depicted Gandhi's overarching political strategy in his 1939 book *War without Violence.*[6]

After Gandhi's death in 1948, numerous biographies were published. Yet, given the widespread sentiment that violence was necessary to end Nazi aggression, Gandhi's ideas took a backseat to the expanded patriotism and celebration of war that followed World War II. Interest in Gandhi was revived, however, as the U.S. civil rights movement gained momentum and Martin Luther King, Jr. spoke repeatedly about the power of nonviolence. King's first book, *Stride Toward Freedom*[7] (1958), detailed King's own journey to embracing nonviolence; he claimed that Gandhi's successes convinced him that these techniques could be highly effective and morally superior to violent struggle. That same year, Joan Bondurant published her groundbreaking work, *Conquest of Violence: The Gandhian Philosophy of Conflict,*[8] with Princeton University Press. Bondurant's work situated Gandhian ideas within Western political thought and brought these ideas into mainstream academic circles. Hence interest in Gandhi continued through this period.

Gene Sharp and Pragmatic Nonviolence (1970s–1990s)

For the first several decades, then, the field was mostly devoted to academic analyses of Gandhian ideas and practices. This changed in the 1970s when Gene Sharp put forth his landmark book, *The Politics of Nonviolent Action.*[9] Sharp, who was initially Gandhian, became convinced that a principled commitment to nonviolence was not necessary. Instead, he proposed a purely pragmatic approach that could be employed by anyone, not only pacifists.[10] Drawing on political theory, he argued that rulers cannot rule without the consent and cooperation of the broader population. Once citizens *actively* withdraw their cooperation, a regime can no longer function and will consequently collapse. Hence Sharp called for a new paradigm of nonviolence that was not grounded in moral or religious principles; rather, it was grounded in the conviction that strategic nonviolence is simply more effective than violence.

With his emphasis on military-style strategic nonviolence, Sharp quickly earned the nickname "the Clausewitz of nonviolent warfare."[11] In the years that followed, a group of scholars began documenting cases and publishing descriptive accounts of successful nonviolent movements to prove that, in fact, this nonviolent strategy works.[12] These researchers did an important service by uncovering a largely overlooked part of history, since historical accounts are generally oriented toward the chronicling of wars. Yet much of the literature during this period had a proselytizing character: the goal was to convince others that nonviolence works.

Empirically Based Theory Building and Testing (approximately 2000–present)

In recent years, researchers have focused less on documenting successful nonviolent movements and more on developing and testing nonviolence theories. One significant step in this direction was when scholars began taking a comparative approach, analyzing successful and failed nonviolent movements. Most previous studies had only examined successful cases of civil resistance. Without the failed cases for comparison, however, it is impossible to definitively discern the factors that are critical to movement outcomes.

One of the earliest works to take such a comparative approach was Ackerman and Kruegler's 1994 book *Strategic Nonviolent Conflict*.[13] Ackerman and Kruegler limit their analysis to strategic factors that influence whether a nonviolent movement wins or loses because they believe that a sound strategy can be the basis for victory regardless of the political and social context. Subsequent comparative works, namely Schock's *Unarmed Insurrections* (2005)[14] and my own *Nonviolent Revolutions* (2011)[15], include an examination of strategic *and* structural factors in nonviolent movements—such as organizational support, access to global media sources, and shifting political relations.

Chenoweth and Stephan provide another important comparative work in their 2011 book *Why Civil Resistance Works: The Strategic Logic of Nonviolent Conflict*.[16] They compare successful and failed nonviolent movements but, perhaps most importantly, they also offer a comparison of armed and unarmed campaigns. Drawing upon a database of over three hundred campaigns, they evaluate the relative effectiveness of each form of conflict and also explore how a variety of factors shape outcomes—from the level of participation to the reactions of security forces.

The study of nonviolent movement outcomes has received more attention than any other theoretical question in this latest generation of civil
resistance scholarship. Yet researchers are now exploring a variety of
issues. Some study the factors shaping tactical choices, including decisions to shift from violent to nonviolent forms of conflict and vice versa.[17]
Other scholars are analyzing the global diffusion of nonviolent strategies,
the dynamics of repression and "backfire," and the role that international
communities can play in nonviolent conflicts. In short, there is a rapidly
growing body of literature that has advanced this field of study, both theo-
retically and empirically.[18]

PURPOSE OF THE BOOK

Despite all this scholarship, there has been no single text that introduces,
surveys, and evaluates the field of nonviolence or civil resistance studies.
Now more than ever, such a book is needed as more researchers are exploring nonviolence and a growing number of instructors are teaching college
courses on this topic. Hence I have written this book with several key
goals in mind. First, I introduce key concepts, theories, terms, and debates
within the field. (I also provide a glossary that offers succinct definitions
of many terms within the field.) Second, I summarize the main empirical
findings to date. Third, I take stock of the field, evaluating the gaps in our
knowledge and identifying areas that merit further research and theoretical development.

OUTLINE OF THE BOOK

To achieve these three goals, I have organized the book in the following
manner. The first part (Chapters 1–4) is largely explanatory, offering an
overview of basic concepts and principles. Chapter 1 explains what nonviolence is and what it is not, dispelling many misconceptions about civil
resistance. It also emphasizes the differences between pacifism and nonviolence. Chapter 2 offers a brief overview of several ethical and religious
traditions that have endorsed and inspired civil resistance. Chapter 3 focuses on the basic strategy of nonviolent conflict. Chapter 4 delineates
nine different forms that nonviolence action can take, ranging from the
covert to the overt, from everyday actions to revolutionary movements.

The second part of the book (Chapters 5–8) summarizes empirical findings on a variety of nonviolent movement dynamics. Chapter 5 looks at

the factors that lead to the emergence of such movements. It also depicts the offensive and defensive interplay between resisters and the authorities they challenge. Chapter 6 summarizes the research on movement outcomes. I offer an overview of the factors that influence whether civil resisters win or lose. I also survey the research that examines the longer-term consequences of using violent or nonviolent resistance; specifically, I summarize the findings on postconflict democratic consolidation, economic development, and the likelihood of civil war. Chapter 7 looks at one particular aspect of nonviolent struggle: persuading the security forces to shift their allegiance from the state to the opposition. This chapter looks at the variety of factors that can increase or decrease the likelihood of defections. Chapter 8 summarizes the literature on diffusion, or the global spread of nonviolent tactics and ideas from one movement to another.

The final part of the book, Chapter 9, points out areas within the field that need further development. This concluding chapter provides an overview of topics that have not yet been sufficiently examined. It is intended to offer direction for future empirical and theoretical inquiry.

In short, it is my hope is that this book will enable scholars to quickly get up to speed with the field and situate their own work within this literature. I also hope that this book can provide essential background information and analytical frameworks for students who are learning these ideas for the first time in undergraduate and graduate seminars. Finally, I hope this book gives readers a deeper and more nuanced understanding of the philosophy, strategy, and tradition of nonviolent civil resistance.

ACKNOWLEDGMENTS

I have been thinking and reading about nonviolent struggle and civil resistance since I was eighteen years old. My interest in the topic began when I was a freshman in college and took a philosophy course on the ethics of peace and war. In that class, for the first time I saw footage of Hiroshima and Nagasaki after the United States dropped nuclear bombs. It was unforgettable. I was deeply distraught by the immense human suffering caused by those weapons. Although my political knowledge was minimal at that time, I was convinced that there had to be other ways to solve our conflicts. That conviction launched me on a journey to find alternatives. Not knowing where to begin, I picked up Gandhi's autobiography, *The Story of My Experiments with Truth*. Although I had always seen Gandhi depicted as an Eastern mystic who talked about the power of truth and love, I discovered a savvy political strategist who was not intimidated by a country that had vastly greater military capacities and material resources. Encouraged, I then read Martin Luther King, Jr., followed by Thoreau, and Gene Sharp. Reading these works not only fulfilled my personal interest in finding an alternative to violence but also generated a strong intellectual interest in the dynamics, philosophy, and strategy of nonviolent change. I wish to thank two individuals who guided me on this journey: Stanley Anderson, who taught that course on the ethics of peace and war, and Paul Wehr, my doctoral advisor, who introduced me to the academic literature on nonviolence. One sparked my interest in the topic; the other taught me how to become a researcher within the field.

When I started graduate school in the early 1990s, eager to build my knowledge on this topic, I found that the existing research on civil resistance was minimal. But over the last decade, that has changed. There are numerous movements throughout the world that are experimenting with these techniques, some with remarkable success. There are also a growing number of scholars who are studying these struggles, collecting empirical data to analyze these nonviolent conflicts. These researchers have brought life and energy into this field, generating new theories, debates, and insights. As a result, the time has come to introduce, summarize, and evaluate this interdisciplinary area of study for a broader audience.

As I proposed this book idea to James Cook, my editor at Oxford University Press, he was immediately supportive. He has been an instrumental force behind this book from the beginning, expeditiously guiding my manuscript through the review process and encouraging me to make it the best book possible. I am truly thankful for his commitment to the project. He is quite simply the best editor an author could hope for.

I am also grateful to various people who read the manuscript and offered me constructive feedback. The book is significantly stronger and more accurate due to the comments of three anonymous reviewers. I especially wish to thank Brian Martin, who read the manuscript closely, providing detailed recommendations on the book's content and form. I also wish to thank Wendy Walker, whose fine copy editing skills have improved the readability of the text. Of course, any remaining errors in the book are my sole responsibility.

Somehow, I manage to compose and revise this book while I served as the chair of the sociology department at the University of New Mexico. When I reluctantly took on this position, numerous people warned me that I would get little to no scholarship done. There are three reasons why I was able to keep writing. One reason is because my astonishingly capable staff person, Dorothy Esquivel, kept things operating smoothly and protected my research time. I am truly indebted. The second reason is because my colleagues are a remarkably productive, responsible, and collegial group, which made my job rewarding and manageable. I thank you all. The third reason is because of a generous grant I received from the United States Institute of Peace. With their financial support, I was able to reduce my teaching load so I could continue my research and complete the manuscript. I thank the grant program officers at USIP for their faith in my abilities and their willingness to support this project.

Most of all, I'm grateful to my loved ones, who endured my endless hours of reading, writing, and talking about civil resistance. My daughters, Linnea and Malaya, and my stepsons, Dante and Aldo, are a source of immeasurable joy. They keep me grounded when I'm tempted to get lost in a world of ideas and research. I thank my parents, Millard and Virginia Erickson, and my sisters, Kathryn Inoferio and Sandra Erickson Nepstad, who encouraged my intellectual interests from the earliest days. And I thank my husband, Claude Morelli, for his love, support, and countless acts of kindness. While Gandhi taught me about the power of truth and love in social and political struggles, these are the people who have shown me the power of love in daily life.

S.E.N.
Albuquerque, New Mexico

CHAPTER 1

ᴄᴌᴏ

What Nonviolence Is and What It Is Not

"Nonviolence is not inaction. It is not discussion. It is not for the timid or weak. Nonviolence is hard work. . . . In some cases, nonviolence requires more militancy than violence."

César Chávez

The word "nonviolence" evokes many images. Some envision the thousands of Indians who marched with Gandhi to the Arabian Sea to make salt, an act prohibited by Britain's Salt Acts. Others think of civil rights activists who endured harassment, assault, and jail for sitting at segregated lunch counters in the southern United States. For others, the term conjures up thoughts of Amish communities who withdraw from the world to isolate themselves from societal violence. And some may think of the recent citizen uprisings in Tunisia and Egypt that ushered in the "Arab Spring." Indeed, nonviolence is embodied in different forms and its adherents hold a variety of philosophies, beliefs, and strategic orientations. Yet many assume that all who embrace nonviolence are more or less the same since they all reject the use of physical force. The confusion about nonviolence is compounded by the various terms that people use—from pacifism to civil resistance, people power, unarmed insurrections, strategic nonviolence, and more.

In this chapter, I offer an overview of these terms. In particular, I highlight the differences between pacifism and nonviolence as well as the distinction between principled nonviolence and pragmatic nonviolence. I also address common misconceptions and criticisms that arise in discussions of nonviolence, demonstrating how they frequently reflect an inadequate or inaccurate understanding of all these terms.

PACIFISM AND NONVIOLENCE

Often, the concepts of pacifism and nonviolent action are erroneously conflated and treated synonymously. On the one hand, pacifism is the principled opposition to war and the use of violence for political purposes.[1] Nonviolent action, on the other hand, is a set of tactics and strategies used for pursuing social and political goals.[2] In other words, pacifism is a moral or ideological stance on war while nonviolent action is a method of fighting oppression and injustice. Yet these are simple distinctions. In reality, there are numerous types of pacifists and various approaches to nonviolent action. Moreover, some pacifists use nonviolent action while others do not, preferring to withdraw from a violent situation rather than actively addressing it. Similarly, within a nonviolent movement, pacifists are often in the vanguard while the majority of activists may not be pacifists at all but are simply using nonviolent tactics and strategies because they believe that is the best option under the circumstances. To fully understand these distinctions, we need to explore the different categories of pacifism and nonviolence.

Types of Pacifism

While pacifists share the conviction that war is unethical, the reasons behind their convictions vary. Scholars have distinguished several different types of pacifism, as listed in Table 1.1.[3] First is *absolute pacifism*. In its pure form, absolute pacifists maintain that the use of violent force against another human being is always wrong. This conviction typically stems from religious or ethical opposition to physical violence—whether it is used in political conflicts or in personal self-defense. In reality,

Table 1.1. TYPES OF PACIFISM

1. Absolute
2. Realistic pacifism
3. Technological pacifism (previously known as nuclear pacifism)
4. Fallibility pacifism

absolute pacifism is rare. Many pacifists believe that a person has a right to use physical power to free herself, for example, from a sexual predator. Thus, as Duane Cady notes, pacifists "may oppose violence – a violating act with the intent to injure or destroy – but not need thereby oppose force, the use of physical strength. Of course all war involves violence but not all violence involves war. Since pacifism is the moral opposition to war, there may be pacifists tolerating some instances of violence while opposing all war."[4]

Those who are unwilling to accept absolutist views often embrace another form of pacifism known as *realistic pacifism*. David Cortright describes realistic pacifism as "predicated on a presumption against armed violence, but acknowledges that the use of force, constrained by rigorous ethical standards, may be necessary at times for self-defense and the protection of the innocent."[5] In other words, this type of pacifist opposes violence for political goals, tempered by the recognition that limited force may be necessary in certain circumstances. Mohandas Gandhi held similar views, stating, "If the capacity for non-violent self-defense is lacking, there need be no hesitation in using violent means"[6] (although he did emphasize that there is always a way to defend oneself without violence).

A third type of pacifism is *technological pacifism* (previously called *nuclear pacifism*). This refers to those who believe that war may have been justifiable in the past but new weapons now make warfare immoral due to their immense destructive power. Warfare once involved combatants meeting face to face on battlefields. Modern war, in contrast, is waged by aerial bombings and drone attacks. And when nuclear and chemical weapons are used, unarmed civilians of all ages are harmed, even when they have nothing to do with the political conflict. Thus innocent lives are taken, which technological pacifists argue is unjustifiable. As one theologian stated, "the evil brought by obliteration is certain injury and death . . . to hundreds of thousands, and an incalculable destruction of their property. The ultimate good which is supposed to compensate for this evil is of a very speculative character."[7] Some technological pacifists also highlight the environmental devastation that is likely to result from war. Some scientists have predicted that the use of weapons of mass destruction could lead to a nuclear winter, potentially causing the extinction of the entire human, plant, and animal worlds.[8] In short, technological pacifists may not be opposed in principle to war but they hold that contemporary weapons of mass destruction have the capacity to do so much devastation, to combatants and noncombatants alike, that no war is justifiable in the modern era.

The fourth and final category of pacifism is called *fallibility pacifism* (sometimes called *epistemological pacifism*). Those who subscribe to this view argue that humans are fallible and thus there is always a possibility that people may not have full or accurate knowledge about a conflict. If war is waged on the basis of false or partial information, there is a risk of harming innocent individuals or promoting an unjust cause. In other words, this type of pacifist believes that

> Given the subtlety and complexity of issues between nations, the history of tensions, the biases of involved parties, the propaganda, the vested interests, the manipulation of demographic inequities, our knowledge cannot be sufficiently secure to justify war, even if it were conceded that war is theoretically justifiable.[9]

Hence fallibility pacifists refuse to wage war since the consequences—including potentially large death rates, infrastructural damage, and economic devastation—are too great a price to pay if one cannot be certain that armed conflict is the correct course of action.

TYPES OF NONVIOLENCE: PRINCIPLED AND PRAGMATIC

One can be a pacifist but not ever engage in nonviolent action. Some pacifist groups, such as the Amish, take a position of nonresistance. The reverse is also true: one can use nonviolent tactics without being a pacifist. Scholarly documentation indicates that nonviolent campaigns have been implemented in virtually every corner of the world.[10] Yet in the majority of these movements, most participants were not pacifists.[11] Accounts of the U.S. civil rights movement, for example, indicate that many African Americans were willing to use violence and had to be convinced to refrain from it during campaigns.[12] So why do nonpacifists use nonviolence? The answer is simple: people employ nonviolent techniques because they believe they can work.

So just as there are variations on pacifism, there is also a distinction between (a) those who make a strategic choice to employ nonviolence because they believe it is more effective than violence and (b) those who choose this method of struggle because they ethically oppose the use of violence. The first category is called *pragmatic nonviolence* (also known as *strategic nonviolence*)[13] while the latter is called *principled nonviolence*.[14] Movements that use pragmatic nonviolence may be filled with nonpacifists but who intentionally refrain from violence as a way to maximize the effect of their tactics. Those who advocate for principled nonviolence are typically pacifists.

Does it matter whether the use of nonviolence is driven by principled or pragmatic motives? Although this is a matter of debate, some argue that these two types of nonviolence represent distinct motives, goals, philosophies, and techniques.[15] I summarize some of these differences in Table 1.2.

Nonviolent activists can be driven by different motives. Those who come from a principled perspective typically choose nonviolent resistance because they believe that violence is wrong—a belief that is frequently grounded in a religious or moral perspective.[16] Indeed, as Chapter 2 shows, every major world religion has some tradition of nonviolence. Thus activists committed to a principled approach maintain that the most ethical, humane way to address conflicts is in a nonviolent manner, which may also bring spiritual or moral benefits. For Gandhi, the individual most associated with principled nonviolence, the ethical imperative comes from the spiritual notion of *ahimsa*, or the refusal to harm life—an important

Table 1.2. DISTINCTIONS BETWEEN PRINCIPLED AND PRAGMATIC NONVIOLENCE

Principled (Gandhi)	Pragmatic (Sharp)
Motive	Motive
1. Ethics: violence is wrong; nonviolence is the most ethical response to conflict	1. Practicality: violence is ineffective or too costly
2. Often has a religious or ideological basis	2. Secular basis
3. Key question: What is the moral way to respond?	3. Key question: What will work?
Goals	Goals
4. Changing the opponent's heart and mind	4. Changing the opponent's behavior
5. Personal and social transformation	5. Transformation of a social institution
6. Ending all violence and establishing social justice	6. Ending a particular violent situation or injustice
7. Seeks a win–win solution; opponents are seen as partners in the struggle to meet the needs of all parties	7. Is satisfied with a win–lose outcome; opponents are seen as antagonists with incompatible interests
Techniques	Techniques
8. Avoids coercion, emphasizes persuasion and understanding	8. Willing to use nonviolent coercion
9. Moral jiu-jitsu: suffering is a means of transforming self and others	9. May try to avoid suffering but emphasizes political jiu-jitsu

concept in Hinduism, Buddhism, and Jainism. Hence proponents of principled nonviolence typically ask: What is the most ethical way to address a conflict? What is the morally correct response?

For those coming from a pragmatic perspective, nonviolent forms of resistance are typically chosen because violence is too costly or unlikely to be effective. Movement organizers use this method of struggle because they believe it offers the best chance for winning. Their motive, therefore, is typically secular and the questions they pose are: Will this form of struggle work? Will it enable us to achieve our goal?[17] While they may also believe that nonviolence is the most ethical response, advocates of strategic nonviolence argue that nonviolence as a set of political techniques can be separated from nonviolence as a moral belief system.[18]

Goals

In the struggle for social transformation, principled nonviolent activists have three primary goals. The first two goals are intrinsically linked: (1) to change the hearts and minds of one's opponents so that they will voluntarily end the conflict at hand and (2) to transform oneself to achieve a higher degree of understanding and integrity. These ideas are embodied in Gandhi's concept of *satyagraha*, which literally translates to "clinging to the truth." Dissatisfied with the term "passive resistance," Gandhi put out a call for a new term. Someone in the Indian independence movement suggested *sadagraha*, which translates as "firmness in a good cause." Gandhi changed this to *satya* (truth) and *ā-graha* (firmness).[19] Thus "truth force" became his means of resolving conflict, but the pursuit of truth also was a goal in itself—a goal with spiritual ramifications. As Gandhi stated, "God and Truth are convertible terms . . . [T]o me, Truth is God and there is no way to find Truth except the way of nonviolence. . . . Truth is the end, Love a means thereto."[20] Thus, while Gandhi aimed to win Indian sovereignty by persuading the British that independence was in everyone's best interest, this goal was intertwined with the personal transformation that comes from discovering truth and fighting with "truth force."

The third goal of principled nonviolence is to create a more just society overall. While it may be imperative to address specific injustices—such as British rule in India—Gandhi felt that India's economic system, political institutions, and cultural practices also needed to change. This is what he referred to as a "constructive program": the development of economic independence by creating meaningful local work, implementing land reform, and establishing quality education and health services for all, among other things.[21] Martin Luther King, Jr. also discussed the importance of comprehensively transforming society to reflect the "beloved community." He defined this as a society guided by the principles of *agape*, a Greek term denoting love for all humanity.[22] The beloved community is a society where the economic, social, and political needs of all citizens are addressed. It is a society where people are concerned about the well-being of all, not just their personal enrichment. Bigotry is replaced with understanding and hatred is overcome through reconciliation.[23] In short, advocates of principled nonviolence argue that action should be taken to address immediate injustices but the larger goal is to radically alter social and human relations.[24]

Advocates of pragmatic nonviolence have a much more focused agenda—namely, the resolution of a specific conflict or the transformation of a particular regime or institution. Thus pragmatic nonviolence has often been used to overturn authoritarian regimes and autocratic rulers. This includes the Philippine "people power" movement of 1986, the Serbian movement that removed Slobodan Milošević from office,[25] and the Ukraine's "orange revolution," to name just a few. In these cases, the goal is not to transform the dictator's heart but to change the dictator's behavior—that is, to end regime repression, corruption, and injustices. In contrast to principled nonviolence, advocates of pragmatic nonviolence generally give little attention to the personal transformation of resisters, although they acknowledge that this can happen in the process. Also, they do not typically emphasize a comprehensive transformation of social structures and human relationships. The goal is to mobilize citizens to remove an unjust ruler or foreign occupier but to do so without resorting to armed warfare.

As they work toward these goals, principled and pragmatic nonviolence practitioners take distinct approaches to the opponent. For those in the principled tradition, conflict is seen as a joint problem to be solved collectively. Hence the opponent is viewed as a partner in this endeavor and the goal is to achieve an outcome where all parties are satisfied. For pragmatic nonviolent practitioners, the opponent is seen as an antagonist. A win–win outcome is not very feasible since they believe that the antagonist holds interests that are inherently incompatible with their own interests.[26]

Techniques

To outside observers, the techniques of nonviolent resistance may look identical regardless of whether the movement is primarily motivated by a principled or strategic interest. Both types of movements use boycotts, mass demonstrations, civil disobedience, and noncooperation. Yet there are some key differences in how these techniques are implemented.

In the principled tradition, nonviolent techniques are used to persuade or convert the opponent. In her interpretation of Gandhian thought, Joan Bondurant wrote, "He who claims a different version of truth from the satyagrahi's must be converted by gentleness. Meanwhile, the satyagrahi must re-examine continuously his own position—for his opponent may be closer to the truth than he. . . . The objective of satyagraha is to win the victory over the conflict situation—to discover further truths and to persuade the opponent, not triumph over him."[27]

Yet the opponent is unlikely to be converted if hostility or disdain is expressed; therefore, principled nonviolent activists are deeply concerned about the spirit in which campaigns are waged. Gandhi asserted that civil resistance must be waged without anger, revenge, or a desire to humiliate the opponent. Gandhi stated, "The essence of non-violence technique is that it seeks to liquidate antagonisms but not antagonists themselves . . . [I]t is often forgotten that it is never the intention of the satyagrahi to embarrass the wrong doer. . . . It is the acid test of non-violence that, in a nonviolent conflict, there is no rancour left behind, and in the end the enemies are converted into friends."[28]

To emphasize this point, Gandhi contrasted principled nonviolent action (*satyagraha*) with *duragraha*—stubborn or coercive force. Bondurant wrote, "Duragraha in its most common form amounts to the intensification of pressure or shifting points of attack until a settlement is reached through capitulation or compromise. . . . Duragraha seeks concessions; satyagraha sets out to develop alternatives which will satisfy antagonists on all sides."[29] Indeed, for Gandhi, it is this truth-seeking commitment that makes nonviolent action effective. He wrote, "There is a causal connection between the purity of the intention and the extent of effectiveness of nonviolent action."[30] In short, a principled approach to nonviolence avoids coercion and aims to convert the opponent.

Another way that civil resisters may convert their opponents is by voluntarily suffering for their cause. Gandhi called this *tapasya* or self-sacrifice. Sometimes, nonviolent resisters fail to persuade because their adversaries have developed elaborate justifications for the injustice. For instance, colonial powers often argued that they were not exploiting their colonial subjects but rather helping them by bringing modern advances that would promote economic prosperity and educational improvement. When opponents deeply believe such justifications, it is difficult to win them over. However, when opponents witness a person suffering for his or her beliefs, their response is visceral and emotional. As Bondurant put it, "suffering acts as a shock treatment – a dramatization of the satyagrahi position."[31] This shock may reach the heart of the opponent, who feels ashamed of his or her role in this suffering and who gains respect for the civil resisters, based on their willingness to make sacrifices for their beliefs.

The transformative capacity of suffering is elaborated by Richard Gregg, one of the early Western interpreters of Gandhi. In Gregg's 1935 book *The Power of Nonviolence,* he argues that suffering creates a dynamic called "moral jiu-jitsu."[32] Comparing it to the martial arts technique of redirecting the opponents' force so that they lose physical balance during an attack, Gregg argued that nonviolence is a technique that makes violent opponents lose their moral balance. Moral jiu-jitsu, then, is primarily a psychological dynamic. If civil resisters voluntarily suffer for their cause—without striking back or expressing hatred—then they induce shame in their attackers, who can no longer justify their oppressive acts.[33]

In contrast to the principled emphasis on winning understanding through sacrifice and suffering, practitioners of pragmatic nonviolence take a different approach, which is best exemplified in the work of American political theorist Gene Sharp. Sharp argues that nonviolence can be purely a political technique rather than a moral philosophy or ethical imperative.[34] According to Sharp, nonviolence is similar to armed combat in that it requires sound strategy, numerous "weapons," and courageous, well-disciplined, nonviolent soldiers.[35] From his perspective, the goal of nonviolent action is to defeat oppressive rulers, not to transform their hearts and minds.

As depicted in Table 1.3, Sharp argues that there are four mechanisms whereby civil resisters can attain their aims: conversion, accommodation, nonviolent coercion, and disintegration.[36] In conversion, civil resisters persuade their opponents to accept their view, leading to the resolution of the conflict. This, of course, is the goal of principled nonviolent activists. In accommodation, opponents concede to civil resisters' demands, yet they never fundamentally change their beliefs and views. As Sharp

Table 1.3. NONVIOLENT MECHANISMS OF CHANGE

1. Conversion
2. Accommodation
3. Coercion
4. Disintegration

explains, "The opponents do this because they calculate that it is the best they can do. Their aim may be to undercut internal dissension, minimize losses, avoid a larger disaster, or save face."[37] In the third mechanism of change, nonviolent coercion, civil resisters win without the consent or agreement of their adversary. The opponent may retain some level of power but is unable to implement his or her will due to widespread noncooperation. The fourth mechanism of change entails disintegration. This means that the opponent's entire system collapses so that no organization remains, even to accept defeat. Based on this overview, we can see that practitioners of pragmatic civil resistance are willing to use nonviolent coercion to achieve their goals. It is not essential to convert the opponent; the goal is to nonviolently defeat the opponent.[38]

Since political goals can be achieved without converting the opponent, suffering and sacrifice may not be necessary in a pragmatic nonviolent struggle.[39] Undoubtedly, suffering can occur in a nonviolent campaign since states often respond with violent repression. But many advocates of pragmatic nonviolence argue that suffering should be avoided. Ackerman and Kruegler, for instance, encourage movement organizers to take every precaution to keep activists out of harm's way since repression can be demoralizing, causing the movement to dissipate.[40] Thus suffering and self-sacrifice are key elements of principled nonviolence but not pragmatic nonviolence.

Are These Differences Important?

After delineating the differences between principled and pragmatic nonviolence, one might ask: Do these distinctions matter? Are they merely philosophical differences or are there actual variations in practice and outcomes? Some in the principled camp think that these distinctions are important. They propose that the type of paradigm shift needed for authentic social transformation can only occur through a principled strategy that changes social structures as well as human attitudes and relationships.[41] As one individual put it, "The [nonviolent] revolution . . . is not about putting a different kind of person in power; it is about awakening a different kind of power in the people."[42] They are also concerned that pragmatic nonviolent resisters may be so oriented toward removing an oppressive political system that they fail to address other enduring problems, such as exploitive economic and cultural systems. They have asked: What if strategic civil resistance removes unjust rulers but sets the stage for violent ways of life associated with neoliberalism, free market capitalism, and consumerist individualism?[43] They propose that only a principled approach that incorporates a Gandhian "constructive program" will establish enduring justice. A final concern is that a singular emphasis on pragmatic nonviolence, without an accompanying emphasis on moral principles, means that anyone could use these methods—even oppressors. Without the Gandhian commitment to truth, this strategy could be used for just goals or unjust purposes.[44] Proponents of pragmatic nonviolence may inadvertently be supplying oppressors with additional "weapons."

Some in the pragmatic camp also think this distinction matters, primarily because they find it is unrealistic to expect civil resisters to embrace the philosophy and ethics of principled nonviolence, particularly in the face of highly repressive systems. Gene Sharp argued that the broader population must first believe that nonviolence is a viable alternative to political violence; once that happens, then people can "consider and deal with the finer ethical problems which arise in the application of nonviolent sanctions."[45] Any requirements that activists accept principled nonviolence can potentially alienate practitioners, thereby impeding (rather than promoting) the adoption of nonviolent methods.[46] In short, they hold that activists do not need to transform hearts before throwing off their chains.[47]

Yet others dispute the notion that these two types of nonviolence are dichotomous or opposing categories.[48] They note that principled and pragmatic nonviolent resisters are often fighting side by side in the same campaigns. In these circumstances, they are united by a common commitment to nonviolent methods of action, even if their underlying belief systems and philosophies differ. Moreover, as nonpacifists join a pragmatic nonviolent struggle, they may become more interested in the philosophical roots of principled nonviolence. As Cynthia Boaz wrote, "Nonviolent action, when done well, can achieve results. When people come to see its efficacy and power through its use, they may develop more appreciation for [its] principles. . . . But whether activists get to the principle prior to action or through it does not matter."[49] Thus a commitment to principled nonviolence may evolve from the practices of pragmatic nonviolent action.

Moreover, a close look at Gandhi and Sharp reveals that they defy simple categorization as representatives of the principled and pragmatic traditions. Gandhi, for example, was quite pragmatic. He made the distinction of nonviolence as a policy, which can be abandoned if it does not work, and nonviolence as a spiritual creed or vow. Yet he considered himself a realist and thus stated, "[B]eing a practical man, I do not wait till India recognizes the practicability of the spiritual life in the political world. . . . A policy can be changed, a creed cannot. But either is as good as the other whilst it is held."[50] He expressed the same sentiment in a letter to the British government of India: "I do not at all need believers in the theory of nonviolence, full or imperfect. It is enough if people carry out the rules of non-violent action."[51]

In addition, both Gandhi and Martin Luther King, Jr. were highly strategic as well as highly principled. Gandhi articulated multiple steps to systematically withhold key sources of power from the British, demonstrating that they had no capacity to rule India. King devised a battle plan for the U.S. civil rights movement. As one analyst has argued, he achieved victory by orchestrating dramatic crises, which provoked violent responses from racists. This led to media coverage that revealed the oppressive circumstances that African Americans faced; it also compelled federal authorities to intervene to uphold their constitutional rights.[52] To designate Gandhi and King as representatives of the principled tradition can sometimes obscure the fact that they, too, were strategic and goal-oriented.

Furthermore, those in the pragmatic tradition often endorse practices that are typically associated with principled nonviolence. For example, Sharp strongly encourages strategic civil resisters not to succumb to hate. Although he does not demand that civil resisters love their opponents, he argues that the techniques are more effective if practitioners are not hostile.[53] In addition, it is completely possible for pragmatic nonviolent resisters to incorporate a constructive program into their movement campaigns. In fact, Sharp notes that building parallel institutions, such as alternative economies and independent governmental organizations, is well within the pragmatic tradition.

To summarize, the bifurcated view of principled and pragmatic nonviolence does not adequately convey the areas of overlap between these two traditions. While the distinctions may be important, we should not falsely characterize them as polar opposites.

REASONS FOR CHOOSING NONVIOLENCE

Regardless of whether civil resisters take a pragmatic or principled approach, the question remains: Why do people choose nonviolent direct action? In most cases of injustice or conflict, citizens often assume they have only two choices: (1) do nothing and resign themselves to the situation or (2) use traditional channels (such as petitions, lobbying, and writing political leaders) to instigate change. Yet often these conventional political forms of action are insufficient, ineffective, or too slow. Other methods are needed beyond those permitted by the government.[54] While some feel the injustice is severe enough that only armed struggle will be effective, others turn to unarmed forms of struggle. There are many reasons why they choose nonviolence over violence. I will list a few of these.[55]

Some groups choose nonviolence because it gives them a greater chance of winning public support—from both fellow citizens and the broader international community.[56] When people take up arms, they are often depicted as terrorists or extremists. If a movement is labeled as terrorist, many governments expressly prohibit citizens from sending financial and material support to it. Moreover, people often condemn their methods without ever learning what the group's grievances and goals are. Thus violent forms of struggle can marginalize and isolate a movement.

A second reason for selecting nonviolence is because it allows for widespread participation. People of all ages and backgrounds can be involved in tactics such as boycotts and noncooperation. Gandhi famously stated, "In nonviolence the masses have a weapon which enables a child, a woman, or even a decrepit old man to resist the mightiest government successfully."[57] In contrast, violent forms of struggle often exclude those who are unable to meet the physical demands of fighting or who are unable to leave behind their jobs and family responsibilities. Chenoweth and Stephan elaborate on this point:

> The physical risks and costs of participation in a violent resistance campaign may be prohibitively high for many potential members. Actively joining a violent campaign may require physical skills such as agility and endurance, willingness to train, ability to handle and use weapons, and often isolation from society at large . . . [T]he typical guerrilla regimen may appeal only to a small portion of any given population.[58]

Moreover, when a cross-cutting sector of the population is involved with a nonviolent struggle, the chances of winning increase and citizens' commitment to a new society deepens.

A third reason for choosing nonviolent methods is that they are compatible with the goal of creating a nonviolent civil society. Gandhi argued ardently that a movement's methods of resistance affect the end result. Thus resisters should select tactics that are consistent with their desired goals—a concept known as "prefigurative politics." By using civil forms of resistance, movement participants acquire experience in interacting and functioning nonviolently. Thus the methods advance the goal, even before the end goal is fully attained. However, if resisters use violence, they shape their current and future society to be more accepting of physical force in political matters. In an armed struggle, the leaders who are most likely to gain prominence are those who are most willing to use violence. As Gandhi noted, these same leaders are unlikely to give up violence after they obtain power. Thus citizens may find that they have merely replaced one oppressive regime with a new but equally oppressive regime.

A fourth reason for choosing nonviolence is because violent forms of struggle can have devastating and lingering consequences. While one might achieve the goal of a new government using armed struggle, new problems may be created in the process—such as massive loss of human life, infrastructural damage, significant reparation costs, environmental destruction, and so forth. Robert Burrowes stated the following:

> Violence is grossly dysfunctional . . . [W]henever it has been used in the service
> of major political goals, it has led to suffering and death, often on a massive
> scale. Critics of nonviolence often overlook these points.[59]

A fifth reason that groups use nonviolence is because violence may be highly impractical. Oppressed groups often do not have access to armaments. If they do possess weapons, they are likely to be ill equipped compared to the state; hence chances are good that armed resisters will be quickly defeated when they rise up against a government that has superior military capacities. Of course, resisters who are out-armed can resort to other forms of political violence, such as terrorism. Yet there is growing empirical evidence that terrorism is not effective in achieving political goals.[60]

COMMON MISCONCEPTIONS AND CRITIQUES OF NONVIOLENCE

Despite the advantages of nonviolence, there are still many skeptics and critics. Some criticisms address important concerns but others are grounded in misconceptions. Specifically, many critics conflate principled and pragmatic approaches. I will summarize a dozen common misconceptions[61] and respond to a few prevalent critiques.

The first misconception is that nonviolence is about neutrality and passivity. This misunderstanding generally stems from a lack of knowledge about the distinctions between pacifism and nonviolent resistance. While some pacifists have historically subscribed to a position of nonresistance, those who embrace nonviolent action are committed to fighting injustice, albeit through alternative means. Thus nonviolence, whether it comes from a principled or pragmatic approach, is about fighting oppression; indeed, it is the opposite of passivity or submissiveness. Nonviolent struggle is about engaging in provocative, sometimes disruptive, action to facilitate change.

A second misconception is that nonviolent action entails nothing more than institutional methods of change, such as petitioning, letter writing, educational campaigns, and voter mobilization efforts. In reality, nonviolent resistance techniques often fall outside the parameters of conventional political action.[62] For example, a nonviolent movement may engage in economic boycotts or general strikes. It may mobilize people to commit civil disobedience—that is, the deliberate violation of a law deemed unjust. Those living under Nazi occupation who hid Jews and smuggled them to safety were breaking the law and nonviolently resisting the worst form of institutionalized anti-Semitism.

Third, some people assume incorrectly that nonviolent action is limited to negotiation and verbal persuasion. In reality, nonviolent movements use a variety of tactics, mobilizing an aggrieved population's social, economic, and political forms of power. While negotiation may be part of a nonviolent strategy, it is not the only technique used. Nonviolence entails resistance, often with the purpose of pressuring authorities to negotiate. In the 1963 civil rights campaign in Birmingham, Alabama, for example, movement leaders negotiated with the city's business owners. The merchants made concessions, agreeing to remove all racially degrading signs, but it was soon apparent that these were insincere promises. Martin Luther King, Jr. describes why they resorted to nonviolent action:

> As the weeks and months went by, we realized that we were the victims of a broken promise. A few signs, briefly removed, returned; the others remained. As in so many past experiences, our hopes had been blasted. . . . We had no alternative except to prepare for direct action, whereby we would present our very bodies as a means of laying our case before the conscience of the local and the national community. . . . [Negotiation] is the very purpose of direct action. *Nonviolent direct action seeks to create such a crisis and fosters such a tension that a community which has constantly refused to negotiate is forced to confront the issue. It seeks so to dramatize the issue that it can no longer be ignored* [italics mine].[63]

Thus direct action can compel opponents to negotiate but it can also enhance a movement's leverage at the negotiation table.

Fourth, some believe that nonviolence is only applicable to reformist movements seeking moderate goals. In reality, nonviolence can also be the primary strategy and method for revolutionary movements seeking radical, transformative goals. Civil resisters have used nonviolent methods to oust authoritarian regimes and implement democracy.[64] Nonviolence has also been used to challenge and transform economic systems such as capitalism[65] as well as cultural systems such as patriarchy.[66] In the words of Kurt Schock, "Challenging groups can be militant, radical, *and* nonviolent."[67]

Fifth, some people maintain that nonviolence can only be used in democratic contexts where states are reluctant to use force against their own citizens. The truth is that nonviolence has successfully been used against dictators, such as Bolivia's Sánchez de Lozada or Haiti's Jean-Claude Duvalier.[68] It has also been used to challenge hybrid regimes, such as in Ukraine, where elections are held but autocratic methods were implemented to ensure that high-ranking political leaders retained power.[69] Regardless of the type of regime that is challenged, nonviolent resisters can never assume that the state will respond peacefully. Governments often use repression to quell civil resistance struggles but, as we will see in Chapter 3, such repression may actually help rather than hurt a nonviolent movement.

A sixth misconception is that nonviolence requires moral pressure or the conversion of the opponent in order to succeed. While principled nonviolence aims for change through conversion, pragmatic nonviolence sees that as only one option. As Sharp has argued, change can also come through nonviolent pressure that forces the opponent to accommodate to the challengers' demands, even if there is no change of heart. Similarly, nonviolent resisters can coerce their opponent to capitulate by simply undercutting key sources of power. The nonviolent withholding of cooperation and resources may also cause an entire system to disintegrate and collapse. Thus conversion is only one mechanism for bringing about change nonviolently.

Seventh, nonviolent action does not necessarily require that civil resisters suffer. Certainly, all serious struggles for social justice can entail significant costs and risks. And suffering may at times enhance a nonviolent movement's leverage and power. But, from a pragmatic nonviolent perspective, it is not necessary to achieve one's goals. In fact, some estimate that nonviolent struggles are far less likely to incur physical casualties than violent struggles.[70]

Eighth, participation in a nonviolent struggle does not require individuals to adhere to any particular religious, moral, or ideological beliefs. Nonviolent techniques can be used by anyone—secular or religious, of any ideological or political orientation. Even nonviolent leaders who have embraced a religious and moral worldview, such as Gandhi and King, acknowledged that not everyone in their movements shared their convictions. Most nonviolent movements are composed of people with various religious and philosophical commitments.

The ninth misconception about nonviolence is that it requires a charismatic leader in order to be successful. Since nonviolent movements are more effective when they mobilize large numbers of citizens, some assume that only a highly charismatic individual could accomplish this. Yet many civil resistance struggles have not had such figures. There was no single leader, for instance, in the East German uprising of 1989 or in the Egyptian revolt of 2011. Indeed, movements led by charismatic figures face their own challenges, since such leaders become easy targets for repression. It is no coincidence that Gandhi and King were assassinated. When these figures are gone, the movement may struggle to stay on course.[71]

A tenth misconception is that nonviolence is a bourgeoisie tactic that is only used by the privileged. People from all class backgrounds have used nonviolent resistance—from slaves to elites.[72] Those who are economically and politically marginalized have most frequently used nonviolence. Since they have little access to institutional sources of power, they resort to "people power" tactics. Therefore, the belief that nonviolence is a privilege that only white, middle-class citizens can use does not reflect historical reality: it has been used by African Americans in the U.S. civil rights movement,[73] by "untouchables" in the Indian independence struggle,[74] by labor unions and indigenous groups in El Salvador,[75] and by landless peasants in Brazil[76]—to name just a few examples.

Eleventh, many people believe that nonviolence is inherently slow. The (unsubstantiated) assumption is that violence can quickly and efficiently rip power from a ruler's grip while nonviolent action slowly wears down opponents over time or gradually convinces them to change. Like other misconceptions, this view does not hold up against historical evidence.[77] It is true that Gandhi's movement for Indian independence took decades to win its victory. Yet the Chinese and Vietnamese revolutions, which relied upon armed struggle, also took decades. Moreover, there are examples where violent movements fought for many years without ever attaining their goals: the Irish Republican Army's struggle in Northern Ireland, the Revolutionary Armed Forces of Colombia (FARC), or the New People's Army of the Philippines, among others. In contrast, many nonviolent movements—such as the Philippine "people power" movement, Ukraine's "orange revolution," and the Arab Spring uprisings in Tunisia and Egypt—have brought down regimes rather quickly, in a matter of months or years. In fact, Chenoweth and Stephan's study shows that successful violent struggles took an average of eight years to achieve their goals whereas successful nonviolent struggles took an average of just two years.[78] Thus nonviolence is not inevitably slower.[79]

Twelfth, many people assume that nonviolence is a nice idea but cannot work in a violent world. In other words, many people assume that violence is more effective than nonviolence. Empirical evidence soundly debunks this myth. In a recent study, Chenoweth and Stephan examined 323 movements occurring between 1900 and 2006; they found that 53 percent of nonviolent movements obtained their goals while only 26 percent of violent movements did.[80] And several studies have found that revolutionary movements that established democracies through nonviolent means were more stable and enduring than democracies put in place by violent methods.[81] In short, these studies find that nonviolent forms of struggle are typically more effective than violent struggles.

CRITIQUES OF NONVIOLENCE

These misconceptions have led many people to prematurely dismiss nonviolence as irrelevant in the modern world. Others have claimed that nonviolence is problematic, detrimental, and even pathological. Since several recent books have criticized nonviolence, it is worth taking a closer look to discern which critiques are rooted in misunderstandings and which critiques raise legitimate issues. These recent books include Ward Churchill's *Pacifism as Pathology*[82] and Peter Gelderloos' *How Nonviolence Protects the State*.[83] Since their arguments are similar, I address their main criticisms together.

Criticism #1: Nonviolence Is Incapable of Achieving Wide-Scale Social Change

The first criticism that these authors raise is that nonviolence is not an effective method for significantly transforming social structures. Even in Gandhi's movement and the U.S. civil rights movement—undoubtedly the most celebrated cases of nonviolent movement success—Gelderloos and Churchill argue that these movements didn't fundamentally change anything. Gelderloos argues that the Indian movement did achieve independence from Great Britain but then it merely replaced a colonial system with a neocolonial one. Similarly, he states that while the civil rights movement did successfully end *de jure* segregation, most forms of structural racism persist in the United States—specifically, people of color still have lower-than-average incomes, less access to health care and housing, and *de facto* segregation.[84] What Gelderloos advocates is tactical diversity—that is, the use of both nonviolent and violent tactics to achieve comprehensive social change. He believes that nonviolent approaches are tactically limited and thus incapable of instigating real, lasting, substantive change. He argues that "[Nonviolent] strategy can only create pressure and leverage; it can never succeed in destroying power or delivering control of society to the people."[85]

Churchill and Gelderloos make a related point that nonviolent movements are rarely completely nonviolent. Movement participants may periodically erupt into violence. Or a parallel group (often referred to as the "radical flank") may emerge that uses violence or threatens to take up arms in pursuit of the cause. Thus, these critics claim that violence (or the threat of violence) is ultimately what brings change. In their perspective, the gains of the civil rights struggle were achieved because of periodic riots and the threat of Black Power groups. Similarly, they argue that the Vietnam War eventually ended because of the Vietnamese armed struggle and the lethal resistance of ground troops within the U.S. military—not because of the U.S. antiwar movement. They argue that it is "historical manipulation and whitewashing" to claim that nonviolent movements achieved civil rights and brought an end to the Vietnam War.[86]

A closer look at Gelderloos and Churchill's points reveals that they are operating with a number of double standards.[87] Regarding the first point, it is a legitimate and accurate critique that many nonviolent movements have not gone far enough in transforming societies.[88] Yet the exact same criticism can be raised regarding armed movements—something that advocates of violence such as Gelderloos seldom acknowledge. As Brian Martin argues:

> Gelderloos doesn't give a single example of an armed struggle leading to the sort of liberated society that he espouses. Why not? Undoubtedly because successful armed struggles—such as in China, Cuba, Algeria and Vietnam—have not abolished the state but rather, if anything, have strengthened it. Armed struggle encourages militarization of the movement, making it more hierarchical and authoritarian. These features seldom wither away after revolutionary victories.[89]

An additional double standard is found in their assertion that nonviolent movement gains are actually attributable to violent impulses that accompany the struggle. Yet most violent conflicts entail both armed and unarmed forms of resistance. Hence a guerrilla group may violently attack the state while civic groups simultaneously engage in general strikes, boycotts, and demonstrations. So which type of action is ultimately responsible for undermining a regime? If nonviolent activists engage in historical whitewashing to credit nonviolent movements for victories, one can easily argue that Gelderloos and Churchill are doing the same thing in reverse: they attribute victory to violent actions when it may well be the nonviolent ones that were decisive.

The primary problem is these criticisms are typically not grounded in any empirical evidence. Hence critics' claims are little more than personal opinions about the factors that have the greatest impact. How do we know, for instance, that the real reason the Vietnam War ended was because of the armed resistance in Vietnam and mutiny within the U.S. military? Gelderloos and Churchill are guilty of the exact flaws that they accuse nonviolent activists of: namely, selectively picking historical examples and attributing power to one type of tactic over others without concrete evidence to support their claim. But there are empirical data available on the relative efficacy of armed versus unarmed struggle. When one looks at the careful and comprehensive evidence presented by Chenoweth and Stephan, it clearly indicates that nonviolence is generally more effective in achieving political goals than violence is.[90] And other studies have documented that violence is growing less and less effective in the contemporary era.[91]

Critique #2: Nonviolence Is Paternalistic and Imperialist

Gelderloos and Churchill also claim, inaccurately, that nonviolence is primarily a tool of white, privileged people from the Global North who counsel oppressed groups to patiently suffer for the cause. Gelderloos goes even further, arguing that nonviolent groups are racist since they take real power away from oppressed racial and ethnic groups by calling upon them to not strike back violently but to gently persuade opponents. Moreover, he argues that nonviolent advocates are sexist because they have not done enough to fight patriarchal systems.

These criticisms are a mixed bag. On the one hand, there is no doubt that many nonviolent movements could and should do more to challenge patriarchal and racist systems and attitudes. However, the same is also true for violent groups.[92] But does this critique of individual activists' shortcomings mean that we should dismiss an entire strategy and tactical repertoire? On the other hand, some of these premises clearly reflect misconceptions about nonviolence. For example, there is an assumption that suffering is an intrinsic part of a nonviolent struggle. While this may be true for principled nonviolent movements, it is not true for pragmatic nonviolent movements. Similarly, this criticism is grounded in the assumption that nonviolence is primarily about converting one's opponents when, as discussed earlier, many pragmatic nonviolent practitioners are willing to bring about social change through nonviolent coercion or structural disintegration.

Another related criticism is that nonviolence has been used for imperialistic purposes. Specifically, Gelderloos points to the recent nonviolent revolts in former communist regions such as Serbia, Georgia, and Ukraine. He argues that these nonviolent revolts "were actually orchestrated and financed by the U.S. to install more market-friendly, pro-U.S. politicians."[93] The U.S. government did provide financial support to key opposition groups, such as the Serbian movement Otpor that ousted President Slobodan Milošević. But, as Otpor organizers have emphatically stated, this was an indigenous movement, not a puppet organization for foreign interests. Stephen Zunes underscores how unrealistic such accusations are:

> In reality, the limited amount of financial support provided to opposition groups by the United States and other Western governments in recent years cannot *cause* a nonviolent liberal democratic revolution to take place any more than the limited Soviet financial and material support for leftist movements in previous decades could *cause* an armed socialist revolution to take place. As Marxists and others familiar with popular movements have long recognized, revolutions are the result of certain objective conditions. Indeed, no amount of money could force hundreds of thousands of people to leave their jobs, homes, schools, and families to face down heavily armed police and tanks and put their bodies on the line unless they had a sincere motivation to do so.[94]

It is unrealistic to claim that an entire population would take up an unarmed struggle against the state, something that might entail significant costs, simply because an outside nation tells them to do so. That view—that nonviolence is a weapon for U.S. imperial interests—paints a highly unflattering and paternalistic picture of citizens overseas who, like sheep, mindlessly do what the U.S. government dictates.[95] Nevertheless, these cases have generated debate among practitioners and scholars in the nonviolence field, many of whom have argued against the acceptance of outside funds precisely because it puts movements at risk for such accusations.

Criticism #3: Nonviolence Ensures a State Monopoly on Violence

Finally, critics contend that nonviolence will ultimately be ineffective since it preserves the state's violent capacities, ensuring that the government will always win since it has the ability to use force to preserve itself. But this premise is rooted in the misperception that nonviolent movements are largely passive and mostly rely on techniques of verbal persuasion. Such inaccuracies are evident in the following comments by Gelderloos: "nonviolence . . . glorifies passivity"[96] and

> Pacifism is a form of learned helplessness, through which dissidents retain the goodwill of the state by signifying that they have not usurped powers the state exclusively claims. . . . In this way, a pacifist behaves like a well-trained dog who is beaten by his master: rather than bite his attacker, he lowers his tail and signifies harmlessness, resigning himself to the beatings . . .[97]

What these critics do not understand is that civil resisters have the capacity to use force as well, but force of a different nature. By wielding the "weapons of nonviolence"—including social, political, and economic noncooperation—they can coerce the collapse of the state, which cannot function without the assistance and obedience of its citizens. There is absolutely nothing passive about boycotts, strikes, and civil disobedience.

CONCLUSION

In this chapter, I have clarified the distinctions between pacifism and nonviolence. I have explained several types of pacifism as well as the differences between principled and pragmatic nonviolence. Such conceptual clarifications reveal that many critics of nonviolence have dismissed or attacked this set of ideas and practices based on misconceptions and stereotypes that are not supported by empirical data. While there are still legitimate reasons to be skeptical of nonviolence, people must be familiar with the varied traditions, ideas, and practices before evaluating them.

CHAPTER 2

಄

Religious and Ethical Positions
on Violence and Nonviolence

"Truth is my God. Nonviolence is the means of realizing Him."
Mohandas Gandhi

"I tell you: love your enemies and pray for those who persecute you."
Gospel of Matthew 5:44

"Islam teaches tolerance, not hatred; universal brotherhood, not enmity; peace, and
not violence."

Parwez Musharraf

Religion has been a force for both war and peace. Religious leaders have sanctified wars, calling upon the faithful to fight for God's will on earth.[1] Religion has also served a tempering role, prescribing rules that will minimize retaliation and revenge. The Jewish Talmud, for instance, allows an injured person to have measure-for-measure retribution: "Your rule should be life for life, eye for eye, tooth for tooth, hand for hand, foot for foot."[2] Religion has additionally constrained war by specifying the circumstances under which war is justified. In the Christian just war tradition, for example, war can only be waged when all nonviolent means have been exhausted, when the goal is to restore peace, and when there is reasonable chance of winning. Finally, religion has been a force for nonviolence and peace. In short, most major religions have a history of holy wars and just wars as well as pacifism and nonviolence. Much has been written about religious-inspired terrorism as well as just war traditions. In this chapter, I briefly summarize some of this information. The bulk of this chapter, however, is devoted to an overview of the religious and ethical traditions that promote nonviolence. While many world religions do permit warfare under certain conditions, and thus cannot be classified as pacifist, every major religious tradition has sacred teachings, values, and practices that encourage nonviolence.

HOLY WARS

Religious elements are present in many wars. However, it is important to distinguish between "wars with religion" and "religious wars." The former term, "wars with religion," refers to cases in which religion supports wars that have secular goals. Thus chaplains may pray for soldiers being deployed to the battlefront and presidents may proclaim that God has blessed the nation with a victory. Yet such wars are fought for political purposes, such as defense against invasion (as in World War II) or promoting or opposing revolution (as in the Indochina war of the 1960s and 1970s). The latter term, "religious wars," is synonymous with holy wars; it refers to battles that have religious end goals, such as the establishment of a theocracy or gaining control over sacred places and territories.[3] Examples of religious wars include the Christian Crusades (eleventh through thirteenth centuries CE) and the Taliban's war against the Soviet invasion of Afghanistan.

Holy wars have several traits, listed in Table 2.1. First, as stated earlier, the end goal of the war is explicitly religious. The battle is seen as a necessary mechanism for implementing God's will. Second, religious leaders initiate holy wars, not political leaders. Third, soldiers are viewed as instruments of God. Thus combat is an act of religious devotion and all military acts are sacred, regardless of how brutal they may be. Fourth, since soldiers believe they are doing God's will, there are no limits on fighting; troops must do whatever is necessary to complete the task. Compromise is

---

Table 2.1. TRAITS OF HOLY WARS

1. War is motivated by a religious objective.
2. War is initiated by religious leaders.
3. Combat is an act of religious devotion.
4. There are no limits on fighting.
5. Those who die in battle are rewarded in the afterlife.

---

not an option since it is tantamount to compromising God's will. Fifth, death on the battlefield is valorized and those who die fighting for the cause are typically assured some type of celestial reward, such as salvation.[4]

RELIGION AND THE JUST WAR TRADITION

Religion has also played a key role in establishing the criteria that make war a justifiable option. In Western traditions, Greek philosopher Aristotle and Roman philosopher Cicero formally articulated just war principles. Similar policies are established in the Hebrew scriptures and the Qu'ran. Religious groups developed such principles to address a contradiction they faced: on the one hand, most of the major world religions teach that the taking of human life is wrong; on the other hand, states have a duty to protect their citizens and therefore require some type of defense system. To reconcile these opposing positions, theologians and philosophers developed criteria to discern what constitutes a just war, how combat should be conducted, and how wars should be concluded.[5]

There are numerous just war theories derived from various religious and philosophical positions. While there are variations, most approximate the following principles, established in the Catholic tradition by Augustine of Hippo (354–430) and Ambrose (340–397) and refined by Thomas Aquinas.[6] These principles specify (1) the conditions that justify the declaration of war (*jus ad bellum*); (2) how combat should be conducted (*jus in bello*); and (3) how to establish justice in the aftermath of war (*jus post bellum*).

I begin by exploring the conditions for declaring war. The first condition is *just cause*: war can only be used as a means of addressing a serious public threat, such as an invasion of an outside force or a massive human rights violation such as genocide. Second, only *legitimate state authorities* (i.e., those responsible for protecting their citizens) can declare war since war is only to be used for public purposes, not private ones. Third, a war must be motivated by *right intentions*. War cannot be motivated by ethnic hatred, revenge, material gain, or power. Moreover, combatants must not hold an attitude of self-righteousness; they must be fully cognizant of their opponents' humanity and regretful for the loss of life. Fourth, war cannot be declared unless there is a *probable chance of success*. It is not appropriate to wage war, which inevitably leads to suffering and loss, if the likelihood of winning is very low. Fifth is the principle of *proportionality*. This refers to the standard in which the good that will be accomplished through war must outweigh the totality of destruction and suffering that it will cause. If the evil generated through combat is greater than the good to be achieved, then war is not justified. Sixth, war can only be waged as a *last resort*. The use of military force is not permissible until all other options (including negotiations, diplomacy, and nonviolent pressure) have been exhausted.

Religious leaders within the just war tradition view war as a necessary evil. However, to minimize the evil, they set standards regarding how war should be waged. First, soldiers must act in accordance with the principle of *distinction*, which requires that civilians not be targeted. Second, all actions must comply with the principle of *minimum force*. The force of any attack must be limited to the amount that will achieve the military's objective—nothing more. Third, soldiers must act according to the principle of *proportionality*: no attacks should occur if the degree of civilian casualties outweighs any military advantages that are gained. Fourth, there must be *fair treatment for prisoners of war*. Any soldiers from the opposing side who surrender or are captured do not pose a threat and therefore torture, neglect, and other forms of mistreatment are not permitted. Fifth and finally, no weapons may be used that are evil or atrocious (*malum in se*)—for example, mass rape or weapons whose effects cannot be controlled.

In the contemporary era, ethicists have extended the just war tradition to guide the conclusion of wars.[7] To end war, there must be *a just cause for termination*—namely, that the injustices have been reasonably vindicated. Next, the opposing side must be willing to negotiate the terms of surrender, which can include compensation for damages, permission for war crime trials, and rehabilitative acts. All terms of surrender must comply with the *principle of proportionality*, meaning that no excessive or draconian measures can be taken against the defeated side. Also, victorious nations must distinguish between political and military leaders, combatants and civilians; punitive actions can only be taken against those who are directly responsible for the conflict. There must also be *right intention*, which specifies that victors may not exact revenge and they must also permit investigations into any war crimes that they may have committed. Finally, *legitimate political authorities* on both sides must accept the declaration of war's end and the peace agreements.

Although just war traditions have predominated most Western thinking and religious positions, there are many who have critiqued it (see Table 2.2). For instance, some have questioned whether we can accurately determine if a just cause truly exists since truth and accurate information is often the first casualty of conflict. Thus the U.S. invasion of Iraq was justified on the basis that Iraq purportedly had weapons of mass destruction—something that was later disproven. Others have asked how we measure

---

Table 2.2. PRINCIPLES AND CRITIQUES OF THE JUST WAR TRADITION

On Declaring War

Principles:

- The only just cause is addressing a serious public threat.
- Only legitimate state authorities can declare war.
- War must be motivated by "right intentions."
- War can only be waged if there is a probable chance of success.
- Proportionality: The good accomplished through war must outweigh the suffering it causes.
- War must be a last resort.

Critiques:

- Issues can be presented as a public threat when, in reality, they are not.
- "Right intentions" get easily lost in warfare.
- It is difficult to accurately assess the chance of success.
- Weapons of mass destruction render the principle of proportionality obsolete.
- It is difficult to determine whether all other means of addressing the conflict have been thoroughly exhausted.

On Conducting War

Principles:

- Distinction: No civilians should be targeted.
- Minimum force: Force should be limited to the amount needed to achieve the goal.
- Proportionality: Civilian casualties should not outweigh military advantages.
- Prisoners of war must be treated fairly.
- No evil or atrocious weapons can be used.

Critiques:

- Weapons of mass destruction violate the principles of distinction, minimum force, and proportionality.

On the Conclusion of War

- Just cause for termination: Injustices have been vindicated.
- Proportionality: No excessive measures can be imposed on the defeated.
- Punitive actions can only be imposed on those directly responsible for the conflict.
- Right intention: No revenge allowed.
- Legitimate political authorities must accept the peace agreement.

Critiques:

- Who determines what "excessive measures" are?

"last resort." How do we know if all alternatives have been exhausted? How long do we wait before declaring negotiations or sanctions a failure? And numerous critics have argued that war can never be just in today's world since there is no way to wage war in compliance with the principles of *jus in bello*. Nuclear, chemical, and biological weapons impose excessive consequences and cannot distinguish between combatants and civilians. Similarly, the principle of proportionality is nearly impossible to accurately assess. As one commentator noted, "How does one measure into the future the continuing hazard of exploding landmines and bombs, drug addiction, alcoholism, mental illness, physical crippling, suicide?"[8] Finally, critics maintain that once war begins, it is virtually impossible to uphold these humanitarian principles and ensure right intention. Thus some individuals have turned to nonviolence since they find that war is no longer a viable option. For others, the just war position is not acceptable because it compromises the original teachings of their religious traditions. These groups hearken back to the nonviolent teachings in various scriptures. In the next section, I summarize the traditions of nonviolence in several major world religions.

NONVIOLENCE IN EASTERN RELIGIONS

Nonviolence is a religious virtue in several Eastern religions, including Buddhism, Jainism, and Hinduism. In these three traditions, nonviolence is rooted in the concept of *ahimsa*—non-injury, or more accurately, the denunciation of the will to harm others.

Hinduism

The Hindu religion does not have one sacred text, deity, or teacher who is considered authoritative by all adherents. Hinduism comprises hundreds of sectarian groups and communities, each with its own spiritual texts and deities. Although there are some common texts that most Hindus consider canon (such as the *Vedas, Upanishads,* and the *Bhagavad Gītā*), Hinduism is essentially a fusion of religious traditions that are indigenous to the Indian subcontinent.[9] Nonetheless, there are some key concepts within Hinduism that support nonviolence.

To understand Hindu philosophy and beliefs, we need to introduce some central ideas. First, Hinduism promotes a belief in *karma.* In its literal form, karma means action. Within the texts known as the *Upanishads,* karma is described as a system of rewards and punishments that result from one's actions, a pattern of cause and effects. This is also linked to the Hindu belief in reincarnation. Karmic consequences can span multiple lifetimes. Thus the only way to end the cycle of death and rebirth is to achieve the transforming wisdom that comes when one experiences the relationship between the human soul (Ātman) and the supreme universal power known as *Brahman*.

The Vedic texts teach that all living beings are a manifestation of *Brahman*. Through this divine force, everything is interconnected and interdependent. When we forget this, a sense of separateness or duality arises that can lead to hatred and violence. Thus, to establish and maintain peace, individuals should renounce any sense of otherness and treat all people as one's own self. This point is underscored in the *Upanishads*, which implore people to "see one's own self in everything and everything in one's own self; then we will not hate anyone. In loving others we are loving ourselves, and when hurting others we are hurting ourselves, because we all carry the same divinity."[10] As individuals become aware of the unity of life, their consciousness progressively changes, approaching this supreme reality known as *Brahman*. It is through this new state of consciousness and spirituality that the human soul achieves immortality.[11]

The concept of *ahimsa*, or non-injury, is linked to this belief in treating others as one's own self. In fact, *ahimsa* is so central to the Hindu faith that it is listed as one of the five ethical virtues that adherents ought to embrace (along with austerity, righteousness, almsgiving, and truthfulness).[12] Several scholars note that *ahimsa* is not synonymous with Western notions of pacifism, conscientious objection to war, or civil disobedience. It is an ethical and philosophical concept that entails much more the refusal to harm or kill. Indeed, *ahimsa* refers to the antidote to all types of violence—physical harm, hatred, humiliation, and economic and cultural oppression. *Ahimsa* denounces selfishness and "otherness" and promotes the unity of all living beings. *Ahimsa* is a doctrine of equality, love, and compassion; it is a commitment to pursuing social good and preserving life.[13]

These Hindu concepts encourage adherents to live nonviolently. This is also evident in sacred Hindu texts. For example, the epic known as *Mahabharata*, which includes the *Bhagavad Gītā*, states that the practice of *ahimsa* enables individuals to free themselves from sin while acts of violence destroy faith and bring bad karmic consequences. The *Bhagavad Gītā* emphasizes that *ahimsa* is a divine quality that all should practice as it generates good karmic consequences.[14]

It is true that Hinduism, generally speaking, does permit warfare if combat can end injustice without creating greater evil or suffering. Indeed, for many Hindus, waging war under this circumstance is seen as a duty, based on the *Gita* story of Lord Krishna and the great military leader Arjuna. In the opening lines of the *Gita*, Arjuna finds himself on the front lines of a battlefield between forces of good and evil. He is reluctant to fight because he realizes that many relatives and friends are on the other side. He cannot bear to kill those he loves. Krishna, his charioteer, who is actually the Hindu god Vishnu, orders him not to be cowardly but to carry out his duty as a member of the warrior caste. As Arjuna's family and friends slaughter one another on the battlefield, Arjuna weeps.

This text, which is often seen as supporting war, is the very same text that heavily shaped Gandhi's thinking. Gandhi and other Hindu scholars interpret this story as an allegory in which the battlefield represents the soul.[15] Gandhi stated:

> I venture to submit that the *Bhagavad Gītā* is a gospel of noncooperation between the forces of darkness and those of light. . . . I do not believe that the *Gita* teaches violence for doing good. It is pre-eminently a description of the duel that goes on in our own hearts. The divine author has used a historical incident for inculcating the lesson of doing one's duty even at the peril of one's life. It inculcates performances of duty irrespective of the consequences, for, we mortals, limited by our physical frames, are incapable of controlling actions save our own. The *Gita* distinguishes between the powers of light and darkness and demonstrates their incompatibility.[16]

Moreover, Gandhi emphasized how the epic ended: with nearly everyone dead. He believed that one moral of this story is the futility of violence. Thus he encouraged Hindus to choose the exalted path of nonviolence since "*ahimsa* is the highest form of religion, virtue, and duty."[17]

Jainism

Religious mandates for nonviolence are also found in the Jain religion, which dates back to roughly 800 BCE.[18] Jainism is currently practiced by more than four million, most of whom live in India, where the religion was born. One of the most influential historically verifiable figures within Jainism is Pārśvanatha, who was part of India's renouncer tradition. Pārśvanatha was the twenty-third *tīrthaṅkara*, or person who has overcome the cycle of death and rebirth and can provide guidance to other Jains seeking liberation. Pārśvanatha preached the doctrine of *ahimsa*, the refusal to do any physical or emotional harm to other beings, and thus it became one of the religion's key defining traits. As the religion developed, observant Jains were expected to adhere to the following five vows: (1) nonviolence (*ahimsa*); (2) truthfulness (*satya*); (3) refusal to steal (*asteya*); (4) sexual restraint (*brahmacarya*); and (5) non-possession (*apari-graha*). These values influenced other Indian religious groups, including Buddhism and yoga traditions.[19]

The earliest texts within the Jain tradition include the first part of the *Acaranga Sutra*, dating to the fourth or fifth century BCE.[20] Several passages from this text support the Jain commitment to nonviolence. These include:

> All breathing, existing, living, sentient creatures should not be slain, nor treated with violence, nor abused, nor tormented, nor driven away. This is the pure, unchangeable, eternal law. (I.4.1)

> Injurious activities inspired by self-interest lead to evil and darkness. This is what is called bondage, delusion, death, and hell. To do harm to others is to do harm to oneself. You are the one whom you intend to kill! You are the one you intend to tyrannize over! We corrupt ourselves as soon as we intend to corrupt others. We kill ourselves as soon as we intend to kill others. (I.5.5)

> With due consideration preaching the law of the mendicants, one should do no injury to one's self, nor to anybody else, not to any of the four kinds of living beings. (I.6.5.4)

These scriptural passages indicate that nonviolence and the concept of *ahimsa* are central to this religious tradition. In fact, the Jain tradition is often summarized with the Hindu *Mahabharata* phrase *Ahimsā paramo dharmah*[21]—"nonviolence is the highest form of religious conduct."[22] By the second century of the Common Era, Jain scholar Umasvati taught that spiritual liberation can only be achieved in abiding by the five major vows of the religion, the first of which is nonviolence.

In more contemporary times, Jain scholars have elaborated the principle of *ahimsa* and its implications for daily living. Modern Jains are expected to be vegetarians and not wear silk, which kills countless silk worms in the production process. Jains must choose professions that minimize harm to animals and humans, and they show reverence for all life forms by carrying a small broom to sweep aside any insects before sitting or sleeping and by carrying a mouth-cloth to protect small air-borne organisms from their hot breath—to name just a few examples.[23]

Jainism has historically focused on personal discipline, asceticism, and strict individual practices in pursuit of spiritual development. Consequently, most Jains have been largely disengaged from the world, reflecting a position of nonresistance. However, a few Jain leaders have emphasized that nonviolence requires social engagement. For instance,

Acarya Tulsi (1917–1997) traveled throughout India, encouraging Jains to nonviolently fight against environmental degradation, ostracism of widows, child marriages, and Hindu–Sikh tensions.[24] He and others have helped pushed traditional Jain nonresistance toward a socially engaged faith.

Buddhism

The religious tradition of Buddhism was also born in India, approximately in the sixth century BCE. Not surprisingly, Buddhist beliefs were influenced by the presence of other Indian traditions, such as Hinduism. Buddhism, for instance, shares a belief in karma and reincarnation. Yet at the heart of Buddhist teachings are the "Four Noble Truths" and the "Eight-fold Path." Some Buddhists use medical imagery to depict these teachings: the Four Noble Truths diagnose the human condition while the Eight-fold Path describes the therapeutic action needed to address the condition.

In the legend of the Buddha's life, the young prince Siddhartha Gautama reached enlightenment after meditating under the Bodhi tree. Afterwards, he articulated what is now referred to as the Four Noble Truths. The first truth is that life is filled with suffering. All humans will encounter suffering through illness, death, experiences of failure and loss, and so forth. The second truth explains the origin of this suffering, which is our constant craving of comfort and security. Such craving and suffering can only be eliminated, according to the third truth, through the extinction of our desires. The fourth noble truth holds that humans can eliminate their desires and make personal improvements by following the Eight-fold Path.[25]

The Eight-fold Path defines the practices that Buddhists should pursue: right views, right thought, right speech, right conduct, right livelihood, right effort, right mindfulness, and right meditation. Although much of Buddhist practice focuses on the emotional and psychological elements of individual practitioners, Buddhist teachings also have a social dimension, particularly in regards to "right action." Right action is understood by many Buddhists to denote the refusal to kill (*ahimsa*) or steal and avoidance of sexual misconduct, false speech, and the use of intoxicants.[26] Thus nonviolence is an essential part of Buddhist practice.[27]

Buddhism also promotes nonviolence via its teachings on the antidotes to violence. This religion holds that the root causes of violence are hatred, greed, and delusion. Compassion can counter hatred, generosity can counter greed, and wisdom can counter delusion. Compassion develops through meditation, which can offer insight into the cause of another's behavior. [28] It also enables people to understand and address the true source of social conflicts rather than punitively responding to the symptoms. Buddhist monk Thich Nhat Hanh illustrates this through a meditation on a horrible event that happened to a refugee child in Southeast Asia:

> There are many young girls, boat people, who are raped by sea pirates. Even though the United Nations and many countries try to help the government of Thailand prevent that kind of piracy, sea pirates continue to inflict much suffering on the refugees. One day we received a letter telling us about a young girl on a small boat who was raped by a Thai pirate. She was only twelve, and she jumped into the ocean and drowned herself.

> When you first learn of something like that, you get angry at the pirate. You naturally take the side of the girl. As you look more deeply you will see it differently. If you take the side of the little girl, then it is easy. You only have to take a gun and shoot the pirate. But we cannot do that. In my meditation I saw that if I had been born in the village of the pirate and raised in the same conditions as he was, I am now the pirate. There is a great likelihood that I would become a pirate. I cannot condemn myself so easily. In my meditation, I saw that many babies are born along the Gulf of Siam, hundreds every day, and if we educators, social workers, politicians, and others do not do something about the situation, in 25 years a number of them will become sea pirates. That is certain. If you and I were born today in those fishing villages, we might become sea pirates in 25 years. If you take a gun and shoot the pirate, you shoot all of us, because all of us are to some extent responsible for this state of affairs.[29]

The Buddhist emphasis on overcoming delusion through the wisdom of interconnectedness is also linked to nonviolence. Interconnectedness stems from the Buddhist concept of non-dualism: all things, even so-called opposites, are intrinsically linked. There is no shadow without light, no death without life. One of the primary delusions that foster conflict and oppression is the self–other distinction, which privileges "us" over "them." Such divisions are present in numerous conflicts: in ethnic oppression, religious conflicts, class wars, nationalist movements, and ideologically based struggles. Such divisions fuel enmity and dehumanization that, in turn, make it easier to carry out violence. Moreover, as groups fight to achieve advantages for their own side, they fail to see how such violent conflicts have negative ramifications for all in the long run, even if

Jews also warned that they would die before they would allow the statue of Caligula to be installed. When Petronius asked if they were planning to wage war against Caesar, they replied:

> "We will not by any means make war with him; but still we will die before we will see our laws transgressed." So they threw themselves down upon their faces, and stretched out their throats, and said that they were ready to be slain; and this they did for forty days together, and in the meantime left off the tilling of the ground, and that while the season of the year required them to sow it. Thus they continued firm in their resolution, and proposed to themselves to die willingly, rather than to see the dedication of the statue.[45]

Hebrew scriptures also reveal that there is a long history of Jewish civil disobedience—that is, the deliberate decision to nonviolently break a law that one deems unconscionable. For instance, in the conflict between King Saul and David in the First Book of Samuel, Saul ordered his guards to kill the priests who aided and abetted David's escape. The guards refused. Also, in the Books of Maccabees in the Apocrypha, we see numerous instances where Jews continued to comply with Jewish dietary laws and circumcision practices, even though they were prohibited during the Hellenization period. Thus civil disobedience—one of the key tactics used in nonviolent struggle—has historically been part of the Jewish tradition.[46]

In summary, most Jewish scholars hold that violence is permissible for defensive purposes, yet many agree that the concept of *shalom* (peace) is the highest expression of Jewish morality.[47] In fact, some argue that it is the true essence of Judaism while the acceptance of war is a reflection of particular historical circumstances—namely, Jewish nationalism in the period of kingdoms and twentieth-century anti-Semitism.[48]

Christianity

Pacifism and nonviolent resistance have been part of the Christian religion from its inception. Up until the fourth century, Christians were pacifists.[49] The writings of church fathers—including Origen, Ireneaus, Tertullian, Hippolytus of Rome, Cyprianus, Arnobius, and Lactantius—indicate that they opposed Christian participation in war.[50] For example, early theologian Tertullian wrote, "Only without the sword can the Christian wage war: for the Lord has abolished the sword." And Justin, in dialogue with Trypho in approximately 160 CE, stated, "We ourselves were well conversant with war, murder, and everything evil, but all of us throughout the whole wide earth have traded in our weapons of war. We have exchanged our swords for plowshares, our spears for farm tools." And Maximilianus of Tebessa, the first documented Christian conscientious objector, was executed for his refusal to serve in the military in 295.[51] In short, many church historians have argued that the evidence substantiates the claim that, up until the time of Constantine, the early Christians were pacifist.[52]

But did Jesus advocate pacifist nonresistance? Or did he teach his followers to engage in nonviolent struggle? The answers to these questions reflect various interpretations of the "Sermon on the Mount"—the longest passage of Christ's teachings found in the Gospels. It reads:

> You have heard it was said, "An eye for an eye and a tooth for a tooth." But I say to you, do not resist one who is evil. But if anyone strikes you on the right cheek, turn to him the other also; and if anyone would sue you and take your coat, let him have your cloak as well; and if anyone forces you to go one mile, go with him two miles. . . . You have heard that it was said, "Love your neighbor and hate your enemy." But I tell you: love your enemies and pray for those who persecute you.[53]

Many have interpreted this passage as endorsing passivity and nonengagement in the face of conflict and oppression. Indeed, many Christian pacifist groups have based their nonresistance stance on this passage. Yet several theologians have argued that this is not an accurate interpretation of Christ's teachings.

This misunderstanding of the Sermon on the Mount stems from two sources: (1) trying to understand Christian scripture without any sociohistorical or cultural knowledge of first-century Palestine and its inhabitants[54] and (2) a mistranslation that occurred when King James commissioned an English version of the Bible. Regarding the latter point, theologian Walter Wink has argued that King James' translators made a grave error:

> When the court translators working in the hire of King James chose to translate antistenai as "Resist not evil," they were doing something more than rendering Greek into English. They were translating nonviolent resistance into docility. . . . The Greek word is made up of two parts: anti, a word still used in English for "against," and histemi, a verb which in it noun form (stasis) means violent rebellion, armed revolt. . . . The term generally refers to a potentially lethal disturbance or armed revolution. A proper translation of Jesus' teaching would then be, "Do not strike back at evil in kind. . . .. Do not retaliate against violence with violence.[55]

In other words, Christ is not telling his followers to passively accept oppression; rather, he is stating that resistance to injustice should be conducted without violence. This comports with the Scholars Version
translation: "Don't react violently against the one who is evil."

So how should Christians react to injustice and conflict? According to
Wink, Jesus advocates creative nonviolent resistance that catches the oppressors off guard and forces them to view the situation in a new light. He
bases this claim on the examples that Jesus offers in the Sermon on the
Mount. In the first example, Christ states, "If anyone strikes you on the
right cheek, turn to him the other also." Drawing upon sociohistorical information about Jesus' era and culture, Wink reveals that using one's left
hand for routine purposes was strictly forbidden; the left hand was desig-
nated solely for "unclean tasks." But how does one strike an adversary's
right cheek using only the right hand? A fist punch isn't possible. Neither
is a slap. The only viable way to carry out such a blow is through a backhanded slap. As Wink puts it: "We are dealing here with insult, not a fist
fight. The intention is clearly not to injure but to humiliate, to put someone in his or her place. . . . A backhand slap was the usual way of admonish-
ing inferiors. Masters backhanded slaves; husbands, wives; parents,
children; Romans, Jews."[56]

Why would Christ encourage those who are backhanded (i.e., the oppressed) to turn the other cheek? Because in turning their cheek, they
undermine the oppressor's ability to humiliate. The only way to strike the
other cheek is with your fist or open palm—either of which was limited to
those considered peers. In other words, in turning the other cheek, people
are refusing to comply with the stratification system that grants one
group power over the other. In turning the other cheek, people force their
opponents to deal with them as equals. In turning the other cheek, they
undermine the adversary's power to humiliate and denigrate.

The second example in the Sermon on the Mount can also be interpreted as advocating nonviolent resistance. "If anyone would sue you
and take your coat, let him have your cloak as well." This reflected the
pervasive problem of indebtedness in Palestine, which was partially due
to Roman imperialism that heavily taxed the rich. To generate more
funds, the rich raised interest rates on loans. Thus Christ was speaking
to the many people who found themselves so far in debt that they only
had the clothes on their backs to offer as collateral. If they failed to
repay the loans and were brought to court to forfeit their coats, Jesus
advised them to hand over their shirts as well. This is not to be interpreted as surrendering to an exploitive system; rather, by stripping off
their clothes, they brought shame to the moneylenders. Nudity was

prohibited in Judaism; however, shame did not fall on the naked party but rather the person viewing or causing it. Thus, in Wink's words, "The creditor is revealed to not be a 'respectable' moneylender but a party in the reduction of an entire social class to landlessness and destitution. . . . [I]t offers the creditor a chance to see . . . what his practices cause and to repent."[57]

Christ underscores his point with a third and final example: "if anyone forces you to go one mile, go with him two miles." Here Jesus is referring to a common practice during the Roman occupation of Palestine. Roman law dictated the amount of forced labor that its military was permitted to impose on local inhabitants. Specifically, Roman troops could stop Palestinians and force them to carry the soldier's backpack for up to one mile. This law had a two-fold purpose: on the one hand, the practice of forcing local residents to carry a backpack served as a reminder that they are a subjected people living under occupation; on the other hand, the law enabled the empire's troops to remain mobile but, by limiting the distance, it minimized the amount of resentment that this practice might generate. So why, then, would Jesus admonish his followers to help an exploitive foreign force? According to Wink's analysis, Christ is offering a subjected people a way to assert their dignity and reclaim their power. By voluntarily going the second mile, the decision-making power shifts from the soldier to the pack carrier. This action would force the Roman soldier to see the pack carrier as a person of agency, not a powerless victim. As Wink states, even if this type of nonviolent confrontation did little to subvert the Roman empire, it nonetheless empowered the oppressed.[58]

This tradition of Christian pacifism and nonviolent resistance was radically altered in the fourth century, when Constantine converted to Christianity. Given his political leadership, he wanted to reconcile Christ's teachings to love one's enemy with his duty to protect the citizens of his empire. This led to the development of the just war tradition, which has been the dominant Christian position ever since. Yet various Christian groups, such as the Franciscans and the historic peace churches (Quakers, Mennonites, and Church of the Brethren), have kept the nonviolent legacy alive over the centuries.[59]

Islam

Since the 2001 al Qaeda attacks on New York City's World Trade Towers and the Pentagon, much attention has been given to the Islamic concept of *jihad*. Journalists often stated that the term denotes an armed holy war in

SECULAR HUMANISM

Nonviolent principles and values are found in all the major world religions, yet religious faith is not a prerequisite for embracing nonviolent action. Indeed, secular groups and individuals have advocated for nonviolence based on ethical values that transcend any religious teachings.[72] Many of these organizations propose that basic respect for human life requires that we treat all people equally and find methods of resolving conflict that do not involve violence. For instance, the American Anti-Slavery Society, led by Frederick Douglass and William Lloyd Garrison, held that both slavery and war were immoral since they used people for economic and political purposes.[73] Women in the suffrage movement called for not only equal treatment of women but also an end to war. Early feminists, such as Jane Addams and Carrie Chapman Catt, formed the Women's Peace Party in 1915 to provide a platform for addressing gender equality and the nonviolent resolution of world conflicts. Representatives from this group formed the Women's International League for Peace and Freedom, one of the earliest transnational nonviolence organizations.[74]

Perhaps the clearest example of a secular humanist organization committed to nonviolence is the War Resisters League (WRL). In fact, several scholars have argued that the WRL epitomizes the "secularization of conscience" that emerged after World War I, as people from varied backgrounds became disillusioned with war.[75] Jessie Wallace Hughan founded WRL in 1923.[76] Hughan had been involved in both suffragist and pacifist groups. Yet she sought to form a mixed-sex organization that was open to all who opposed war, regardless of their religious or political orientation. Her proposal to create WRL was endorsed by the Fellowship of Reconciliation, a religiously based nonviolence organization, who saw the new organization as an important secular partner. The creed of WRL members is quite simple: "War is a crime against humanity. I, therefore, am determined not to support any kind of war, international or civil, and to strive for the removal of all the causes of war."[77] With its officially pluralist stance, this organization drew members from a broader array of backgrounds and motives, although a large number were socialists, anarchists, and secular radicals from other traditions.[78] Yet their opposition to war was rooted in the conviction that such violence is a violation of human dignity.

During the 1960s and 1970s, Barbara Deming—a well-known American feminist—also endorsed nonviolence on a purely secular basis. Deming argued that basic humanist values, such as justice, are at the heart of civil resistance. Moreover, nonviolence is rooted in the value of respect, which every person deserves by virtue of being human. Respect, she argued, means allowing people to have basic rights and freedoms. Deming believed that nonviolence does not deprive individuals of any of the freedoms that they are entitled to, yet it does deprive opponents of their ability to oppress and exploit others—which they had no right to do in the first place. Moreover, like Gandhi, Deming believed that the means of social change affect the end result. Therefore, if civil resisters are working toward a society that respects all people and affords them justice and equal rights, the movement must embody this in its interactions with opponents. Nonviolence, she argued, is the only method of resistance that does this: it is a means of demanding one's own rights while simultaneously respecting the rights of adversaries. She wrote, "We assert the respect due ourselves, when it is denied, through noncooperation; we assert the respect due all others, through our refusal to be violent."[79]

To achieve a society in which all people are treated justly and respectfully, Deming assumed that some coercive capacity was needed to force oppressors to change their policies and practices. Yet she maintained that nonviolent resistance was the most effective coercive power, precisely because it is disruptive but shows respect for the opponent. She stated,

> This is the heart of my argument: We can put *more* pressure on the antagonist for whom we show human concern. It is precisely solicitude for his person in combination with a stubborn interference with his actions that can give us a very special degree of control (precisely in our acting both with love, if you will—in the sense that we respect his human rights—and truthfulness, in the sense that we act out fully our objections to his violating our rights). We put upon him two pressures—the pressure of our defiance of him and the pressure of our respect for his life—and it happens that in combination these two pressures are uniquely effective.[80]

In short, Deming felt that the humanist values of justice and respect are a sufficient ethical basis for committing oneself to nonviolent methods of change.

CONCLUSION

Ethical and moral commitments to nonviolence may be rooted in religious teachings or secular values. As this chapter shows, the scriptures of major world religions can be interpreted as endorsing nonviolent action. However, these same scriptures have also been interpreted as resources into campaigns for political office, as was the case of Ross Perot, who ran in the 1992 presidential election, and Steve Forbes, who ran in the 2008 presidential primary.[2] High-ranking military leaders, such as General Dwight Eisenhower or General Colin Powell, have readily stepped out of military positions and into political positions. And retired politicians often land corporate lobbying jobs after rewarding businesses with government and military contracts.

Moreover, those within this power elite use their influence to help each other out. This was evident in the United Farm Workers' (UFW) struggle of the 1960s. In a campaign to win union recognition, fair wages, and safer working conditions, the UFW launched a boycott of California grapes.[3] As a result of savvy organizing and campaigning, the farm workers made a serious dent in the growers' profits: grape sales declined 12 percent on the national level and were down as much as 50 percent in some of the major cities.[4] When intimidation and threats failed to stop the movement, the California growers turned to their governor, Ronald Reagan. Reagan appealed to President Richard Nixon, who assisted the growers by persuading the Department of Defense to purchase the grapes for soldiers serving in Vietnam. In short, the *state* intervened to save a *big business* by getting the *military* to buy their product. Over the course of several years, the U.S. armed forces purchased nearly ten million pounds of grapes to bail out agribusiness elites.[5] As Mills stated, the ties between business, federal government, and the military are strong and reinforcing. Thus labor activists, fighting a local business, found themselves up against powerful national leaders and institutions.

Citizen-Based Power

Yet a closer look at the farm workers' movement illustrates that the power elite is not undefeatable. Although the UFW members were up against formidable opponents, they eventually won the struggle. Although Mills may well be correct that members of the power elite structure their institutions to reinforce their privilege and influence, this does not mean that citizens are powerless. Indeed, nonviolent strategies—such as those used by the UFW—are rooted in an alternative view of power. In contrast to the elite-based theory, this "pluralistic" or citizen-based theory[6] holds that the real source of power is found in the population, not elites. Citizens have numerous forms of power that they can use to support a state or to undermine it. If people are determined and committed, then they simply need to develop a strategy to systematically withhold key sources of citizen-based power that a government needs in order to function.

Several political thinkers have emphasized that citizens' primary form of power is their obedience and consent. If people obey a government and cooperate with it, then they give their power to political rulers. But when they refuse to do so, they undermine and obstruct state power. Sixteenth-century French philosopher Étienne de la Boétie articulated this concept in his work *The Politics of Obedience: The Discourse of Voluntary Servitude.* His primary argument is that most people obey governments, and such compliance enables rulers to sustain power. But even a dictator is but a single individual, and there is no way that he or she could command the obedience of others; rather, as Boétie argues, citizens make a choice (sometimes begrudgingly) to comply with tyrants. Boétie writes:

> I should like merely to understand how it happens that so many men, so many villages, so many cities, so many nations, sometimes suffer under a single tyrant who has no other power than the power they give him; who is able to harm them only to the extent to which they have the willingness to bear with him; who could do them absolutely no injury unless they preferred to put up with him rather than contradict him. Surely a striking situation! Yet it is so common that one must grieve the more and wonder the less at the spectacle of a million men serving in wretchedness, their necks under the yoke, not constrained by a greater multitude than they . . .[7]

According to Boétie, if people wish to get rid of oppressive rulers, then war is not needed; the solution is simply to stop cooperating and obeying:

> Resolve to serve no more, and you are at once freed. I do not ask that you place hands upon the tyrant to topple him over, but simply that you support him no longer; then you will behold him, like a great Colossus whose pedestal has been pulled away, fall of his own weight and break in pieces.[8]

American writer Henry David Thoreau articulated the same idea. In his 1849 essay "On Civil Disobedience," Thoreau wrote about the Mexican–American War, which he felt was immoral and motivated by purely material interests. He argued that if people opposed the war, then they had an obligation to withdraw all forms of support from it. He stated:

> It is not a man's duty, as a matter of course, to devote himself to the eradication of any, even the most enormous, wrong; he may still properly have other

concerns to engage him; but it is his duty, at least, to wash his hands of it, and, if he gives it no thought longer, not to give it practically his support. . . . Unjust laws exist: shall we be content to obey them, or shall we endeavor to amend them, and obey them until we have succeeded, or shall we transgress them at once? Men generally, under such a government as this, think that they ought to wait until they have persuaded the majority to alter them. . . . If the injustice is part of the necessary friction of the machine of government, let it go, let it go: perchance it will wear smooth—certainly the machine will wear out. If the injustice has a spring, or a pulley, or a rope, or a crank, exclusively for itself, then perhaps you may consider whether the remedy will not be worse than the evil; but if it is of such a nature that it requires you to be the agent of injustice to another, then, I say, break the law. Let your life be a counter-friction to stop the machine. What I have to do is to see, at any rate, that I do not lend myself to the wrong which I condemn.[9]

Yet if the solution is simply refusing to cooperate with an unjust system, why are so many people compliant? Why do they obey ruthless and corrupt leaders? There are numerous reasons why citizens comply with oppressive systems. To begin with, people are taught to be obedient from a young age. We are told to obey our parents, teachers, religious leaders, and the law. By the time we reach adulthood, it is a deeply ingrained habit. Others are obedient for instrumental purposes since authorities often reward compliant individuals. Another reason for obedience is the fear of sanctions. Citizens may not want to risk arrest, imprisonment, or other punishments. Others may believe that they have a moral or religious obligation to comply. Finally, citizens may feel a sense of resignation. They may not believe that resistance will make a difference; indeed, they may have no hope that the future can be better.

Due to widespread obedience, a significant part of any resistance struggle—whether it is violent or nonviolent—is to break through these cultural and ideological barriers that keep people compliant. In the next section, I look at how this theory of citizen-based power has been translated into movements of civil resistance. I first look at the strategy of principled nonviolence. Then I turn to the strategy behind pragmatic nonviolence.

STRATEGIES OF NONVIOLENT ACTION

Precisely how does this notion of citizen-based power translate into nonviolent action for social change? Gandhi was the first to articulate a systematic strategy that is grounded in this conceptualization of power. He blended ideas about disobedience with his own philosophy of *satyagraha* ("truth force") to create a battle plan to win political independence through principled nonviolent resistance.

Gandhian Strategy of Principled Nonviolent Action

Paralleling Boétie and Thoreau's ideas, Gandhi argued that it would simply be impossible for the British to control and dominate India's three hundred million citizens if those citizens refused to cooperate. Thus, as the struggle for Indian independence began, he developed an overarching strategy that consisted of nine steps, listed in Table 3.1.

The first step is *negotiating* with one's opponent. Before any action is taken, citizen resisters need to do preliminary work that includes collecting and analyzing facts, speaking with their adversaries, and attempting to identify common interests and concerns. Civil resisters must also explain their concerns and propose clear solutions. This step is designed to develop personal and cooperative relationships with the opponent, and it gives the other side a chance to voluntarily make changes.[10] In many instances, however, the adversaries are unlikely to agree to the proposed changes since they will not want to relinquish the power, privilege, and benefits that result from their domination. Thus, if they refuse to change, civil resisters move to the second step: *preparing the group for direct action.*

Since Gandhi insisted that the fight for Indian independence must be conducted in the spirit of *satyagraha*, it was imperative to train participants to maintain a nonviolent approach in their thoughts, words, and deeds. Part of this training is encouraging *satyagrahis* to discern their motives,

---

Table 3.1. GANDHI'S STRATEGIC STEPS IN CIVIL RESISTANCE[11]

---

1. Negotiate with the opponent.
2. Prepare resisters for direct action.
3. Engage in acts of agitation (to demonstrate level of opposition).
4. Issue an ultimatum.
5. Implement economic boycotts and strikes (to undermine the state's finances).
6. Implement campaigns of noncooperation (to demonstrate the state's lack of power).
7. Implement campaigns of civil disobedience.
8. Usurp government functions.
9. Build parallel government institutions.

---

since any desire to defeat or humiliate the opponent would undermine the campaign's effectiveness.[12] Gandhi also wanted participants to be fully aware of the consequences they faced; they needed to be capable of accepting suffering without retaliating.

Once cadres of *satyagrahis* were prepared, the third step—*agitation*—could be implemented. Agitation can consist of demonstrations, marches, protests, pickets, and other methods of showing adversaries the level of opposition that they face. Yet such actions are merely expressions of opposition, not acts of resistance.

Before resistance is implemented, Gandhi argued that opponents should be given another chance to meet the movement's demands. Thus the fourth step is *issuing an ultimatum*. Resisters make a final appeal, explaining that changes need to be made immediately or the state will face direct action campaigns. If the ultimatum is ignored or refused, then civil resisters can begin to incrementally undermine various elements of state support.

The next steps entail acts of resistance. In the fifth step, civil resisters *undermine the state's financial base* through labor strikes and economic boycotts. In the sixth step, citizens *refuse to cooperate;* this includes withdrawal from public institutions, social practices, and business as usual. It also includes encouraging soldiers to refuse orders to arrest or repress resisters. In the seventh step, civil resisters *refuse to comply with unjust laws.* This may entail the refusal to pay taxes or carry government-issued identity cards. After these steps have been implemented, the population becomes ungovernable, thereby showing state leaders that they have no capability of ruling without popular consent.

In the final steps, civil resisters begin *taking over government functions* (step 8) and *building an independent parallel government* (step 9), rendering the unjust or illegitimate state obsolete. Thus citizens are encouraged, for example, to stay out of government courts, choosing instead to bring their disputes to a movement-based arbiter. Instead of attending public schools, citizens are encouraged to form their own independent schools.

The key idea behind Gandhi's strategy was to demonstrate to political elites that they have no intrinsic power and cannot govern a people who choose not to cooperate. The strategy is also designed to withhold any incentives for retaining political power, such as the economic benefits achieved through taxation and sale of government services to the broader population. The final steps, of building a parallel government, facilitate the transition to a new state by creating foundational institutions before the old regime has been overthrown. It also shows political elites that they are not needed; indeed, their positions have become unnecessary. Each

step, therefore, works to incrementally undermine the incumbent political system and build a new one.

Gandhi's strategy gained credibility and visibility when it was used to
win Indian independence from Great Britain. Enthusiastic observers emulated it in various contexts around the world.[13] Yet Gandhi argued that
these steps should not be used as a purely pragmatic way to win one's
goals. He emphasized that this strategy must be carried out in a nonviolent spirit—that is, in the spirit of *satyagraha* or the pursuit of truth. If
nonviolent campaigns are implemented with a coercive or hate-driven
spirit, they would not be successful, he posited, even if the opponents
were forced to capitulate.

To ensure that the movement held to the spirit of *satyagraha*, he developed a code of conduct, specifying how civil resisters should behave. This
code is listed in Table 3.2.

This code serves a number of functions within a civil resistance campaign. When observed by all participants, it ensures nonviolent discipline
and respect for the opponent. Without adherence to this code, anger can
easily escalate, making it difficult for opponents to see the justness of the
cause. Also, any deviation from nonviolent discipline can provide fodder
for the conflict and justification for a state crackdown. This code is also
designed to maintain internal cohesion, minimizing the chance for adversaries to exploit divisions within the movement. Most importantly,
the code ensures that a *satyagraha* campaign promotes the search for
truth and a mutually acceptable outcome. In Gandhi's principled approach, coercing the opponent is not desirable. The goal, he argued, is to

---

Table 3.2. GANDHI'S CODE OF CONDUCT FOR *SATYAGRAHIS*[14]

---

1. Harbor no anger but suffer the anger of the opponent. Refuse to return the assault of an opponent.
2. Do not submit to any order given in anger, even if doing so may risk severe punishment.
3. Refrain from insults and swearing.
4. Protect opponents from insults and physical attacks, even if it means risking your own life.
5. Do not resist arrest.
6. Refuse to surrender any property that is being held in trust.
7. If you are taken prisoner, behave in an exemplary manner.
8. Comply with the orders of *satyagraha* leaders; resign from the group in the event of a serious disagreement.
9. Do not expect any guarantees for the maintenance of your dependents.
10. Persistently search for avenues of cooperation with the opponent on honorable terms.
11. Refuse to surrender or compromise essentials in negotiation.

---

get the other side to understand your concerns, to see that your goals are just, and eventually to come to an agreement. That is why Gandhi emphasized that *satyagrahis* should explore avenues for helping opponents; this demonstrates the desire to reach agreement, not simply to defeat one's adversary.[15]

A related aspect of a *satyagraha* campaign is that Gandhi discouraged civil resisters from compromising on essential goals.[16] To capture the reasons why, several scholars have developed the idea of a "Gandhian dialectic." The dialectic dynamic was articulated by Greek philosophers, who noted that advancement occurs through an interaction of opposites: one side makes an assertion (or thesis) while the other side makes an opposite claim (or antithesis). Through this exchange, the best insights of both can be integrated, leading to a more informed position (synthesis). A *satyagraha* campaign also begins with the premise of limited truths since Gandhi believed that no human was capable of possessing absolute truth. Hence *satyagrahis* must cling to truth as they know it, refusing to compromise, while simultaneously recognizing that they might be in error. They actively persuade the opponent of their truth claims—for example, that Indian independence is the best solution—while simultaneously inviting adversaries to do the same. *Satyagrahis* must be unceasingly open to others' views but they should never compromise on key matters unless they become convinced that it is the most just and truthful thing to do. The premise of the Gandhian dialectic, therefore, is that an open-minded exchange will lead both sides to a more informed and accurate understanding of the conflict. As their views are synthesized, *satyagrahis* and their opponents come closer to a shared perspective and solution. In short, nonviolent conflict is a truth-creating process.

Paul Wehr cogently describes how the Gandhian dialectic differs from compromise. He writes:

> [O]nce conflict materializes, the Gandhian technique proceeds in a manner qualitatively different from compromise. What results from the dialectical process of conflict of opposite positions as acted upon by satyagraha, is a synthesis, not a compromise. The satyagrahi is never prepared to yield any position which he holds to be the truth. He is, however, prepared—and this is essential—to be persuaded by his opponent that the opponent's is the true, or the more nearly true, position. In the working out of the Gandhian dialectical approach, each side may, of course, yield through dissuasion any part of its position. But this is **not** compromise. When persuasion has been effected, what was once the opponent's position is now the position of both antagonist and protagonist. There is no sacrificing of position, no concession to

the opponent with the idea of buying him over. Non-violent resistance and persuasion must continue until mutually agreeable adjustment. Such adjustment will be a synthesis of the two positions and will be an adjustment satisfactory to both parties in the conflict. There is no victory in the sense of triumph of one side over the other. Yet, there is no compromise, in the sense in which each side would concede parts of its previous position solely to effect a settlement. There is no "lowering" of demands, but an aiming at a "higher" level of adjustment which creates a new, mutually satisfactory, resolution. (Bondurant, 1965:197) What unfolded in the Gandhian dialectic was a process similar in many ways to the consensus formation traditionally used by Quaker bodies and in certain traditional political systems (Bourdieu, 1962). No one wins or loses. Antagonists arrive at a "meeting of the minds," so to speak.[17]

Another hallmark of a *satyagraha* campaign is that acts of civil resistance are accompanied by a "constructive program." While civil resistance is aimed at the opponent, constructive programs are aimed at building one's own community. In the Indian independence movement, the constructive program included improving basic education and health and promoting economic development and social equality.[18] While civil resistance removes structures of oppression, the constructive program builds new structures of affirmation.

To illustrate the strategy of principled nonviolence, I offer a summary of the Gandhian Indian independence movement.[19] The movement had three major phases: noncooperation (1919–1922); civil disobedience and the salt *satyagraha* campaign (1930–1931); and the Quit India campaign (1940–1942). The first phase began when the British passed legislation that allowed the colonial regime to take unprecedented measures against any Indian suspected of sedition. Under these measures, Indians could be arrested without warrant and had no rights to legal counsel. Anyone's home could be searched, and traditional standards, such as evidence of wrongdoing, were not observed. In response, Gandhi and his followers engaged in a general strike. A British military leader, Brigadier-General Reginald Dyer, upped the ante by banning all public meetings. Drawing upon the tactic of civil disobedience, a crowd gathered in the town of Amritsar to defy the ban and to plan a course of resistance. Dyer decided to crack down, ordering his troops to shoot into the crowd. Within ten minutes, they had killed 379 civilians and wounded an additional 1,137. Subsequently, martial law was imposed and hundreds were arrested and imprisoned.

Yet the massacre created a backlash, ultimately leading to an investigation. To subdue public outrage, the British colonial government made a few concessions. Gandhi and other Indian leaders called these actions inadequate and unsatisfactory. In the spirit of *satyagraha*, they were not willing to compromise on their essential demands; they moved forward with their goal of convincing the British to leave India voluntarily, thereby winning complete independence. Thus Gandhi called for a new campaign that entailed four stages of noncooperation: (1) resignation of titles and honors (to symbolize the illegitimacy of British control); (2) resignation from civil service (to withhold the skills and labor needed to operate the state); (3) resignation from the police and military (to undermine the state's repressive power); and (4) refusal to pay taxes (to undermine the state's financial basis).

This noncooperation phase ended when Gandhi was thrown in prison, having pled guilty to charges of sedition since he readily admitted that he aimed to overthrow the British government. During his incarceration and immediately upon his release, Gandhi focused on the implementation of a "constructive program" in India. In particular, he emphasized the importance of Hindu–Muslim unity since he knew that the British had historically exploited this tension to maintain control over India. He also worked to end untouchability, the discriminatory practices against India's lowest caste. And he promoted spinning and the wearing of the traditional Indian clothing. This was designed to instill pride in Indian traditions and customs. Moreover, in encouraging people to wear homespun clothing, he challenged the global trade system whereby Indians imported expensive Western clothing that profited the English but put Indians into debt. In short, it was a way to promote economic self-sufficiency and limit foreign debt.

The second phase of resistance began in 1930. True to the principled strategy, the movement, represented by the Indian National Congress, issued an ultimatum to the British: grant the demands (dealing with various taxes, tariffs, and currency exchange rates, among others) or face a civil disobedience campaign. When the British refused to make any changes, Gandhi implemented the salt campaign. He focused on salt because the salt tax affected all Indians and because British control of it reflected the colonial dynamics of controlling a resource that belonged to Indians, not the British.

Gandhi began his civil disobedience salt campaign with a traditional Asian practice: the *padayatra* or long spiritual march. As he marched through villages on his way to the sea, a trek of nearly 250 miles, thousands of participants joined in. When he reached the Indian Ocean, on the anniversary of the Amritsar massacre, he took a handful of mud from the sea and declared that the movement would free Indians from

British rule. He then boiled the sea water to make salt, an illegal act that defied the British monopoly on salt production. Tens of thousands of Indians followed his example. Other campaigns of resistance followed, including the picketing of stores that sold foreign clothing, the burning of British-made clothing, and withholding of rent to British landlords. With every action, Gandhi also encouraged a constructive program whereby members of the untouchable caste (known as "dalits") worked alongside members of higher castes. Similarly, he insisted that Hindus and Muslims work together. Although some criticized this as a distraction from the goal of winning independence, Gandhi emphasized that personal and cultural transformation was the end goal as much as political transformation.

During the salt campaign, Gandhi was arrested. The British believed that the movement would falter without his leadership, but they were wrong. Civil resisters persisted, launching a nonviolent raid on the Dharasana salt works. With Western journalist Webb Miller documenting the event, wave after wave of *satyagrahis* marched up to the salt production facility. Wielding steel-tipped poles, soldiers clubbed them down but the civil resisters did not strike back. The sheer brutality of the attacks generated backlash as many began to sympathize with the Indian movement and question the legitimacy of British control. The salt campaign ended when the British invited Gandhi to London to discuss Indian independence.

The London talks were a disappointment, however, so Gandhi returned to India and launched the movement's third and final phase in August 1942.[20] This phase, known as the Quit India campaign, began with an inaugural speech whereby Gandhi warned that "We shall either free India or die in the attempt; we will not live to see the perpetuation of our slavery."[21] Shortly after his speech, Gandhi and other National Congress leaders were imprisoned, but civil resistance continued unabated. Although the British government had banned protest marches, *satyagrahis* held major demonstrations, processions, and general strikes. During these events, they hoisted the flag of free India, symbolically proclaiming their freedom. In response, British officials made mass arrests, incarcerating roughly 100,000 civil resisters and even publicly flogging demonstrators.[22] The arrests did not weaken the movement: civil resisters persisted, nonviolently raiding municipal government facilities and developing local parallel government institutions.

The Quit India campaign had largely subsided by March 1943, but the resistance had generated such international pressure that the British felt compelled to end the conflict. Moreover, British political leaders were aware that they would never regain control or authority since Indians had proven that they were capable of making the country ungovernable. Also, Indian boycotts of British textiles meant that this colony was no longer economically beneficial for the United Kingdom. Consequently, the British granted India independence in 1947. The *satyagrahis* had defeated one of the greatest military powers in the world, and they did so without picking up arms.

Pragmatic Strategy of Nonviolent Action

Gandhi's approach to nonviolent resistance is highly strategic yet it also entails the discovery of a deeper, spiritual "truth force" that is personally transformative. Eventually, some nonviolent strategists, most notably Gene Sharp, proposed an alternative model: they called for a pragmatic approach that removes the moral and spiritual aspects of Gandhi's *satyagraha* and promotes nonviolence as simply an alternative way of fighting. In many ways, Sharp's pragmatic strategy closely resembles Gandhi's principled strategy since it is derived from the same premise of citizen-based power. Moreover, Sharp's methods of action are largely drawn from his analysis of Gandhi's campaigns. Thus he builds off Gandhi's ideas but extends them in distinct ways.

Sharp introduces his nonviolent strategy by identifying the various power sources that citizens possess. He discusses six types of power that the population controls.[23] First, citizens can refuse to grant leaders *legitimacy or authority*. Authority is not intrinsic to an individual; as Max Weber noted long ago, authority is bestowed upon a leader when the population decides this individual has the legitimate right to rule. Yet there are numerous examples when leaders proclaim authority and people refuse to acknowledge it—such as after the fraudulent 1986 elections in the Philippines or Ukraine in 2004. Outraged citizens simply rejected the election results.

A second source of citizen-based power is *obedience and cooperation*.[24] While political rulers may legislate laws and implement policies, citizens always have a choice of whether they will comply with these edicts. In Nazi-occupied Europe, for example, many people refused to cooperate with the policy of detaining Jews and sending them to concentration camps. Instead, people in the Netherlands, France, Poland, and other countries warned Jewish friends and neighbors, hid them in their homes, and helped them escape.[25] The state may have the power to approve laws but people have the power to obey or disobey them.

The third source of citizen-based power is *skills and knowledge*. Every political system is dependent upon citizens' talents to keep society functioning. No single ruler is able to maintain communications and transportation systems, financial markets, industrial factories, sanitation and health care facilities, and the criminal justice system. It is only when citizens provide these forms of labor that a society can operate. If they choose to withhold their skills through a general strike, then the population can paralyze an entire nation.

Material resources is the fourth source of citizen-based power. Put simply, states need money to function. They get their funds from different sources, including taxes, sale of government services, the export of national resources controlled by the state, and international aid and loans. Citizens directly control some of these financial resources: for example, people may refuse to pay taxes or purchase government goods and services. In other instances, they may persuade international donors to withhold aid and foreign countries to boycott exported items. In various ways, then, citizens can drain the state's coffers, making it difficult for a government to operate.

Cultural and ideological factors are the fifth source of citizen-based power. Political leaders may use religious and cultural beliefs to encourage obedience to the state. For instance, some rulers have proclaimed a divine right to rule. If they are able to convince people that they are God's appointed leader on earth, then there is a lower chance of rebellion since this would be viewed as rebellion against God's will. Ideologies of patriotism can also be used to encourage submission to the government, even a corrupt one. Yet political leaders do not have a monopoly on these ideas, and thus citizens can shift cultural beliefs to support resistance. Hence Martin Luther King, Jr.'s "Letter from a Birmingham Jail" argued that civil disobedience, or the intentional breaking of unjust laws, is completely consistent with biblical teachings. Similarly, liberation theologians often cited the example of Moses leading the Hebrews out of enslavement in Egypt, proclaiming that God is a God of justice who does not tolerate oppression but actively intervenes to end it. In short, citizens can challenge and transform attitudes to foster an ideology of resistance.

The final source of power is *sanctions*. When citizens strike, break laws, and refuse to cooperate, the state may try to punish them as a way to undermine the movement and deter others from joining. Yet political leaders themselves do not make arrests or attack protesters; they send their armed forces to do this work. And while soldiers and police officers work for the state, they can be persuaded by the population to not carry out repressive orders. In some cases, they even defect. When this occurs, the state loses its ability to punish the population.

Since citizens have control of all these power sources, every government is highly vulnerable. If citizens refuse to cooperate, then rulers are rendered powerless and have no capacity to govern. Thus Sharp's strategy for overthrowing the state entails the systematic withdrawal of each power source until the government is no longer operable. He writes,

> When people refuse their cooperation, withhold help, and persist in their disobedience and defiance, they are denying their opponent the basic human assistance and cooperation that any government or hierarchical system requires. . . . Subjects may disobey laws that they reject. Workers may halt work, which may paralyze the economy. The bureaucracy may refuse to carry out instructions. Soldiers and police may become lax in inflicting repression; they may even mutiny. If people and institutions do this in sufficient numbers for long enough, that government or hierarchical system will no longer have power. . . . Its power has dissolved.[26]

In addition to systematically withdrawing cooperation, Sharp's pragmatic strategy directly targets the government's main pillars of support.[27] This might include the media (especially if it is state-controlled), religious leaders and institutions, the educational system, businesses and economic elites, and the military, among others. Strategically, the movement must undermine the loyalty of these traditional state supporters, persuading them to shift allegiance to the opposition. Civil resisters may erode soldiers' loyalty, for instance, by talking with troops in the street, establishing rapport, and persuading them that a new regime will benefit them more than the current one. However, if civil resisters insult troops, threaten them, or throw rocks, it is likely to reinforce troops' loyalty to the state. Similarly, civil resisters ought to develop ties to those in the media in hopes of getting news coverage from their perspective rather than the official government view. They should also try to win the support of religious leaders, who can provide an opposition movement with moral legitimacy, resources, and international ties.[28] Efforts should be made to reach out to sympathetic civil servants, who may conduct work slowdowns or strikes, further impairing the government's ability to function. And business leaders can be critical allies; indeed, many studies indicate that the state is unlikely to fall if economic elites support it.[29] As several nonviolent strategists observed, "Their main interest is profit, so they are quite pragmatic and often view support for a nonviolent movement or a government as an investment. [Civil resisters'] challenge is to convince this

---

Table 3.3. STEPS IN A PRAGMATIC CIVIL RESISTANCE CAMPAIGN[30]

1. Identify supporters and recruit them into the movement.
2. Train participants.
3. Implement a series of campaigns that withdraw key sources of power from the system.
4. Weaken the authorities' traditional support systems, drawing key allies away from the state and into the opposition.
5. Increase the movement's intensity and pressure until authorities capitulate or accommodate, or the system merely falls apart.

---

community that supporting your vision . . . is a wiser investment than supporting your opponent."[31]

The strategic steps of pragmatic nonviolence are summarized in Table 3.3. First, organizers identify supporters and recruit them into the movement. The largest effort comes in the beginning, when organizers must convince a sizeable group to undertake the initial actions. As successful campaigns are waged, more recruits will join in. Second, these supporters need to be trained in civil resistance techniques. Third, movement leaders must plan and implement a series of campaigns that withhold key sources of citizen-based power. Fourth, civil resisters must undermine the state's traditional bases of support. Fifth, the movement must expand its actions, intensifying the pressure over time.

Precisely what types of actions are implemented? Civil resistance campaigns draw on three categories of nonviolent "weapons," summarized in Table 3.4.[32] The first is *protest and persuasion*. This category includes

---

Table 3.4. CATEGORIES OF NONVIOLENT WEAPONS

1. *Protest and persuasion*
   (includes demonstrations, vigils, petitions, deputations, etc.)
2. *Noncooperation*
   - Economic (boycotts, strikes, etc.)
   - Social (refusal to participate in social events, customs, and institutions)
   - Political (election boycotts, political resignations, expulsion from international institutions)
3. *Intervention*
   - Psychological (fasts, nonviolent harassment)
   - Physical (sit-ins, nonviolent obstruction or blockades)
   - Social (building alternative social institutions)
   - Economic (defiance of blockades)
   - Political (building parallel government, disclosing confidential political information, etc.)

---

demonstrations, pickets, vigils, petitions, or synchronized moments of silence or noise—such as the classic Latin American technique of clanging pots and pans. Such acts are primarily symbolic and designed to communicate that citizens are aggrieved, outraged, and ready to mobilize. Protest alone will rarely topple a regime, but it does help to erode state legitimacy and build a coalition of people committed to further campaigns of resistance.

The second category is *noncooperation*, which can take various forms. *Social noncooperation* refers to the rebuffing of cultural practices or social institutions. For example, resisters may refuse to salute the flag of an occupying force. *Economic noncooperation* includes tactics such as boycotts or work slowdowns. As was evident in the Montgomery bus boycott and the divestment campaigns against the South African apartheid regime, this weapon can rapidly deplete a target's financial base, making it highly vulnerable and thus more willing to negotiate. Boycotts are also a relatively low-risk tactic that anyone can participate in, regardless of age, gender, class status, physical ability, and so forth. Hence it can be highly effective. Finally, *political noncooperation* entails the refusal to participate in obviously fraudulent elections or the refusal to comply with political policies such as military conscription.

The final category of nonviolent weapons is *intervention*. Intervention can be *psychological*, such as a hunger strike, which Gandhi used to reach the conscience of his own people, giving them reason to reflect on their actions during the postindependence violence between Muslims and Hindus. Intervention can also *physical*, such as the lunch counter sit-ins in the segregated United States or the blocking of military tanks, as occurred in the 1989 Tiananmen Square protests. Intervention may be *economic*. For instance, solidarity groups have delivered aid to Cuba, refusing to comply with the international embargo against this country. Finally, there is nonviolent *political intervention*. Resisters may, for example, disclose confidential political papers—such as the group Wikileaks—or they may build parallel governments and other institutions.

If done consistently and persistently, the strategic use of these nonviolent weapons can bring about significant social transformation. Opponents may voluntarily make changes due to a genuine change of heart (a process known as *conversion*). In other instances, rulers may capitulate when they realize they have been defeated (*accommodation*) or simply that the nation is ungovernable and they cannot continue (*coercion*). In some cases, the state— or any other targeted institution—may actually collapse (*disintegration*).

To illustrate the strategy of pragmatic nonviolence, I briefly discuss the "bulldozer revolution" in which Serbs nonviolently ousted their president, Slobodan Milošević.[33] Starting in the 1990s, a growing number of Serbs were frustrated with Milošević, who had earned the nickname the "Butcher of the Balkans" as he waged vicious wars with Croatia, Kosovo, and Bosnia. The brutality of these conflicts led to international condemnation and isolation; as a result, Serbia's economy faltered badly. Opposition groups mobilized against Milošević in the early 1990s but without success. By 1998, a student group called Otpor ("Resistance") decided to try again. Otpor leaders organized workshops to teach the basics of strategic nonviolence. Next, the young Serbs identified the power sources that they controlled—such as skills, knowledge, and cooperation—as well as Milošević's traditional "pillars of support." The activists decided to target the military and the media, hoping to win them over to the opposition.

Quickly, Otpor established eighty movement chapters throughout Serbia. Once they had recruited and trained participants, Otpor leaders introduced their strategy: they would pressure the state to hold elections and then mobilize citizens to vote Milošević out. If the president tried to rig the vote, a likely scenario, they would subsequently launch a series of civil resistance campaigns to reveal the fraud and establish new elections that would be observed by the international community.

But big battles begin with smaller actions, and Otpor started by raising awareness of Milošević's corruption and highlighting the imperative need for change. They accomplished this by getting critical news stories aired on alternative media sources. They also used satire to mock Milošević, withholding any authority or legitimacy from him. For example, they mimicked a government initiative that placed donation boxes in stores and public spaces, asking Serbs to donate one dinar (the local currency) to support agricultural work. Alongside these boxes, Otpor placed their own barrels, covered with a photo of Milošević, accompanied by the request to donate one dinar for social change. Those who made the donation were then given a stick to hit the barrel; if they were too poor to donate as a result of Milošević's policies, they were allowed to hit the barrel twice. The police quickly confiscated the barrels, but Otpor sent a press release proclaiming their initiative a huge success: they had collected enough money that Milošević could retire and they trusted the police to deliver the funds directly to the president.[34] Such actions kept the focus on Milošević's questionable reputation while also garnering support for the movement. Although mockery of the opponent would not be acceptable in principled nonviolence, it is part of the arsenal of tactics that pragmatic nonviolent practitioners can use.[35]

As Otpor gained momentum and popularity, the government developed counterstrategies to thwart the expanding movement. First, it arrested Otpor leaders and censored the independent media stations. Next, in June 2000, Milošević passed a law allowing him to run for another term in office. Then in July, he set the elections for September 24, 2000, in hopes that opposition groups would not have sufficient time to organize. Milošević thought he could quickly clinch the election, giving the appearance of democratic legitimacy.

Otpor mobilized rapidly. Using the slogans "He's Finished" and "It's Time," they began registering voters. They also played a key role in uniting the eighteen different (and historically divided) opposition parties. Eventually, with Otpor's help, the parties formed a coalition called the Democratic Opposition of Serbia, which endorsed Vojuslav Kostunica as their candidate. All their organizing efforts paid off: on election day, independent polls showed that Kostunica received 50.2 percent of the vote—a significant win over Milošević's 37.2 percent. But the Federal Election Commission argued that Kostunica did not receive a majority, and thus a runoff election was scheduled.

Otpor anticipated that the election would not be fair, and thus they were prepared for civil resistance. Within three days of the Federal Election Commission's announcement, mass demonstrations began, drawing up to 200,000 participants. Otpor also met with allied police officers, who agreed to not arrest or attack civil resisters if they remained nonviolent. Next, Otpor called for strikes. The first response came from the Kolubara coal miners. This had a significant impact since this mine supplied approximately 50 percent of the country's electricity. Next, the mayor of Belgrade called for a general strike and workers at state-controlled media agencies refused orders to only air pro-Milošević stories. Within a couple of weeks, citizens throughout Serbia had shut down entire cities and built human barricades. Members of the secret police were sent to take over the mines and restart coal production, but 20,000 resisters confronted the police, causing them to leave.

On October 5, 2000, opposition leaders asked civil resisters to convene in Belgrade to nonviolently occupy the federal parliament building until Milošević resigned. A few protesters borrowed a local farmer's bulldozer, which they planned to use to break down any potential barricades. Once hundreds of thousands gathered in Belgrade, the police did not stop them from entering the federal building. The protesters crashed through the doors of parliament and took over the state-run media facilities. The next day, the Constitutional Court reversed the election ruling, pronouncing

Kostunica as the legitimate winner. By October 7, just two weeks after the fraudulent vote, Milošević resigned.

As the new president took power, Otpor continued to nonviolently push for the consolidation of democracy in Serbia. To remind the new government of the power of civil resistance, Otpor plastered Belgrade with posters bearing the emblem of a bulldozer. The posters read, "In Serbia there are 5,675 registered bulldozers and several million potential drivers. . . . WE ARE WATCHING YOU!"[36]

COMPARING THE STRATEGIES OF PRINCIPLED AND PRAGMATIC NONVIOLENCE

Principled nonviolence and pragmatic nonviolence are often presented as distinct and contrasting. However, in practice, these two approaches have many similarities. Adherents of both traditions share similar tactics, developing battle plans that include withdrawing consent, withholding cooperation, and refusing to support an unjust system. Yet pragmatic nonviolent practitioners rely on these tactics to achieve a limited, immediate goal. In contrast, principled nonviolence advocates emphasize the development of a spiritual "truth force" that can instigate comprehensive social and personal transformation. Other differences between principled and pragmatic approaches can be seen in the attitude toward the opponent and the mechanisms of change.

For Gandhi, principled nonviolent activists always aim to reach their opponents' hearts. Through dialogue and action, they hope their adversaries come to see the merits of their position. This can only be achieved when civil resisters treat opponents respectfully, without a tinge of hatred or the desire to humiliate them. Once the opponents have a genuine change of heart, by witnessing civil resisters' willingness to suffer for the cause, they will voluntarily change their behavior. Hence the only acceptable mechanism for change is conversion.

For those operating in Sharp's pragmatic approach, nonviolent resistance is directed at stopping oppressive behavior. Direct action is used to undercut opponents' power, making it impossible for them to continue ruling. While civil resisters must maintain nonviolent discipline in order for the techniques to work, they are not required to seek the good in the opponent. Hence the mechanisms that occur in pragmatic nonviolence movements are primarily accommodation, coercion, and disintegration.

Martin Luther King, Jr. sought to blend these two traditions. On the one hand, King believed that the most enduring change occurs when the opponents recognize the injustices and voluntarily agree to stop the oppression. However, King also recognized that sometimes coercion was needed to stop discriminatory behavior. The Montgomery bus boycott, for example, resulted in bus company owners voluntarily changing their segregation rules, yet they made this change because they were losing money and feared bankruptcy. In other words, it was economic pressure that led them to grant the boycotters' demands, not a change of heart. Nonetheless, King believed that in changing the behavior, society would be establishing new norms that could eventually transform attitudes. As segregation was prohibited, eventually, with time, most people no longer believed that this type of institutionalized racial discrimination was acceptable in a democracy.

Regardless of whether one changes the opponent's heart or behavior first, both the principled and pragmatic traditions of nonviolence rely on a strategy that withholds obedience and cooperation.

CHAPTER 4

⌀⌀

Types of Nonviolent Action

Nonviolent resistance has occurred in many different geographic loca-tions,[1] across different time periods, and in different forms—ranging from hidden acts of everyday resistance to full-scale revolutionary move-ments. Most studies of civil resistance have focused on overt resistance to the state. Yet this gives an overly narrow view, obscuring the many differ-ent ways that people have used nonviolent action. Some people use nonvi-olence to overthrow authoritarian states; others use it to stop the illegal overthrow of a democratic state. Nonviolent action can be used to symbol-ically challenge moral issues such as militarism but it can also be used to physically intervene in militarized conflicts. To gain more awareness of its many forms, I discuss and use historical examples to illustrate nine differ-ent categories of nonviolent action, listed in Table 4.1.

EVERYDAY RESISTANCE

The movements described in the last chapter—the Indian independence struggle and the Serbian effort to oust Milošević—were intentional, open, and well-orchestrated examples of nonviolent action. Yet a great deal of nonviolent resistance occurs in subtle, spontaneous, and hidden ways. It may only occur on the individual level, never culminating in collective action or public protest. It can occur through the subversion of daily prac-tices and customs. This is called "everyday resistance": disguised acts of defiance that require little to no planning and avoid any direct confronta-tion with authorities.[2]

Political scientist James C. Scott has written extensively on everyday resistance. He argues that while oppression is widespread, large-scale

---

Table 4.1. CATEGORIES OF NONVIOLENT
ACTION

---

1. Everyday resistance
2. Covert resistance
3. Symbolic moral witness
4. Reformist nonviolence
5. Negotiated revolutions
6. People power revolutions
7. Electoral revolutions
8. Anti-coup defense
9. Third-party intervention

---

revolts are relatively rare. Since open rebellion is risky, many individuals resist and subvert oppressive structures through covert forms of action in daily life. This includes tactics of foot dragging (intentionally working slowly), feigning ignorance, false compliance, subtle sabotage, evasion, slander, and pilfering. Scott maintains that this type of resistance has been largely overlooked since it is falsely perceived as apolitical or insignificant. Yet everyday acts of resistance can indeed have an impact; moreover, when we fail to give attention to such actions, we create a false impression that oppressed groups are apathetic or resigned to their subordinate status.

Everyday resistance occurred among slaves in the United States.[3] Some feigned illness to miss work. Others pretended to accidentally break tools, damage crops, or misunderstand directions that resulted in a job done incorrectly. Others learned to read and write (which was prohibited for slaves) and used birth control when slave owners expected them to bear children. As Scott points out, such acts *did* have a real impact—primarily on the slave owners' profits. Every day of missed work meant a lower productivity rate. Every damaged tool or crop cut into the plantation's profitability. Contraception undermined slave owners' wealth since slaves were considered property. In short, such actions matter—in terms of real material interests and fostering cultures of resistance.

COVERT RESISTANCE

Like everyday resistance, covert resistance is hidden in hopes of avoiding confrontation with authorities. However, unlike everyday resistance, this second type of nonviolent action is planned and carried out in a coordinated fashion as actors develop strategic plans to subvert oppressive structures. Yet, in contrast to public demonstrations or strikes, the plans are implemented secretly.

The coordinated efforts in Le Chambon, France, during World War II illustrate this type of nonviolent action.[4] The village of Le Chambon has a history of sheltering the persecuted. In the seventeenth century, it took in Huguenots—a small Protestant minority in this overwhelmingly Catholic country. This tradition of helping the persecuted was revived when André Trocmé became pastor of the local church in 1934. Trocmé, a committed pacifist, quickly became a respected community leader, and thus the townspeople looked to him for direction when Nazis occupied the region in May 1940. The Nazis had signed an armistice with the French cabinet, which included an agreement to divide France: the north and west regions were directly under control of German troops while the rest of the country constituted a "free zone" controlled by France's Vichy regime, headed by Marshall Pétain. Pétain fully cooperated with the Nazis, enforcing their anti-Semitic laws.

Trocmé and his assistant, Pastor Édouard Theis, believed that complying with the Nazi-backed Vichy regime was immoral. Determined to find a way to help Jews, they met with Burns Chalmers, a leader of the American Friends Service Committee, a Quaker relief organization that was working in the Marseille internment camps. Burns stated that Marseille physicians were lenient in issuing releases, stating that many Jewish internees were not fit for labor, thereby sparing them from deportation to concentration camps. Although they were not deported, they needed a place to stay; Burns asked Trocmé and Theis if Le Chambon could accommodate them. Moreover, the Marseille internment camp housed Jewish children whose parents were deported; these children needed schooling.

Trocmé and Theis asked Le Chambon residents to take in the Jewish internees. The people agreed. As persecution of French Jews escalated over the next year, an increasing number of people sought refuge in Le Chambon. Within a short time, the town shifted from simply housing Jews to the riskier work of hiding them and helping them escape. As the work became more dangerous, the Chambonnaise people developed a secret system. Theis would send villagers postcards of the Tower of Constance. Everyone was familiar with this symbol since the Tower of Constance was a seventeenth-century shelter for persecuted Huguenots. On the postcard, Theis would write, "I am sending you five Old Testaments [i.e., Jewish refugees] on Thursday." The townspeople hid them in their barns and homes until they could be smuggled into Switzerland. To help with the escape, the secondary school director produced false passports.

Then the refugees traveled at night and only bought tickets to the next station; when they arrived, they stayed in short-term hiding places until they could travel to the next train station. They continued this pattern until they reached the Swiss border. By traveling in incremental spurts, it was difficult to track the refugees since the tickets did not reveal their final destination.

Eventually, French officials learned about Le Chambon's illegal activities. They sent French Secretary General for Youth Georges Lamirand to investigate. When he arrived, Lamirand ordered Trocmé to give him a list of all Jewish refugees. Trocmé refused, stating that he did not know the refugees' names or ethnicities. That evening, the townspeople turned off the streetlights, enabling Trocmé to slip out of town under the cover of darkness. He contacted the town's Boy Scouts and ordered them to spread the word throughout the area that Lamirand was going to arrest all Jews. The Boy Scouts carried out the request, enabling the refugees to escape. The next day, Lamirand's police arrived with a dozen buses to transport the Jews. The police searched for weeks but only made two arrests. Eventually Lamirand gave up. By the time the war ended, the village of Le Chambon had saved the lives of an estimated five thousand Jews.

SYMBOLIC MORAL WITNESS

A third category of nonviolent action is called symbolic moral witness. The term "moral witness" refers to people who express our collective memories of extreme evil and those who are harmed by it.[5] Acts of moral witness are not strategically directed toward winning specific political or material goals. Rather, they are designed to "strip away from our understanding of war and repression romantic or heroic readings of the past."[6] They expose untruths and force us to see the reality of oppression. They require us to think about the ethics of social practices such as warfare.

But what is *symbolic* moral witness? It is a form of resistance that uses symbols for the following reasons. First, symbolism may be used as a visual, graphic, or visceral way of depicting the moral issues at stake. A mock funeral, for instance, may get people to see the human costs of a political conflict. Second, symbolism can be used to indicate a solution. For example, activists may choose alternative labels for themselves to indicate a new consciousness. Some Mexican Americans favor the term "Chicano" over "Hispanic." This is a politically symbolic choice: "Hispanic" emphasizes their Spanish heritage while "Chicano"—which comes from Nahuatl, the native language of Mexico at the time of Spanish conquest—emphasizes their indigenous heritage.[7] Similarly, the Black Power movement rejected white standards of beauty, such as straight hair, and chose to wear their hair naturally to signify pride in their African heritage. Afros were not a way to directly fight racism; rather, they were a symbolic way to resist white standards.

When we combine symbolic resistance with moral witness, we get a distinct form of nonviolent action that exposes the ethical costs of an injustice and/or points the way to an alternative. The Catholic Left–inspired Plowshares movement in the United States illustrates this type of nonviolent resistance. The movement was launched in 1980 at a General Electric (GE) plant that developed highly accurate "first strike" nuclear weapons that had enormous destructive capacity. One activist, John Schuchardt, began to question whether protesting was enough. He thought that holding a vigil at GE was the equivalent of holding a vigil beside the train tracks that transported Jews to concentration camps. Something more needed to be done; an intervention was necessary.

Schuchardt explained how he came up with their distinct tactic of symbolic moral witness. One day, during a vigil, he watched as workers filed into the GE plant for the morning shift. He noticed that there was minimal security around Plant No. 9, where the first-strike weapons were developed. He though it would be fairly simple to enter the facility, disguised as employees. He explained:

> [We knew] these weapons were not defensive; they are criminal and genocidal. I thought, if we believe this, then what is our responsibility? Here we are vigiling but is it possible that a group of us could go in and bring this production line to a halt? These warheads have all these electronic components that would be very vulnerable to a hammer blow. . . . So I said . . . , "Can we live with ourselves if we just stand here and vigil?"[8]

Eventually, Schuchardt found seven others who agreed to disrupt the weapons manufacturing process. As they planned their action, they realized that they would be symbolically enacting the biblical prophecy: "Nations shall beat their swords into plowshares and their spears into pruning hooks; one nation shall not raise the sword against another, nor shall they train for war again" (Isaiah 2:4). Schuchardt's co-conspirators included the radical Catholic activists Philip Berrigan and Father Daniel Berrigan, who had served time for breaking into conscription offices during the Vietnam War and pouring blood on the draft files.[9] So Schuchardt, the Berrigans, and five others took action in September 1980. Wearing fabricated GE employee identification cards, they entered the plant. Two members of the group stayed to speak with the security guard while the others slipped inside. In their jackets were household hammers and baby bottles filled with their own blood. Within minutes, the activists found a room that housed warheads known as missile re-entry vehicles. The door, which was normally secured, was unlocked and the resisters entered easily. Then they pulled out their hammers and pounded on the warheads. Afterwards, they poured blood and then knelt in prayer.

Security guards quickly apprehended and arrested them, but supporters on the outside released the "Plowshares Eight" statement to the press. It read:

> We commit civil disobedience at General Electric because this genocidal entity is the fifth leading producer of weaponry in the U.S. To maintain this position, GE drains $3 million a day from the public treasury, an enormous larceny against the poor. We also wish to challenge the lethal lie spun by GE through its motto, "We bring good things to life." As manufacturers of the Mark 12A reentry vehicle, GE actually brings good things to death. Through the Mark 12A, the threat of first-strike nuclear war grows more imminent. Thus GE advances the possible destruction of millions of innocent lives. . . . In confronting GE, we choose to obey God's law of life, rather than a corporate summons to death. Our beating of swords into plowshares is a way to enflesh this biblical call. . . . We are filled with hope for our world and for our children as we join in this act of resistance.[10]

The eight were charged and convicted of various crimes, including burglary, conspiracy, and criminal mischief. They received sentences ranging from eighteen months to ten years. But the movement has continued well into the twenty-first century, with more than eighty similar symbolic disarmament campaigns.[11]

The Plowshares movement has received heavy criticism. The most common critique is that the movement hasn't achieved anything. These activists did not stop the arms race or abolish nuclear weapons; they paid a high price for virtually no gains. Yet for those in the movement, the act itself is important because it symbolically reveals what these weapons are about: death. One Plowshares activist recounted:

> War has been sanitized . . . because we mostly do it through our technology and satellite surveillance. Back when people [fought] hand-to-hand, you would see the blood and gore and you would see the consequences. Now we're so far removed and we watch war coverage on TV like it's a miniseries. That's so

desensitizing, deadening. So when we use blood, it has a very powerful effect. It says, "This is what we're talking about—human life. All this technology is made to destroy it, to spill human blood."[12]

Symbolic action in the Plowshares movement is also about calling people to create an alternative society where people beat their swords into plowshares (i.e., shift away from a warrior society to one that emphasizes life). Thus hammering on missiles is not an instrumental act; it is a call for people to demand disarmament.

REFORMIST NONVIOLENCE

Some nonviolent action is aimed at reforms—that is, improvements in social institutions rather than the overthrow of those institutions. Thus the U.S. civil rights movement was not trying to destroy the U.S. government but improve it. It called on the state to embrace the ideals of democracy and the Constitution by ensuring that all citizens had equal rights.[13] However, not at all nonviolent movements target the government. Sometimes civil resisters challenge cultural norms, corporations, nonprofit institutions, or religious organizations. For instance, resisters organized a movement to boycott the Boy Scouts, a nonprofit group, until it admitted gay youth.[14] Another example is the movement of Catholics who formed Voice of the Faithful to pressure the Catholic Church into changing its policies toward priests engaged in sexual abuse.[15]

One movement that reflects this category of reformist nonviolence is the United Farm Workers (UFW), led by Cesar Chavez.[16] The UFW was a union of agricultural workers in California formed in 1962. In 1965, the UFW launched a major strike against grape growers because the farmworkers sought the following reforms. First, they wanted higher wages. Due to the provisions of the guest worker *Bracero* program that brought in needed labor from Mexico, agricultural workers were not included in U.S. labor laws that guarantee safe conditions and a minimum wage. Thus, the farm workers made poverty-level wages, averaging about $1,400 per year. They also worked in unsanitary and unsafe conditions; they labored long hours in the fields without latrines or clean drinking water. The housing provided to them was substandard, mostly dilapidated shacks or tents in overcrowded camps with no running water. Moreover, they received no benefits or even the stability of a contract.

When the grape growers cut wages, the farmworkers launched a strike and picket. The strength of a nonviolent strategy is that it can target the sources of power that an opponent needs most. In the case of corporate-oriented reform movements, nonviolent action that under-cuts business profits can evoke a quick reaction. In this campaign, the opponents' immediate reaction was repression. Picketers were harassed and assaulted. Grape growers used the courts, convincing judges to issue injunctions. The local sheriff even began arresting people on the grounds that they *might* picket.

The farmworkers did not back down.[17] Instead, they brought national and international attention to the issues. They gained the support of Sena-tor Robert F. Kennedy, who gave great visibility to the plight of the farm-workers as news media crews filmed his visit to the grape fields. This gave Chavez a chance to win the support of other groups. A couple of months into the strike, longshoremen in Oakland intentionally let a thousand ten-ton crates of grapes rot instead of processing them in a timely manner. Next, the UFW launched a consumer boycott of grapes in 1966. To draw attention to the boycott, Chavez led a pilgrimage, fashioned after Gan-dhi's salt march. He marched from Delano—a small farming community that was the home of the UFW—to Sacramento, California's capitol. Each evening, the marchers held rallies in local communities. When they even-tually reached the capitol, the march had expanded to thousands. Press coverage of the pilgrimage made the grape growers worried about their public image; consequently, they signed a contract that included a wage increase of thirty-five cents per hour. While this was an important vic-tory, the wage increase only covered roughly 2 percent of California's farmworkers, and so the struggle continued.

By 1968, the boycott shifted from specific companies to an across-the-board consumer boycott of grapes. This decision was made because the targeted corporations had changed their label to trick boycotters. Thus the UFW set up organizing offices throughout the United States, winning the support of various religious groups, student movements, and civil rights organizations. By 1969, seventeen million people were boycotting table grapes, causing significant losses. To stop the financial impact, forty growers signed contracts. By 1970, the largest grape company signed union contracts and the others followed suit. The farmworkers had at-tained the reforms that they had sought.

NEGOTIATED REVOLUTIONS

A fifth form of nonviolent action is called the negotiated revolution. For many people, the term *revolution* conjures up images of armed guerrillas, mobilizing to overthrow the state through violence. Indeed, many revolutions have occurred this way: the French revolution, the 1979 Nicaraguan revolution, and the Vietnamese revolution, to name but a few. However, revolutions can happen through a variety of mechanisms, including nonviolent ones. Hence a better way of conceptualizing revolutions is as follows:

> [R]evolutions can be seen as: *the rapid, mass, forceful, systemic transformation of a society's principal institutions and organizations.* . . . Ways of doing business and competing politically must change alongside shifts in values and attitudes. . . . Revolutions are not merely about the introduction of elections, the privatization of one or two industries, or the opening up of media outlets to allow mild critiques of the status quo—they are something much more fundamental and comprehensive. Revolutions seek to overturn a society's social, economic, and political structures and recast its international relations, all within a relatively short time.[18]

Yet how is a negotiated revolution different from other types of comprehensive social change? In an armed insurrection, the revolutionary forces try to defeat the state and its military through violence. The victors are able to physically subordinate their opponents or, in a war of attrition, the winner is simply the side that is able to endure the most violence and thus is the only one left standing to seize power. In a coup, elites—from within the political system or armed forces—oust the established leader without the involvement of citizens. In a negotiated revolution, the impetus for social transformation comes from grassroots social movements, not from elites. In addition, the mechanism of change is not violence or the threat of violence; rather, it is nonviolent pressure to implement democratic ideals and a written constitution of rights and policies. Civil resistance is not used to make the existing state collapse; rather, it is used to pressure a regime into negotiations toward genuine democratization.

Negotiated revolutions are also different from armed revolutions in the post-conflict phase. Specifically, negotiated revolutions are based on the principles of restorative justice, not punitive justice. Whenever a revolution succeeds, the new political leaders must find ways to deal with the perpetrators of the old regime's injustices. In many violent revolutions, former oppressors may be executed or imprisoned. In many negotiated revolutions, the past is dealt with through truth commissions that cast a public light on the injustices and give victims the opportunity to confront their former oppressors. In essence, these processes "trade truth for punishment"[19] and, in so doing, they forge a new historical narrative for the new nation.

The transformation of the South African apartheid system illustrates this category of nonviolent action.[20] The origins of South Africa's conflict can be traced to its colonial heritage in which British and Dutch settlers subordinated the local black population. In 1910, South Africa became a self-governing dominion; its constitution excluded blacks from any form of political participation. Blacks responded by forming the African National Congress (ANC) in 1912. Over the next decades, the ANC fought to enfranchise and establish basic rights for black citizens, but petitioning and lobbying resulted in few gains.

Conditions worsened for black South Africans in 1948 when the Christian Nationalist Party, backed by Afrikaners (i.e., ethnic Dutch), won the general election on a platform of "apartheid"—the Afrikaans word for racial segregation. Upon assuming office, the Nationalist Party took several actions. In 1950, it passed the Population Registration Act, which categorized citizens into racial groups and forced all adults to carry an identity card denoting their race. That same year, the Group Areas Act was implemented, designating areas for each racial group to live. In 1953, the Reservation of Separate Amenities Act legalized the division of municipal grounds—such as schools, hospitals, beaches, and parks—for specific races. Not surprisingly, the white amenities were far superior to those for blacks, coloreds, and Indians. Further laws were passed to prohibit interracial marriage and to suppress communism. In reality, the anticommunist measures were applied to any groups that challenged government policies. In short, by the 1950s, the Nationalist Party had fully segregated South Africans and provided the state with the powers to enforce this segregation and suppress any opposition.

In response to these apartheid laws, the ANC shifted from institutional methods of political change to a major civil disobedience campaign in the early 1950s. But after thousands were arrested, the movement subsided for several years. Mass demonstrations erupted again in 1960 in response to new laws that restricted freedom of movement and travel. This time, the Nationalist Party cracked down brutally. In Sharpeville, police fired into a crowd of protesters, killing at least 69 individuals and wounding an estimated 178 protesters.[21] The government declared a state of emergency, banned the ANC, and arrested thousands of black activists. The massacre led Nelson Mandela to co-found Umkhonto we Sizwe (Spear of the Nation), the armed wing of the ANC. Mandela remained underground for a while but was eventually arrested and sentenced to a life term in a labor camp.

By the 1980s, a new wave of anti-apartheid organizations and social movements emerged. One of the largest, the United Democratic Front, was an alliance of nearly six hundred organizations—from labor unions to youth organizations and religious and civic groups. The United Democratic Front used various nonviolent techniques: they implemented election boycotts, consumer boycotts of white businesses, and rent boycotts and developed parallel government organizations on the local level, including alternative schools and health care facilities. The Congress of South African Trade Unions, with more than one million members, joined the resistance by implementing labor strikes; these strikes made an impact since the nation's industrial-based economy was heavily dependent on black labor.[22] These acts of nonviolent resistance meant that the Nationalist Party and the South African state were facing a dire economic situation. But political leaders clung to power, expanding the level of repression and use of torture.

Meanwhile, the ANC concluded that they were unlikely to defeat the South African state militarily. In fact, it was becoming clear that the ANC's armed struggle was having little effect; in contrast, civil resistance was bringing pressure on the state.[23] When the ANC decided that nonviolent action for a democratic transition was the most promising option, it activated its diplomatic offices in more than twenty countries and the United Nations. Through these connections, the ANC mobilized third-party sanctions on the apartheid state, including the divestment movement in which citizens pressured banks and businesses to withdraw from the South African economy.[24]

The result of this pressure was that white elites within South Africa divided. One group, known as the "securocrats," wanted to increase repression. But their leader, P. W. Botha, had failed to contain the resistance through this approach; in fact, his excessive repression appeared to backfire, causing opposition to escalate. Hence another group of elites decided that a new course of action was needed. Without a transition out of apartheid, the South African economy would never recover. This reformist group believed that a negotiated path to democracy was the only way to end the nation's international isolation and pariah status.[25]

The reform-minded elites began to secretly negotiate the transition. From 1987 to 1990, leaders from the Afrikaner nationalist movement clandestinely met with ANC leaders to hammer out the details. In 1989, they replaced Botha with another president, F. W. de Klerk, who would implement this transition. Within months, de Klerk lifted the ban on opposition political groups, dismantled the security apparatus, released Mandela from prison, and called for multiparty elections. Not surprisingly,

Afrikaner nationalists devised various methods to maintain control, such as promoting an anti-ANC coalition. But when elections were finally held in 1994, South Africans elected ANC candidate Mandela as the first president of their new nonracial democratic state.[26]

Shortly after his inauguration, President Mandela set up a "Truth and Reconciliation Commission" that enabled perpetrators of violence, either from the state security forces or from armed rebel groups, to apply for amnesty. The belief was that such a commission was necessary if the country was going to survive, with victims and perpetrators living in the same nation. The condition for amnesty was that the perpetrators must admit their guilt and fully disclose the details of their actions. During these hearings, victims and their families were allowed to question and talk with those responsible for crimes committed against them. The hope was to bring to light the injustices, to expose those responsible, and to allow victims to speak about their experience. It was designed to deal with past atrocities yet enable the country to move forward as an integrated nation.[27]

PEOPLE POWER REVOLUTIONS

The sixth category of nonviolent resistance is termed people power revolutions. Like negotiated revolutions, such movements involve a civilian uprising that uses various nonviolent weapons toward the goal of comprehensive social, political, and economic transformation. Yet nonviolent revolutions happen through a different mechanism. In negotiated revolutions, state actors are pressured into implementing democracy so that free and fair elections will bring about change; in people power revolutions, the change happens when the state either collapses or abdicates power to the opposition. In other words, people power revolutions are citizen-based movements that use the weapons of nonviolence to force rulers out of office. Rulers may cling to power until the end, when they realize they can no longer rule. The outcome is not negotiated, as it was in South Africa; the change occurs through nonviolent coercion or state disintegration.

Reviewing the mechanisms of nonviolent change can illustrate the differences between these types of social transformation. As stated in Chapter 2, Gene Sharp distinguished four mechanisms of nonviolent change.[28] First, in *conversion*, the ruler is moved by civil resisters' willingness to suffer and sacrifice for their cause. Through dialogue and persuasion, accompanied by nonviolent action, the opponents are persuaded that the movement's goals are just and hence they voluntarily agree to civil resisters' demands. Second, in *accommodation*, the opponents voluntarily concede to the movement's demands—not necessarily due to a change of heart but because they see it as the only viable alternative. In the last two mechanisms of change, nonviolent *coercion* and nonviolent *disintegration*, the opponents lose control involuntarily. Civil resisters launch various campaigns that take away an opponent's ability to function. With coercion, the opponents may cling to power until the state (or organization) can no longer function; at that point, they surrender, but against their will. With disintegration, the entire social structure falls apart so that the surrender isn't even possible. It is a situation where the system completely collapses.

The 1986 Philippine movement illustrates the nonviolent coercion that is an inherent dynamic in people power revolutions. The movement was rooted in opposition to President Ferdinand Marcos, who took office in 1965 through largely free and fair elections. However, in 1971, when his second term was nearing completion, he pushed through a constitutional amendment that allowed him a third term. This caused major demonstrations, particularly among students who were disgusted with Marcos's nepotism and use of the presidential office to increase his personal fortune. When Marcos threatened to invoke emergency measures, the demonstrations expanded. He used this as an excuse to declare martial law, suspend the presidential elections, and imprison his opponents, including Senator Benigno "Ninoy" Aquino—his rival for the presidency.

Marcos remained in office but opposition grew in the late 1970s. Marcos's corruption had worsened and his personal wealth had grown exponentially, just as the average Filipino faced growing economic hardships. To keep the upper hand, Marcos expanded his military and the use of repression, including torture. But everything changed in 1983 when Marcos's primary political rival, Aquino, returned to the Philippines. Aquino had spent nearly eight years on death row in Filipino prisons. In 1980, he developed a heart condition and was allowed to travel to the United States for medical care. He stayed in the United States until 1984, when it was announced that legislative elections would be held. He wanted to provide leadership to the fledgling opposition and, after studying Gandhi, he was determined to use civil resistance to push Marcos out of office.

Aquino flew to Manila in August 1983. As he exited the plane, he was shot on the tarmac and died instantly. This brutal act backfired: instead of stopping the opposition, Aquino's assassination galvanized it, bringing roughly two million people into the streets during the funeral procession. The murder was also a turning point for the business class, who had previously felt immune from the violence and were now shocked that one of their own would be killed on government orders. Moreover, economic leaders had grown tired of the downward-spiraling Filipino economy. The assassination was the proverbial last straw, causing many to begin collaborating with the opposition.

The opposition quickly devised plans for a nonviolent revolution. The leader of the Philippine Catholic Church, Cardinal Jaime Sin, invited nonviolence trainers from the International Fellowship of Reconciliation, a pacifist organization, who held workshops throughout the country on civil resistance. Soon thereafter, Filipinos put their training to use, organizing mass demonstrations. The demonstrations brought Marcos under growing international scrutiny, so he decided to hold legislative elections in 1984 in hopes that it would give him new legitimacy and credibility. But to no one's surprise, the elections were marred with irregularities and fraud. This point was raised directly with Marcos when he made an appearance on a U.S. news show. When questioned about the legitimacy of the elections, Marcos grew indignant, proclaiming: "If all these childish claims . . . have to be settled, I think we had better settle it by calling an election right now. I'm ready. I'm ready!"[29] The presidential election was set for February 1986.

The opposition selected Aquino's widow, Corey, to run against Marcos. Then they trained election observers who would guard ballot boxes and accompany voters to polling places. Even though the movement ensured that citizens could fairly cast their votes, they were unable to avoid fraud in the vote-counting process. Despite international observers who declared the election fraudulent, Marcos proclaimed himself the winner.

The movement subsequently shifted to campaigns of civil resistance aimed at forcing Marcos out of office. At a rally of two million people in the capitol city of Manila, Corey Aquino described the plan of action. First, Filipinos would boycott all government-controlled companies, banks, and newspapers. Then, over the course of ten days, additional actions would be implemented, culminating in a general strike on the presidential inaugural date. If Marcos still refused to step down at that point, then businesses would withhold all corporate income taxes, which would severely restrict government resources.

Yet before the campaign could be fully implemented, a key event occurred: soldiers began to defect. The defections started when Marcos's defense minister and the deputy chief of staff for the armed forces made a televised announcement from Camp Aguinaldo. They stated that they could no longer support an illegitimate regime and thus they were resigning. Everyone knew that Marcos would quickly have the two defectors arrested, so Cardinal Sin called on citizens to go to Camp Aguinaldo to protect them. Within a day, around one million people gathered, forming a human barricade. Members of religious orders quickly organized a food brigade to feed the crowds. Then, when the soldiers arrived in tanks, they appealed for restraint. The commander warned the resisters that they had thirty minutes to disperse. When the allotted time passed, the people refused to budge. Nuns dropped to their knees and prayed the rosary in front of the tanks. Unwilling to harm the nuns, priests, and unarmed citizens, a few soldiers climbed out of their tanks and joined the crowd. Then more soldiers defected. And more. Within four days, an estimated 80 to 90 percent of the soldiers had joined the opposition.[30]

On February 25, 1986—the day he was supposed to be inaugurated—Marcos had no ability to rule any more. His soldiers had defected *en masse* and his palace guards deserted. Citizens were not complying with orders to disperse and return to their homes and jobs. Even the television network employees refused to give him any airtime. When he realized that there was no way to assert control, he flew to Hawaii. The Marcos regime had collapsed and Corey Aquino took over the presidency.

ELECTORAL REVOLUTIONS

The seventh category of nonviolent action is electoral revolutions.[31] This type of nonviolent action generally occurs in hybrid regimes where authoritarian leaders work with an elected legislature that has typically been put into office through fraudulent means. Civil resisters mobilize to transform fraudulent electoral practices into fair ones, thereby promoting genuine democratization. Thus a succinct definition of an electoral revolution is "an innovative set of coordinated [nonviolent] strategies and tactics that use elections to mobilize citizens against semi-authoritarian incumbents."[32] Thus social change is not a result of political talks (as in a negotiated revolution); nor does it force a leader out through nonviolent coercion (as in people power movements). Instead, civil resisters use nonviolent action to ensure democratic mechanisms are in place so that change—including the total transformation of a regime—can occur through institutional methods.

The strategy behind an electoral revolution entails the following steps.[33] First, civil resisters build a diverse, cross-class coalition that unites around an opposition candidate. Second, organizers focus on pre-election activities that will enhance citizen participation and electoral fairness. Efforts are concentrated on running voter registration campaigns, improving the accuracy of voter registration records, educating people on the issues at stake, and increasing voter turnout. Third, civil resisters establish some type of independent media to counteract state-controlled media information. Fourth, opposition organizers solicit the help of international election monitors to ensure fairness and to have witnesses to any fraud that might occur. Fifth, on election day, the movement employs pollsters to conduct an independent vote count and exit polls so that they do not have to rely upon government reports. Sixth, civil resisters mobilize mass protests if the election is fraudulent. Such demonstrations reveal to the global community that the regime has no legitimacy. Moreover, these protests pressure authorities to throw out election results and force incumbents to concede defeat.

Many of the so-called color revolutions in the early twenty-first century fall within this category.[34] Ukraine's "orange revolution" clearly illustrates this form of nonviolent action.[35] The movement erupted over growing frustration with the corruption and repression of President Kuchma's administration. Public outrage first surfaced in 2000, when journalist Georgiy Gongadze, who had criticized leading Ukrainian politicians, was murdered. Gongadze's death was widely believed to have happened under Kuchma's orders. Thus, as the 2004 presidential election approached, Kuchma realized that his reputation was severely tarnished and he needed to relinquish the presidency; moreover, he had completed two terms in office, which is the maximum allowed under the Ukrainian constitution. He selected a successor, Prime Minister Viktor Yanukovych, to run.

Convinced that Yanukovych would continue Kuchma's semi-authoritarian tradition, civil resisters contemplated direct action. Consulting civil resisters in other regions, they decided to implement the electoral revolution strategy. The first step, therefore, was to convince the various opposition parties to form a coalition that would back a single candidate. The newly formed coalition, called Force of the People, rallied behind their chosen candidate, Viktor Yushchenko. Next, civil resisters began a significant voter education effort.

As election day neared and as Yushchenko's popularity expanded, the Kuchma regime resorted to intimidation tactics. Yushchenko supporters were arrested on fabricated charges and the state used government-controlled television to promote negative coverage of Yushchenko without giving him airtime to respond. In other instances, his plane was not given permission to land in local airports when he was scheduled to attend major rallies. Then, in early September 2004, Yushchenko was poisoned with dioxin. He became gravely ill and was forced to stop his campaign tour. He survived, although his health suffered and the poison left his face disfigured. After a month, Yushchenko recovered sufficiently that he was able to return to the campaign.

When election day arrived on October 31, 2004, state reports claimed that the two main candidates, Yanukovych and Yushchenko, each won 40 percent of the vote. The opposition, however, had arranged for election observers and independent polls, which provided significant evidence of voter irregularities and fraud. Yet the Ukrainian constitution required that a runoff election must be held if no candidate receives 50 percent or more of the vote. Since challenging the election results probably would not have changed the need for a runoff, civil resisters decided to focus on the next election, scheduled for November 21.

Opposition activists were, of course, convinced that the government would try to steal the runoff election, too, so they devised a plan to combat this. Since the main television stations were controlled by the state, they established alternative media outlets. The Internet became the source of movement news while one independent television station, forced to operate on cable networks, continued to air opposition perspectives. Civil resisters also solicited help from independent pollsters and roughly ten thousand local and international election monitors. As the runoff results came in, independent exit polls revealed that Yushchenko had won with 52 percent of the votes, compared to Yanukovych's 42 percent. However, state polls claimed that Yanukovych won, edging out his competitor with a 2.5 percent lead. There were other issues as well. For instance, tens of thousands of people were bussed from polling station to polling station; they each cast multiple absentee ballots at every stop. And the government's election commission changed its reports overnight to reflect higher voter turnout rates in Yanukovych-favored regimes. By one estimate, "this 'miraculous' last minute upsurge was responsible for 1.2 million new votes—well over 90 percent of which went to the regime's favorite, giving him enough for a comfortable 800,000-vote margin of victory."[36] Even Ukraine's Security Service brought forth evidence that the government had manipulated the election commission's computer server to inflate the votes for Yanukovych.

With widespread evidence of vote rigging and fraud, civil resisters refused to accept the government's claim that Yanukovych had won. Thus they moved into the final step of an electoral revolution: nonviolent resistance. It started with mass demonstrations: the morning after the election, hundreds of thousands gathered in Kiev's Independence Square to protest the stolen election. Most wore orange—the color of Yushchenko's opposition coalition. The protesters camped out in the square, refusing to leave. Over the next few days, they nonviolently occupied the cabinet of ministers, the presidential administration, and even Kuchma's own residence. They also embarked on a general strike.

During this post-election resistance, protesters appealed to members of the security forces, imploring them to side with the movement. No one was sure how the military would respond; indeed, it appeared that they were torn and confused. Whose orders should they take? In that moment, there were three presidents: incumbent President Kuchma, whose term had not yet expired; the state-declared presidential winner, Yanukovych; and Yushchenko, who proclaimed himself the legitimate winner. As the movement expanded over the next few days, the security forces began to fragment, with a significant portion siding with the movement. In fact, as Yanukovych prepared to order an attack on the protesters, security force leaders warned him that they would protect protesters. In short, civil resisters had undercut the state's ability to repress.

As the extra-institutional tactics of nonviolent resistance continued in Kiev's Independence Square, Yushchenko and the movement also pursued an institutional strategy. The opposition appealed to members of the parliament to nullify the vote results. With incontrovertible evidence of fraud, it took only six days for the parliament to declare the state-issued election results invalid. The next step was to get the Supreme Court to annul the runoff election results. By the beginning of December, the Supreme Court agreed and set a date for new elections. When Ukrainians went to the polls for the third time on December 26, 2004, the movement had won so much international coverage that the whole world was watching. With twelve thousand international monitors and constant media scrutiny, the final elections were fair. Hence the movement was not at all surprised when their candidate, Yushchenko, won with 52 percent of the vote, easily defeating Yanukovych, who received 44 percent. The electoral strategy had worked. Hours after the polls closed, Yushchenko made his acceptance speech, declaring that Ukraine was a new country with a new future.

NONVIOLENT ANTI-COUP DEFENSE

An eighth type of nonviolent action is called anti-coup defense.[37] To understand this category of nonviolence requires us first to define what a coup is and then to explain how civil resisters can prevent it. A *coup d'état*, or *putsch*, is the coercive ousting of existing political leaders by a group (often the military) who uses violence or the threat of violence to rapidly seize control of the state. A coup happens quickly, typically within a few hours to a few days—making it distinct from a civil war, which occurs over a longer period of time. Coups have occurred throughout the world and have been used to institute new forms of government (such as a democratic system being replaced by a military junta), while at other times the regime type remains constant (an incumbent military regime replaced by a new military regime). While much academic attention has been devoted to citizen movements that use nonviolence to overthrow their own authoritarian regimes or foreign occupiers, little attention has been given to nonviolent citizen movements that protect their democracies against internal usurpation.

How can civil resisters protect their political institutions and prevent coups? First, they can construct strong barriers to deter those contemplating an illegal government takeover. Second, civil resisters can use nonviolent tactics so that coup leaders may gain physical control of government facilities but not political control of state operations or of the citizenry. As Sharp and Jenkins state,

> Civil servants, bureaucrats, military groupings and other state employees at times steadfastly refused to cooperate with putschists, denying control of state apparatus. Coups have also been imperiled by severance of the link between control of the central state machinery and control of the society—including independent social institutions, local governments, and the population as a whole. Putschists have often narrowly assumed that dominance of state structures equals political and social control. However, without the submission of all these sections of the society, the coup leadership cannot become a lasting government.[38]

In other words, this category of nonviolence reflects preemptive efforts to stop coups before they start *and* efforts to keep the putschists from consolidating power after they oust the incumbent political leaders.

What is the strategy of nonviolent anti-coup movements? If civil resisters can preemptively identify the threat, they can rally international support. Nations can warn that aid, trade agreements, and diplomatic relations will be suspended if a legitimately elected government is ousted through a coup. Civil resisters can also nonviolently obstruct putschist troops from gaining physical control of key government buildings: they can block streets and form human barricades around parliamentary buildings and presidential offices. Although such obstructionist actions may be short-lived, they send a message to the putschists that they do not have citizen support and therefore winning control of the nation will be difficult.

More commonly, civil resisters try to make the country ungovernable after a coup has occurred. From this approach, nonviolent activists have five strategic objectives. First, they must demonstrate to the putschists that they have no legitimacy. Second, they must undermine putschists' control of the state. In other words, civil servants, lower-level political leaders, technocrats, and security forces must refuse to work for the putschists. Third, civil resisters must ensure that they establish and sustain alternative media venues since the putschists are likely to take over state-owned media outlets and control the information that is released. All citizens should refuse to promote putschist propaganda. Fourth, citizens must refuse to cooperate with or obey orders issued by putschist leaders. Finally, civil resisters may block the putschists' efforts to control or neutralize key civil society groups such as religious institutions or labor groups.[39]

The effort to stop a coup against Argentine President Raúl Alfonsín illustrates this category of nonviolent action. Alfonsín was elected to office in 1983, following the period known as the "Dirty War." This war began when a military junta, headed by General Jorge Rafaél Videla, took power in 1976. The junta dissolved the congress and the Supreme Court, prohibited political opposition groups, and announced that dissidents would be eliminated. General Videla stated, "First we will kill all the subversives. Then we will kill their collaborators; then . . . their sympathizers, then . . . those who remain indifferent; and finally we will kill the timid."[40] To root out subversion, the military used kidnappings, interrogations, torture, imprisonment, assassination, and "disappearances." During this time, an estimated thirty thousand civilians disappeared, many of them university students. This prompted a number of opposition movements to mobilize, including a movement of mothers who pestered the regime with the question, "Where are our [adult] children?" Wearing cloth diapers as headscarves, each bearing the name of a kidnapped son or daughter, the "Mothers of the Disappeared" gained international press coverage, particularly during the World Cup soccer games that Argentina hosted in 1983. Global media attention, combined with growing domestic pressure, eventually forced the regime to hold elections in October 1983. Alfonsín won the presidency that year.[41]

Alfonsín immediately faced the issue of whether to prosecute those responsible for human rights abuses during the Dirty War. Before the political transition occurred, the military had taken action to protect itself: it granted blanket amnesty to all soldiers through the "Law of National

Pacification." Upon assuming the presidency, Alfonsín repealed the law and pressed charges against the nine members of the military junta. In April 1985, as their trial neared, news of a coup emerged: to avoid prosecution, the military planned to overthrow the president. When Alfonsín learned that a coup was under way, he went on television and called upon Argentines to defend their democracy. An estimated 250,000 citizens arrived at the presidential palace, demanding that the military respect the elected government. As a result, the military backed off and the trials continued.[42]

THIRD-PARTY NONVIOLENT INTERVENTION

The final form of nonviolence is called third-party nonviolent intervention. Boothe and Smithey define this as "a collection of [nonviolent] tactics and methods used to support, rather than direct, social change work in intense conflict situations. Organizations using this method focus on protecting vulnerable populations and creating or widening the 'space' necessary for nonviolent movements to operate."[43] In practice, this means that interventionists travel to global conflict zones and physically interject themselves between the parties in dispute as a way to prevent harm. This works best when one or both parties have important reasons to avoid harming the interventionist—for example, to avoid news coverage that might provoke negative reactions (such as sanctions) from the international community.

There are three distinct forms of nonviolent intervention.[44] Some actions entail "protective accompaniment" whereby nonviolent interventionists, generally foreign nationals, travel to places where authoritarian political rule has stripped people of democratic freedoms and basic human rights. To create space for organizing and resistance, these foreigners remain in the constant company of those who are at risk for attack or repression, such as political dissidents and activists. The basic idea is that an act of political violence against foreigners is likely to exact higher political costs.[45] Thus groups like Peace Brigades International and Nonviolent Peaceforce have sent volunteers to places such as Guatemala and Sri Lanka, where interventionists accompany human rights workers, labor organizers, and opposition activists throughout their daily activities, hoping to deter kidnappings and arrests.[46]

Another type of third-party intervention is "monitoring and observation." This entails outside groups going to a conflict zone and being a presence with cameras and video equipment. The idea is that any repressive event will be recorded and reported to the global media, quickly bringing international attention to the situation. Often, this technique is used for elections where the chance of fraud is high. With an international presence ready to document any evidence of voting irregularities, the hope is that the observers will deter fraud, enabling genuinely free and fair elections to take place. Monitoring and observation may also include attending trials of opposition leaders to ensure fairness. For example, Western officials were present during Nelson Mandela's court hearing in 1983.[47]

The last type of third-party intervention is called "interpositioning." This is when nonviolent interventionists physically get in the way of conflicting groups. An example of this is Witness for Peace, an organization formed in 1983.[48] Witness for Peace was created when Gail Phares led an ecumenical delegation of U.S. citizens to Nicaragua to witness the effects of the Reagan-sponsored Contra war. She took the entire group to a village in the war zone, which was under attack when they arrived. However, as soon as the Contras saw the delegation arrive, they stopped shooting. Why? The Contras did not want to jeopardize the millions of dollars in aid they received from the United States, and they knew that the U.S. Congress would have a hard time justifying ongoing funding to a group that killed U.S. citizens. So the delegates spent some time in the village, speaking with the local residents about the impact of the war. As they departed, one person asked: If all it takes to stop Contra attacks is the presence of gringos (white North Americans), then why don't we set up a permanent presence here? Before the delegation left Nicaragua, they ran the idea past a few government leaders, who granted the group permission to operate.

Upon returning to the United States, Phares and others officially launched Witness for Peace. This organization had a two-fold strategy. One aspect of their mission was sending long-term international volunteers to live and work in the war zones. These volunteers would engage in "interpositioning"—that is, placing themselves in the war zones to deter Contra attacks. In the early days, this was referred to as a "human shield" between counterrevolutionary guerrillas and citizens. The other aspect of Witness for Peace's strategy was to send short-term volunteers who would tour Nicaragua, speaking with a variety of individuals to learn about the effects of the U.S.-sponsored war. These short-term delegates were then trained to tell others about their experiences through presentations at their churches and synagogues, through writing stories for local newspapers, and by talking with their congressional representatives. During the 1980s, Witness for Peace sent roughly five thousand volunteers to

Nicaragua and became one of the leading organizations that opposed the Reagan–Bush policies toward the region.[49]

Third-party intervention is not without problems, however. As numerous critics have pointed out, this type of nonviolent action may provide short-term protection or assistance in creating space for organizing. Yet it often works precisely because of the privilege of outsiders, mostly white Europeans and North Americans, thereby reinforcing a system of inequality. In his study of Peace Brigades International, Patrick Coy has noted, "While the international accompaniment technique itself may not have racism at its core, it does nevertheless engage the preferential dynamics of racism, and it flirts with colonialism."[50] Although nonviolent third-party intervention groups place an emphasis on empowerment of local movements, they may unintentionally create the opposite outcome. Coy continues, "The truth is . . . that the reliance on the outsider by international and national accompaniment organizations to protect local activists may produce various forms of disempowerment."[51]

Aside from the problems of privilege and inequality, there may be other problems associated with these techniques.[52] For instance, local groups may face accusations that they are lackeys, agitating for political changes that are favorable to Northern interests.[53] Also, some have noted that while "white privilege" may provide immediate protection, it may actually increase the long-term danger to local activists.

Most nonviolent interventionist groups are aware of these problematic dynamics and are addressing them. Some have incorporated anti-oppression awareness in their volunteer training programs. Others, such as Nonviolence International, are recruiting larger numbers of people from the Global South and sharing the privilege across the interventionist team. In other words, if interventionist team members are arrested and imprisoned, global pressure is used to ensure that all are released, not merely those team members who come from privileged positions. Finally, greater emphasis is placed on local leaders determining the direction, strategy, and techniques of action rather than international intervention team leaders. While none of these offers a perfect solution, the idea is to balance the potential power of third-party intervention without reinforcing the structures of inequality and oppression.

CONCLUSION

Nonviolent resistance takes many forms. It can be covert or open. It can be conducted in daily practices or it may be a long-term strategic effort to mobilize mass numbers of people. Nonviolent resistance can be used in tandem with institutional practices, as in the electoral revolution strategy and negotiated revolutions. It can also be used for different types of goals: to make reforms, to bear witness, or to bring international attention to an overlooked injustice. While the goals, strategies, and forms may differ, all these types of resistance rely solely on nonviolent weapons rather than violence.

CHAPTER 5

༄

Dynamics of Nonviolent Struggles

Rosa Parks, refusing to give up her seat on the bus to a white customer in Montgomery, Alabama. A lone Chinese citizen, obstructing a row of tanks headed for Tiananmen Square to crush the democracy movement. Millions of Egyptians defiantly occupying Tahrir Square until their long-standing autocratic ruler resigned. These moments were powerful, leaving an enduring imprint on our cultural consciousness and our history books. They represent significant moments in which regular citizens took brave stances in the name of equality, human rights, and democratic freedoms. Yet these moments can also be misleading as they sometimes give the impression that a heroic act is all one needs to expose injustices and instigate social change. In reality, behind each of these moments was a group of organizers who carefully planned out movement campaigns, including the mundane but necessary tasks of finding meeting spaces, recruiting participants, raising funds, and getting news coverage. For example, in his book *Stride Toward Freedom,* Martin Luther King, Jr. describes all the details that were necessary to sustain the Montgomery bus boycott for an entire year. The city's black citizens had to be convinced to join the boycott, carpools had to be organized to accommodate thousands of bus customers, reduced fares had to be negotiated with black cabbies, and regular meetings had to be held to sustain participants' motivation. Rosa Parks' arrest was simply the proverbial tip of the iceberg.[1]

This chapter sheds light on the various tasks, issues, and dynamics that are part of a nonviolent struggle. Specifically, we will examine the conditions necessary for a nonviolent movement to emerge, the factors involved in building a strong set of campaigns, the typical responses of authorities to civil resistance, and the ways that nonviolent movements respond to repression. This chapter also summarizes the research results on these topics, focusing on overt nonviolent resistance to state authorities.

MOVEMENT EMERGENCE

Civil resistance movements arise when there are *widespread grievances* within a population. Movements often erupt when the economy is in a downward spiral or when there is rampant political corruption or fraudulent elections. Grievances may also result from state restrictions of basic human rights and democratic freedoms. Whatever the precise grievance, a movement is unlikely to erupt unless a sizeable portion of the population is seriously disgruntled and sees the government as the source of the problem.

But the mere presence of an injustice is not enough to spark protest. There must also be *free spaces*[2]—that is, autonomous places that are relatively free of state control where people are able discuss these injustices, determine who is responsible, and decide what should be done. In short, free spaces are necessary to develop an "ideology of rebellion"[3] that encourages citizens to take action to change the situation. Without this, citizens may simply resign themselves to the situation, feeling that nothing can be done.

The third factor that facilitates mobilization is a *cross-class coalition* of people who wish for social change. As numerous studies have pointed out, resistance movements rarely win if elites (including high-profile leaders in business, politics, and the military) remain loyal to the state. However, sometimes elites become frustrated and convinced that the nation cannot make progress without major changes. When elites break ties to the state and shift their support to the opposition, a movement is more likely to emerge.

These three factors—widespread grievances, free spaces that allow for the cultivation of an ideology of rebellion, and a cross-class coalition—set the stage for a resistance movement to emerge. Yet often there is some type of triggering event that galvanizes public sentiment and arouses such indignation that people feel compelled to act. Trigger events may include actions such as the self-immolation of a fruit vendor in Tunisia that sparked the so-called Arab Spring. Or, in the 1986 people power movement in the Philippines, it was the brazen assassination of political opposition leader "Ninoy" Aquino that roused moral outrage and mobilized millions. Such events, called moral shocks, tend to evoke such deep visceral reactions that people feel compelled to act.[4]

New political opportunities may also serve as a triggering event as resisters realize that the time is right to act. For example, in 1989 Chinese democracy activists decided to mobilize protests in Tiananmen Square right after the death of Hu Yaobang, a former Secretary General of the Chinese Communist Party. Hu's funeral offered one of the few moments for citizens to gather in protest. As one dissident stated, "[I]n China, a leader's death serves as an excuse for people to assemble. The Party can't very well tell the people to not mourn a Party leader! Since a funeral is the only situation when people can assemble, you take advantage of the opportunity."[5]

When circumstances are ripe for resistance and a trigger event brings people out to protest, then one more factor helps transform a moment of protest into a sustainable movement: a mobilizing organization. Such organizations offer key resources such as money, meeting places, recruitment networks, and so forth. They also provide an infrastructural basis to the movement. Very often, preexisting organizations—such as labor unions, religious institutions, or other established civil groups—will help launch a movement. Such organizations have been called "movement midwives"[6] because they provide the assistance needed to birth a new movement organization that can strategically direct the erupting acts of resistance.

TAKING THE OFFENSIVE: MOVEMENT ACTIONS

Once civil resisters have mobilized, movement organizers face a variety of tasks to sustain action and achieve their goals. One task is to identify the state's traditional allies, also referred to as its "pillars of support" since they prop up the existing power structure. As Figure 5.1 indicates, such pillars might include religious leaders, business elites, the educational system, judiciary and electoral commissions, and security forces. Civil resisters must decide which pillars are most important to the government's ability to endure; once identified, organizers can devise plans to win these groups over to the opposition or, at a minimum, to neutralize the harm they might do to the movement. How is this accomplished? Civil resisters target individuals in these institutions. As the figure shows, if the movement focuses on the armed forces, activists may speak with the police and soldiers on the street, appealing to their sense of nationalism and assuring them that a new government would benefit them and their families. They can hold meetings with key military officers, winning their trust and securing an agreement to not unfairly attack protesters.[7] If done well,

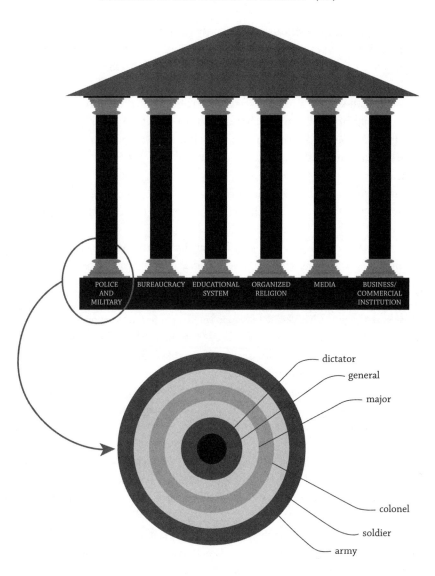

Figure 5.1:
Pillars of State Support[8]

such actions weaken the pillars of state support, making the government more vulnerable.

Another immediate task is to develop a long-term strategy for the struggle. In other words, movement leaders need to move beyond the initial outburst of opposition to a well-formulated "battle plan." Similar to the strategy of nonviolence described in Chapter 3, this battle plan starts with an identification of the crucial forms of power upon which the state relies. For instance, if the state is heavily dependent on foreign aid, resisters may focus their efforts on getting international donors to suspend aid until changes are made. If political rulers cannot function without control of the media, then resisters may create an alternative, independent media network that breaks a regime's hegemonic hold on information. Although it is important to recognize that a conflict situation can rapidly change and thus the best-laid plans may shift, civil resisters need an overarching strategy to give the movement direction and increase their odds of winning.

In developing a battle plan, organizers aim to incrementally build a movement's leverage. Kurt Schock defines *leverage* in the following way:

> The power of civil resistance comes not from hammering away at an opponent through direct armed assaults or asymmetric wars of attrition; rather, it inheres in its ability to undermine the power of the opponent through collective actions that drain power and legitimacy of the opponent or catalyze the withdrawal of support from key actors upon which the opponent depends. Violence works like a hammer, while nonviolence works more like a lever. Through leverage, oppressed and marginalized actors are able to defeat repressive and ostensibly more powerful opponents. In fact, the crucial variable in determining the outcome of nonviolent struggle is not repression, as is commonly assumed, but rather dependence relations that can be leveraged by challengers to undermine the opponent's power.[9]

To increase this leverage, resisters launch a series of campaigns that systematically withhold various forms of citizen-based power from the state until political rulers voluntarily make changes, grant concessions, or are coerced out of office.

The incremental approach typically begins with symbolic acts of resistance. This may entail synchronized moments of silence when the entire population stops in its tracks to show the unity and breadth of opposition. Or it can be the opposite: synchronized moments of noise. A common tactic in Latin America is to clang pots and pans to express dissent. For example, in Panama's movement against General Manuel Noriega in the 1980s, citizens honked horns and clanged pots each day at noon and 6 p.m.[10] The point of such actions is to get many people involved and to send political leaders a message that there is widespread opposition. It also withholds legitimacy from the opponent.

Yet symbolic acts provide little leverage vis-à-vis the state and hence they are rarely sufficient to topple authoritarian systems. Movement organizers must escalate to other types of resistance that withhold more important sources of power. Next might come acts of noncooperation, for example. To build confidence and participation, civil resisters may start with relatively low-risk actions. For instance, in 1980s Chile, civil resisters held rock concerts during voter registration campaigns even though guitars and public singing were banned under General Pinochet's rule.[11] Such actions can embolden resisters toward greater acts of noncooperation.

Finances constitute another crucial point of leverage. Civil resisters must undercut the material resources that governments (or any institution) need to operate. They may refuse to pay taxes or purchase government goods and services. They may institute a consumer boycott of key commodities, thereby reducing the amount of sales tax revenue the government receives. Finally, civil resisters may appeal to the international community, asking them to refuse loans, grants, and trade agreements with the nation in dispute.

As these campaigns are implemented, movement organizers should be mindful of the need for *tactical diversity*.[12] Resisters should vary their tactics for several reasons. First, it keeps the opponent guessing, never quite sure what type of action will come next. This makes it more difficult for the opponent to preemptively neutralize or counter the action.[13] Second, it keeps participants engaged and interested in the movement. As the famous community organizer Saul Alinsky wrote, "a tactic that drags on for too long becomes a drag."[14] Third, different tactics serve different purposes. Robert Burrowes argues that it may be particularly useful for a movement to shift between what he calls "methods of concentration" and "methods of dispersion."[15] The former includes tactics, such as protests and marches, whereby civil resisters are densely congregated in a public space. These actions build solidarity among participants, visibly represent the degree of support the movement has, and can capture global media attention, thereby highlighting the injustices. However, if the state begins to crack down, the movement ought to shift toward methods of dispersion, such as boycotts and general strikes, which are carried out in a physically diffused manner. It is very difficult for authorities to repress boycotters—not only because they are geographically dispersed but also because they are simply exercising their consumer preferences. Thus this type of tactical diversification can sustain the movement during periods of repression while expanding its leverage.[16]

Finally, civil resistance leaders must increase participation, expanding the movement's size and base. As Chenoweth and Stephan have argued, it is generally far easier to get people to participate in a nonviolent struggle compared to a violent one.[17] This is because there are significant physical, informational, moral, and commitment barriers to joining an armed uprising. In terms of the physical barriers, people must have a level of strength, stamina, and weapons skills to engage in guerrilla warfare. Many people—including the very young and the very old, as well anyone with a physical disability—may be simply unable to perform the tasks required in combat. In contrast, just about anyone can participate in a boycott or a strike, thereby expanding the recruitment pool. In terms of informational barriers, armed struggle is conducted covertly, making it difficult to recruit members. In contrast, unarmed struggle is mostly conducted openly, allowing organizers to publicize events and movement activities widely, thereby expanding recruitment possibilities. Potential recruits may also face moral barriers to join an armed struggle since many people are unwilling or reluctant to use violence against their opponents. Finally, violent struggles have a difficult time gaining members because they often require that recruits give up their careers, families, and homes to live underground. Nonviolent movements often do not demand such sacrifices and people can participate in a work slowdown or act of noncooperation as they go about their daily lives and activities. Thus, for all these reasons, it should not be surprising that nonviolent struggles tend to have a larger number of participants compared to their violent counterparts.

Why is it important to have mass participation from diverse sectors of society? Empirical data show that greater participation increases a movement's chances of winning.[18] This is because widespread participation enhances the effectiveness of nonviolent mechanisms. For instance, the more people participate in campaigns that withhold cooperation, skills, and finances from the state, the more comprehensive the impact is. Simply put, greater participation leads to greater movement leverage. Widespread diverse participation can also enhance tactical innovation, since different participants will bring distinct skills and ideas to the struggle. This can increase the number of pressure points and the ability to outmaneuver the opponent. Finally, mass participation enhances the movement's *resilience*—that is, the movement's capacity to "withstand and recover from repression."[19] Chenoweth and Stephan explain:

> The more diverse the participation in the resistance—in terms of gender, age, religion, ethnicity, ideology, profession, and socioeconomic status—the more difficult it is for the adversary to isolate the participants and adopt a repressive strategy short of maximal and indiscriminate repression. Of course, this does not mean that nonviolent campaigns are immune from regime repression— typically they are not—but it does make the opponent's use of violence more likely to backfire.[20]

In short, selective repression is hard to enact with a large movement. Any attacks on resisters are likely to be indiscriminate, harming a wide array of people, thereby eliciting outrage from a sizeable sector of society and expanding opposition to the state. This is a dynamic known as political jiu-jitsu or backfire, which we will explore in greater depth in the next section.

DEFENSIVE MANEUVERS: OPPONENTS' COUNTERSTRATEGIES

Whenever a nonviolent movement threatens the power and control of authorities, those authorities will try to stop civil resisters. They have multiple ways of thwarting movements, ranging from the subtle to the explicit.[21] Hence, to understand civil resistance dynamics, we must pay attention to the chess-like moves between resisters and opponents. Each side has a strategy for achieving its goals, and yet each side must also anticipate the other's strategic steps and try to obstruct them. In this section, we will look at the typical strategies that states use to undermine the power of nonviolent movements.

Tarnishing the Movement's Image

One way that authorities try to undermine a movement is to destroy its credibility. Often, states spread unsavory information about movement leaders. For example, the U.S. Federal Bureau of Investigation (FBI) had Dr. Martin Luther King, Jr. under constant surveillance. They first tried to discredit him by claiming he was associating with communists, thereby bringing his patriotism and loyalty into question. Then they revealed details of King's personal life, including extramarital sexual encounters. The hope was that he would lose credibility with his followers as well as the broader American public.[22] In addition, when media outlets are tightly regulated by the state, political leaders may block information that is favorable to the movement.

Creating a negative image of the movement is a tactic that states frequently employ. Governments may claim that civil resisters are terrorists or a front for terrorist groups. In Serbia, when President Milošević accused the civil resistance group Otpor of being terrorists, the movement quickly capitalized on this, using it as a joke in their street theater satire.[23] Another common smear-campaign tactic is to claim that the movement is a puppet for foreign interests. Milošević claimed that Otpor was a lackey group, carrying out the mission of the U.S. government and various U.S. organizations, such as the National Endowment for Democracy. Such accusations are designed to undercut trust in movement leaders and cast doubt on whether the movement is genuinely pursuing the interests of local citizens.

Generating Internal Movement Tensions

Another common counterstrategy is to create tensions and divisions within the movement. Internal divisions can undermine a movement in a couple ways. In some cases, civil resisters become so embroiled in conflicts that they spend more time and energy working on their differences and thus cannot organize against the opponent. If the tensions are strong enough, the movement may splinter or implode. This dynamic reflects the old adage of "divide and conquer." A second way that internal conflicts undermine movements is that they can create distrust, jealousy, and suspicion among resisters. Regimes have sometimes planted agents within a movement to accuse leading activists of being government informants. In some instances, these individuals become isolated or expelled—a counterstrategy technique of involuntary derecruitment. For those who remain, there is often a lingering suspicion that others are secret informants, making it difficult to carry out campaigns.[24]

Undermining Nonviolent Discipline by Planting Provocateurs

States may also try to undermine civil resisters' international support. Researchers have documented that international groups are more likely to support movements that espouse nonviolence than those who use violence.[25] So if a movement's image and support depend on maintaining nonviolent discipline, then states may take measures to provoke violence among activists. They do this by planting agents who become hostile and aggressive toward police. These *agent provocateurs* may even start riots and induce mob attacks. This discredits the movement, provides justification for state crackdowns, and undermines international support.[26]

Overt Repression and Violence

While governments typically prefer covert counterstrategies, they may resort to overt forms of repression to stop civil resistance. They may ban political opposition groups and eliminate freedom of speech and assembly. If a movement organization is not legally permitted to function, it is difficult for such groups to receive financial donations or hold meetings. A regime may also arrest key leaders and activists. Sometimes these civil resisters are held in prison; at other times, they are tortured or killed. Movement leaders are particularly targeted for violence since states believe that if they remove the leader, they will "decapitate" the movement, leaving it without direction or guidance.[27] Yet violence is also used to intimidate. The belief behind such repression is that people will become too frightened to continue resisting. As more and more people drop out, the movement will lose strength and eventual fade away.

RESPONDING TO REPRESSION: CREATING BACKFIRE

How is a movement to respond to repression? Civil resisters must grapple with this question for a couple of reasons. First, violent repression should be expected. In Chenoweth and Stephan's statistical study of nonviolent movements throughout the twentieth century and the early twenty-first century, they found that 88 percent of movements faced violent repression from their adversaries. Second, a movement's *resilience*—that is, its ability to recover from and persist in the face of repression—is a strong indicator of whether it will succeed. For these reasons, civil resisters ought to anticipate violence and come up with a plan to respond to it.

Some movements have taken a preemptive approach to repression. For instance, in the 2004 orange revolution, members of the opposition met with the security forces for weeks, convincing them not to carry out orders to arrest or attack protesters. But they also had a backup plan: if the police and military broke the agreement and used violence, then civil resisters ensured that it would be captured on video. They placed live streaming video cameras in every corner of Independence Square. Those cameras were linked to various broadcasting agencies, and thus any violence on the state's part would be instantly televised. One diplomat reflected on this strategy, "The move was . . . 'the ultimate trump card' and sent a clear message: 'Come and get us, but if you make us bleed, it will be live on CNN'."[28]

Yet sometimes movements and campaigns unfold quickly and there is little time for preemptive action to minimize repression. In those instances, we often see civil resisters appealing to security forces during a confrontation, persuading them to not attack. This occurred in the 1986 people power movement in the Philippines. When President Marcos ordered his troops to go out in tanks to disperse the crowds, protesters refused to back down. Thus they put the soldiers in a difficult moral quandary: they could either carry out orders, killing thousands of un-armed people in the process, or they could defect. The protesters encour-aged the soldiers to abandon their posts, saying: "You are one of us. You belong to the people. Come back to those to whom you belong."[29]

But what should civil resisters do when troops actually carry out re-pressive orders? How should they respond to violence? Here we must return to the concept of political jiu-jitsu,[30] backfire,[31] or the paradox of repression. At the heart of these concepts is the idea that violence perpe-trated against unarmed resisters can have an unanticipated effect: instead of stopping the movement, civil resisters may experience enhanced par-ticipation and support while the opponent, having revealed its brutality, loses support. There are numerous historical examples where violent re-pression of civil resisters has generated such backlash: the assault on Indian civil resisters during Gandhi's campaign of nonviolent interven-tion at the Dharasana salt works[32]; the beating of 167 student protesters in Czechoslovakia in 1989, which prompted the "Velvet Revolution"[33]; the massacre of pro-democracy demonstrators in Mali in 1991, which caused entire military units to refuse further orders to suppress resisters[34]—to name but a few. Yet this backfire dynamic is not automatic or guaranteed. In fact, in some instances, violent attacks serve their intended purpose of bringing nonviolent struggles to a halt. Hence civil resisters need to work strategically to create the backfire.

According to Hess and Martin, two conditions are needed to turn an attack into backfire. First, the broader public must perceive the attack against civil resisters as unwarranted, unfair, and excessive. This is likely to occur if resisters remain nonviolent and if their grievances are seen as legitimate. Second, information about the attack must reach relevant au-diences. Moreover, the audience must be large enough and influential enough that it can provoke a response from authorities. In other words, violent repression occurs, unfortunately, with relative frequency. Hence civil resisters need to make sure that the attacks generate outrage and that this information is communicated—by way of photographs, video, and news accounts—to an influential group of bystanders.[35]

Yet even if these conditions are met, opponents can quickly diffuse initial expressions of indignation. How? Typically, opponents use five techniques to reduce outrage. First, they try to cover up the atrocity. They may, for instance, attempt to censor any media reports about the attack. Second, they devalue and stigmatize the victims to create the impression that they deserved the treatment they received. Third, they spin the story to create an alternative interpretation—namely, that this was a case in which troops acted in self-defense or that action was necessary to restore law and order. Fourth, authorities may create the appearance of justice by using official channels to address the attack. They may instigate commissions to collect facts and bring in experts to assess the situation. In other words, authorities try to appease the population by making it look like they are doing something to investigate the situation when, in fact, such endeavors are a farce. Fifth, authorities may resort to bribery and intimidation of witnesses so that they recant their testimonies about the attack.

This discussion reveals that every move in a nonviolent conflict evokes a response from the other side. The struggle is a highly iterative process of offensive campaigns by civil resisters and defensive responses from their opponents, which in turn lead to further actions by nonviolent activists. What, then, can resisters do to enhance public outrage and backlash, even as authorities are trying to stop it? Hess and Martin capture this iterative contention around potential backlash in Table 5.1.

As authorities use each technique to quell incipient outrage and backlash, civil resisters must rapidly counter that technique. For instance, as the state censors media reports and evidence of the attack, civil resisters must find other ways to disseminate this information— either through alternative media sources or personal networks (such religious institutional ties, international solidarity groups, and so forth). As authorities devalue the target and claim they were simply

Table 5.1. TECHNIQUES USED TO INHIBIT BACKFIRE AND RESPONSES TO THOSE TACTICS[36]

Technique of inhibiting outrage	Examples	Methods of promoting outrage
Cover-up	Censorship; confiscation of evidence	Communication to movement members and wider society; journalism (stories, photos, videos)
Devaluation of the target	Racial prejudice; framing of repressed as liars or quacks	Humanization through personal stories
Reinterpretation	Lies; spin; frame alignment of elites with public interest	Persuasive accounts by credible witnesses; revealing power or financial interests of repressive elites
Official channels	Official statements; formal inquiries; courts; scientific research and expert panels	Use of alternative, nonofficial channels; exposing biases in formal inquiries
Intimidation and bribery	Threats, arrests, beatings, killings; job loss/demotions	Continued initiative by movement members; initiative by third parties

acting in the nation's best interests, civil resisters must humanize and validate victims through personal stories, demonstrating that they were unjustly attacked. When regimes commission their own fact-gathering studies, civil resisters must use nonofficial channels to independently document the situation.

In short, the outcome of a repressive event depends on the ability of authorities to suppress outrage and the skill of civil resisters in promoting it. If civil resisters can outmaneuver their opponent so that backlash erupts, the movement is likely to be strengthened.[37] They must then use that strength and momentum to pursue their goals with new campaigns and actions. In other words, the resilience they demonstrate—in terms of their ability to withstand and persist in periods of repression—has a strong influence on whether the movement will achieve its goals.

ILLUSTRATIVE CASE: INDONESIA'S STRUGGLE TO OUST PRESIDENT SUHARTO

One can see the iterative nature of a nonviolent conflict in the struggle between Indonesian civil resisters and President Suharto.[38] Indonesia had been a colony of the Netherlands for nearly three centuries. During World War II, the country was occupied by the Japanese. A national revolution broke Japanese control and the country gained independence in 1949. The first president of the newly sovereign Indonesia was Sukarno, who gained popularity based on his anticolonial platform.

In 1965, there was an attempted coup. This led Sukarno to give more power to the military, which quickly took action to stop all threats to the state. Prominent in these efforts was General Suharto, who massacred those rumored to be associated with the Communist Party of Indonesia and others considered politically subversive. By 1966, the military demanded that Sukarno grant greater powers to Suharto, who had become the army's chief of staff. But Suharto was not satisfied with more power; he wanted total power. By 1968, he was appointed as president. To consolidate his control, he banned opposition political groups and student organizations and had his opponents imprisoned or killed. An estimated 500,000 to 1,000,000 citizens died in his anticommunist rampage, making it one of the worst massacres in the twentieth century.[39] Over the next decades, Suharto ruled ruthlessly. Western allies, such as the Australian and U.S. governments, turned a blind eye since they considered him a crucial Cold War ally.

Although it was extremely risky, some individuals openly criticized Suharto. These criticisms focused on the regime's corruption, the expanding repression, and the lack of genuinely democratic election processes. Suharto responded by forcing his opponents within the military into retirement or transferring them to posts abroad. He also set up a parliament, which was largely populated by government-appointed politicians. Yet the parliament was a façade, since the regime heavily controlled legislators' activities. Suharto cultivated a policy of co-opting political leaders and granting rewards for loyalty, while repressing those who refused to be co-opted or opposed his leadership.

For nearly thirty years most Indonesians tolerated Suharto's authoritarianism and corruption—mainly because Suharto was able to stimulate economic growth, decrease poverty rates, and improve the country's health and welfare systems. Literacy and education rates climbed and life expectancies improved dramatically. So how, then, did a movement emerge that eventually led to Suharto's demise?

Ripe Conditions

At the start of the chapter, we learned that several factors enable nonviolent resistance to emerge: widespread grievances, cross-class coalitions, and free spaces where oppositional consciousness can grow. The free spaces were at universities. Suharto had tried to control universities by prohibiting student groups from meeting on campus and appointing administrators and student council leaders who were regime supporters. Yet dissident students had formed underground "study groups" that functioned as a free space where ideologies of rebellion flourished and strategic planning occurred.

Widespread grievances erupted when the economy collapsed in 1997. The collapse was instigated by a fiscal crash in Thailand that spread to several Southeast Asian economies. Indonesia's currency dropped dramatically in value, causing rampant inflation and exploding unemployment rates. Students began to organize protests—tens of thousands demonstrated, first on campus and then later off campus. But those who participated were not just students; the protests included the urban working class as well as middle- and upper-class professionals, who experienced a sharp decline in their lifestyle. Soon, demonstrators addressed issues beyond the failing economy; they also began to challenge Suharto's political corruption and the lack of democratic freedoms.

Like so many movements, the anti-Suharto movement exploded after a "trigger event." This event occurred during a student-led protest on May 12, 1998, at the prestigious Trisakti University in Jakarta. During the protest, security forces killed four students. Indonesians were outraged that troops would callously kill their own citizens, and the four fallen students were quickly transformed into martyrs. The murders prompted widespread protests, which escalated into riots. Nearly two thousand people died in the riots, mostly Indonesians of Chinese descent, while others were raped or injured.[40]

Early on, civil resisters suspected that government undercover agents were instigating the riots to discredit and divide the movement. They called for a fact-finding commission to investigate. When the commission published its findings, there was indeed evidence that members of Suharto's military were responsible for the violence. Hence this effort to repress the movement backfired, largely because civil resisters refused to accept the government's version of the events and pushed for an independent commission to expose who was really responsible. When Indonesian citizens realized that the state was culpable, the repressive act actually harmed Suharto and helped the opposition.

Escalating Resistance: Offensive Maneuvers

After the initial outburst of protest, student organizations served as the "movement midwife," supporting sustained resistance. Immediately, they established an alternative media communication system to guide the movement and air demands. This was essential since the Indonesian press had been highly regulated and censored for many years. The student organizers also used e-mail and the Internet to send news reports to international audiences, including CNN. They received help from the Alliance of Independent Journalists, who offered crash courses on how to clearly convey their ideas and publish news reports.[41] While the Internet helped to broadcast news of the movement overseas, organizers knew that few Indonesians had access to e-mail or the Internet at home. Thus, to communicate within the movement, a group of civil resisters physically occupied several radio stations. Over the airwaves, they called for an election on May 18 to vote in a new president of the national legislature. They also announced that a million-person rally would be held in Jakarta on May 20.

Next, the movement focused on undermining the state's pillars of support and winning them over to the opposition. The murder of the four students had helped on this point: it caused Indonesian elites to break ties with Suharto.[42] This included political elites, who were convinced that the nation could never change course until Suharto was gone. It also included military elites. Divisions had been growing for months within the Indonesian security forces. Before the protests began, Suharto had appointed his son-in-law, Prabowo Subianto, to head the Special Forces known as KOPASSUS. Prabowo was highly ambitious and aimed to gain power over General Wiranto, who headed the armed forces. The conflict between Prabowo and Wiranto culminated after the student killings as each had different ideas about how to handle the situation. Prabowo was ready and willing to use a heavy hand. In contrast, Wiranto advocated for protesters, declaring that students should be granted the right to demonstrate off campus. Meanwhile, the loyalty of many soldiers was waning. There were reports that troops were loading their weapons with blanks (instead of rubber bullets) so that no protesters would be harmed.

The rapidly expanding civil resistance movement intensified the division between the Special Forces and the military. Prabowo allied himself with Vice President Habibie, who promised to promote Prabowo to Commander of the Armed Forces when he became president. Given Suharto's declining health and recent stroke, Habibie thought his chances of becoming the next president were good. He needed Prabowo and he knew that this offer would keep him loyal to the regime. Wiranto also wanted to protect his political future and, convinced that Suharto's demise was imminent, he initiated conversations with the civil resisters.[43]

Student resisters were open to an alliance with the military. After months of protests, they saw little progress toward their goal of ousting Suharto and realized that this connection might enhance their chances by undermining one of the regime's primary pillars of support. Moreover, student activists had been in conversation with the armed forces for years. In the beginning, the conversations were initiated by the military as a way to gather intelligence, but it also gave students an opportunity to learn about the inner workings of the regime. By May 1998, the military and students saw their interests converging. One officer made a proposal: "We share the same vision. We've both been disappointed and we should work together to overthrow Suharto."[44]

After several days of protests without any concessions from the state, the movement organizers decide to shift tactics. On May 18, they sent busloads of students to nonviolently intervene in the national legislature. The alliance with the military was crucial here: as the students approached the building, Wiranto ordered his troops to allow the resisters to freely enter. He further ordered the soldiers to provide transportation and food to the student resisters, thereby facilitating the occupation.[45]

The Regime's Defensive Maneuvers

Nonviolent conflicts entail a set of strategic offensive actions as well as a set of defensive responses. In the Indonesian case, the Suharto regime employed a number of techniques to thwart the expanding resistance movement. In early 1998, the Special Forces (under Prabowo's leadership) kidnapped leading activists. Some were released after being tortured and imprisoned for months. Others were never released or found and are presumed dead.[46] The purpose of this violent repression was twofold: (1) to "decapitate" the movement by removing its key leaders and (2) to raise the costs of activism so that participants would drop out and others would be deterred from joining.

The state also attempted to tarnish the movement by provoking violence. There was clear evidence that the regime planted provocateurs to incite riots, looting, and sexual assault. The government believed this would give the movement a reputation as little more than thugs and criminals. The attacks on ethnic Chinese citizens were another defensive act, intended to increase ethnic tensions and undermine unity within the movement. The regime also planted infiltrators, whose purpose was not only to gather intelligence information but also to fuel divisions between the mostly Muslim civil resisters and religious minority groups.[47]

Resilience and Persistent Action

Despite government attempts to defeat the movement, civil resisters increased their chances of winning by using the deaths of the four martyred students to create a backlash that undermined Suharto's traditional base of support. Moreover, civil resisters demonstrated resilience when they persisted in the face of threats. As students occupied the legislative building, they continued planning for the million-person march, but news of a heavy-handed military crackdown was leaked. Since the crackdown was scheduled for May 19, the students had to time plan their response. They asked foreign journalists and diplomats to gather at the legislature building, protectively encircling the student occupiers. Suharto and Prabowo knew they could not attack without provoking an international outcry. But movement leaders anticipated that the military would try to furtively attack during the rally on May 20. Hence they called off the rally in Jakarta to avoid violence, but nearly five hundred thousand demonstrated in Yogyakarta and Bandung.

At this point, Suharto realized he had no power. He had lost legitimacy in the eyes of Indonesian citizens, who were refusing to cooperate with his rule. His traditional political allies had abandoned him. In fact, the leaders of the legislature announced that they were giving him three days to resign; if he refused, they would start impeachment processes. And he could not even count on his Special Forces, many of whom had defected to the opposition in the last days—most likely to preserve their futures in what seemed to be an inevitably forthcoming post-Suharto era.[48]

But Suharto had one last defensive tactic planned. On the evening of May 20, 1998, he called in General Wiranto, ordering him to impose martial law and endorse a state of emergency. Wiranto refused. The General informed Suharto that the military would not repress the civil resisters, and he asked Suharto to step down. With no one to impose martial law, and without the support of the existing legislators, he had no other choice. On May 21, Suharto resigned.

Why did civil resisters win? First, conditions were favorable for an opposition movement to emerge. The downward-spiraling economy created widespread grievances and helped to form a cross-class coalition since people from all socioeconomic backgrounds were affected. The presence of student organizations provided free spaces. These same organizations served as the "movement midwife," promoting large-scale mobilization after the murder of the four students. Second, civil resisters undermined the state's primary pillars of support: political leaders and, perhaps most importantly, the military. Third, the opposition movement demonstrated resilience. Despite the state's countermoves—including violent attacks and planting infiltrators and provocateurs—civil resisters persisted. They found ways to turn repressive events to their favor, evoking the dynamic of backlash. They also continued to push for their goals, moving from demonstrations to nonviolent occupations. In the end, civil resisters simply outmaneuvered Suharto.

CONCLUSION

Although it often appears that civil resistance struggles erupt spontaneously, when the oppressed simply can't take it anymore, it is generally the case that several favorable conditions are in place that facilitate movement emergence. These include widespread grievances, cross-class coalitions, trigger events, free spaces, and mobilizing organizations that sustain resistance. Within these mobilizing organizations or networks, strategic plans are developed to undermine a government's pillars of support and to withhold crucial forms of citizen-based power. As in any conflict, however, nonviolent struggles include at least two sides that are each responding strategically to the moves of the other. Therefore, while civil resisters may undertake offensive campaigns, the regime will respond defensively, trying to undermine the movement. It is an ongoing, iterative process, and the course of the struggle is shaped by civil resisters' ingenuity and resilience in the face of repression as well as their ability to expand their points of leverage through diverse tactics and campaigns.

CHAPTER 6

✧

Outcomes and Consequences
of Nonviolent Struggles

1989 was the year that Soviet-style socialism collapsed in Eastern Europe. People throughout the world watched in awe as the Berlin Wall came down and dissidents, such as Czechoslovakia's Vaclav Havel, became leaders of new democratic states. The power of civil resistance seemed capable of transforming the most intransigent regimes. Yet 1989 was also the year that civil resisters in China were crushed. Students and workers had occupied Beijing's Tiananmen Square, calling for democratic reforms and human rights. Unlike their Eastern European counterparts, Chinese resisters were not victorious. Instead, the Chinese Communist Party cracked down, massacring an estimated three thousand people as it brutally extinguished the movement. As this case illustrates, not all nonviolent struggles are successful.

In the last chapter, we examined the common dynamics of a nonviolent conflict. Both civil resisters and their opponents plot strategic maneuvers, hoping to be victorious. But what really shapes the outcome of such struggles, both in the short term and the long term? What factors influence whether a nonviolent movement will succeed or fail? And what has research revealed about the other consequences of participating in civil resistance? These are the questions that we explore in this chapter.

IMMEDIATE OUTCOMES

Several studies have examined why some nonviolent resistance movements succeed while others fail. Not surprisingly, a sound strategy that systematically severs various forms of power from the opponent is essential. Yet a savvy strategy alone is insufficient to ensure a victory.[1] Recent empirical research has delineated several additional factors that can influence whether civil resisters achieve their immediate goals. However, this research does not represent a recipe for success. Even if civil resisters manage to achieve all of the following, the outcome is never predetermined; shifting political circumstances and unanticipated developments can always alter a conflict situation. Nonetheless, these factors, listed in Table 6.1, can increase the odds of success or derail a promising movement.

Type of Campaign

Not all movements have the same goal. As Chapter 4 highlights, civil resistance struggles may be focused on obtaining higher wages and improved working conditions; they may seek to end discrimination against religious, ethnic, or sexual minorities; or they may aim to overthrow a domestic dictatorship. Do all types of movements fare equally well using nonviolent tactics and strategies?

In a study that compares hundreds of violent and nonviolent campaigns from 1900 to 2006, Chenoweth and Stephan examine movements with three distinct aims: (1) anti-regime struggles (aiming to overthrow an incumbent domestic political system); (2) anti-occupation or self-determination struggles (aiming for national independence and autonomy from foreign control); and (3) secessionist struggles (aiming to break away from a nation to form an independent territory). What they found is that anti-regime

Table 6.1. FACTORS POTENTIALLY SHAPING OUTCOMES
FOR IMMEDIATE GOALS

Factor	Effect on Likelihood of Success
Type of goal	Mixed
Duration of campaign/movement	Negative (longer campaigns = less success)
Resilience	Positive
Radical (violent) flank effect	No effect
Size and diversity of participation	Positive
Maintaining nonviolent discipline	Positive
Degree of movement cohesion	Positive
Security force defections	Positive
International pressures	Mixed

movements using nonviolence were successful in nearly 60 percent of the cases. (In an interesting contrast, anti-regime movements that used violence were successful less than 30 percent of the time.) For anti-occupation or nationalist movements, roughly 30 percent that were nonviolent achieved their goals; their armed counterparts won in an estimated 25 percent of the cases. But nonviolence was not effective in secessionist struggles: not a single nonviolent secessionist movement in their database achieved its goal. Their violent counterparts did not fare much better: less than 10 percent of armed secessionist groups won their goals.[2]

Why do we see a difference in the success rates among different types of nonviolent struggles? Chenoweth and Stephan do not provide us with a definitive answer, but they do provide remarkable empirical evidence that nonviolence is strategically superior to violence in all but secessionist struggles. Beyond that, we know very little, and thus there is a great need for more systematic research to understand how nonviolent dynamics operate differently based on movement goals.

Duration

The length of time that it takes for a movement to wage its struggle also has an effect on whether civil resisters reach their goals. In general, the longer a movement goes on, the lower the chances that nonviolent activists will fully achieve success. Why? Civil resisters may lose faith in the efficacy of nonviolence and shift toward armed struggle.[3] Movement participants may simply grow weary of the costs of activism and drop out. Also, given more time, regimes can figure out new methods for thwarting the nonviolent movement; in contrast, when civil resisters move quickly, political rulers are often caught off guard and may not find effective counterstrategies. There are, of course, some notable exceptions to this trend. Nonetheless, the empirical data from Chenoweth and Stephan's study find that a general pattern exists: the longer a movement drags on, the lower its chances for full success.

Resilience

Another factor shaping nonviolent movement outcomes is resilience. Resilience is defined as a movement's capacity to sustain resistance in the face of repression.[4] It is typically measured by a movement's ability to retain its members, recruit new ones, and launch additional campaigns despite concerted efforts by opponents to crush civil resistance.[5] Numerous studies have documented that resilience is a critical factor for a successful outcome in nonviolent struggles.[6]

But what enables a movement to endure through repressive periods? Why are some groups devastated while others persist? Some argue that tactical shifts help movement participants to evade the effects of repression—particularly shifts between tactics of concentration (where movement participants are in the same geographic location and close physical proximity) and tactics of dispersion (where participants engage in resistance in a variety of locations with little to no physical proximity). In other words, tactical diversity and tactical shifts can minimize repression. While mass demonstrations serve the important function of showing the breadth of opposition and building solidarity, such actions make it easier for the state to repress civil resisters since they are all in one location and easily identifiable. Thus, as the likelihood of a crackdown increases, movement leaders may shift to tactics of dispersion to shield resisters from the brutality of an attack. They may launch a boycott or a symbolic action—such as synchronized moments of silence or noise—to sustain action and motivation while decreasing the chance of direct repression.

Ackerman and Kruegler also argue that resilience is enhanced when civil resisters mute the impact of repression. This can be done in several ways.[7] First, whenever possible, movement organizers should devise plans to keep resisters out of harm's way. For example, Argentina's Mothers of the Disappeared took measures to minimize the chance of being caught by security forces. To spread the word about upcoming actions, the Mothers met during Mass in Catholic Churches. They would sit next to one another, pretending to pray, but secretly passing information about upcoming campaigns. When the Mothers held demonstrations in front of Congress—holding signs that asked, "Where are our children?"—they anticipated that the police might harass or arrest them. As soon as it appeared the police would act, they would disperse in pairs, leaving by various routes and blending into the pedestrian crowds, making it difficult to apprehend them.[8]

A second method for muting the effects of repression is to "take the sting out of the agents of violence."[9] This may include the highly controversial tactic of disabling opponents' weapons through demolition. Ackerman and Kruegler make a careful distinction between sabotage and demolition. They argue that demolition is a subset of sabotage and simply refers to "all acts which render inoperative the material resources of an opponent."[10] In their view, there is violent sabotage and nonviolent sabotage. Although they duly caution civil resisters about the problems with this technique, they argue that nonviolent sabotage can useful.[11] This includes tampering with opponents' weapons to make them unusable, disrupting the production of weapons at the factory level, or jamming electronics and overloading computer systems to render them inoperable. Illustrations of this can be seen in the Nazi occupation of Denmark, where Danes sometimes took weapons from Nazi troops. Danish factory workers also engaged in a work slowdown so that the warships they were ordered to build for the Nazis were never completed and thus never put into use.[12]

Yet sometimes repression still happens, despite the best efforts to avoid or mute it. When a movement suffers a loss, resisters must try to recover from it. This means fostering the backlash dynamic (as described in Chapter 5) to generate international outrage, win broader support, and push elites to break ties to the state. Leaders can also pursue ways of restoring any critical assets they lost. Ronald Francisco argues that if a movement cannot rebuild its organizational and leadership base, its capacity for resilience and survival is severely restricted.[13] Movement leaders must also provide support for victims and survivors. Finally, leaders need to frame the repression in a way that mobilizes further action rather than promoting a defeatist mentality. For instance, civil resisters can frame the repression as an indication that the movement is effective and posing a real threat to the regime.

If the movement is able to generate backlash, tangibly support the victims of repression, regenerate its key assets, and frame the repression in a motivational manner, it can sustain resistance. If it concedes defeat after a crackdown, then defeat is ensured. Resilience is critical, yet we must underscore the fact that resilience is not an innate trait but something actively cultivated by civil resistance organizers.

Radical or Violent Flank Effect

In many countries, armed and unarmed movements are mobilizing at the same time. It is quite common to see guerrilla groups and civil resistance groups working simultaneously for the same goals. What effect do violent movements have on nonviolent struggles? This is what social scientists call the "radical flank effect" question. In reality, "radical flank" is a misnomer since civil resistance groups can be equally radical in calling for comprehensive change. A more accurate term would be the "violent flank effect." Nonetheless, I use the standard nomenclature in the discussion below to remain consistent with the commonly accepted and known terminology within the social sciences.

Some argue that there is a *negative* radical flank effect: that is, the presence of an armed movement undermines civil resistance because the violence has a tainting effect in which all oppositional groups lose credibility in the eyes of national and international audiences. Moreover, this tainting may mean that a state will crack down on all dissidents, regardless of whether they are violent or nonviolent. This happened during the "Troubles" in Northern Ireland. In the late 1960s, a civil rights movement emerged in which Catholics were fighting for equality in voting, housing, employment, and education. When the armed Irish Republican Army (IRA) reemerged and joined the fight for Catholic rights, virtually all Catholic activists in Northern Ireland were repressed and perceived as terrorists, whether they advocated violence or nonviolence.[14]

Others, however, have noted that the radical flank effect can be *positive*: the presence of a militant, armed wing may make the nonviolent group appear more moderate and less threatening, thereby generating pressure on the state to negotiate or grant their demands. In other words, the presence of violent groups may actually enhance the power, credibility, and leverage of nonviolent groups. Some have argued that this dynamic was present in the anti-apartheid struggle in South Africa (with the armed wing of the African National Congress) as well as the U.S. civil rights struggle (with accompanying Black Power groups). In fact, according to James Cone, Malcolm X was aware of this dynamic and intentionally played off it in the last months of his life. While Congress was deliberating over the proposed civil rights bill, Malcolm X warned the U.S. government that if it continued to obstruct African Americans' struggle for equality and justice, then they might be forced to resort to armed struggle. As he famously stated, "If we don't do something real soon, I think you'll have to agree that we're going to be forced either to use the ballot or the bullet. It's one or the other."[15] Malcolm X reportedly felt that the best thing he could do to help Martin Luther King, Jr. was to continue his fiery, militant rhetoric. He purportedly even asked Coretta Scott King to convey this information to her husband.[16]

What does the empirical evidence tell us about how an armed wing affects civil resistance movements?[17] Schock and Chenoweth examined this question using 108 nonviolent movements that occurred worldwide from 1900 to 2005. Their conclusion was that the presence of an armed movement does not improve civil resisters' power and leverage.[18] Referring to Table 6.2, Chenoweth wrote, "What is evident here is that having an armed wing has a slight negative effect on the probability of success. However, this effect is not statistically significant—a finding that is confirmed in other statistical tests. There is definitely no evidence to support the

Table 6.2. THE RADICAL (VIOLENT) FLANK EFFECT ON CIVIL
RESISTANCE MOVEMENTS

	Presence of Violent Campaign	Absence of Violent Campaign
Successful	22 (46%)	35 (60%)
Unsuccessful	26 (54%)	23 (40%)
	48 (100%)	58 (100%)

$N = 106, X^2 = 2.23; p < 0.136.$
Bivariate cross-tabulation of the relationship between nonviolent movement outcomes and the presence or absence of an armed group.
From Schock and Chenoweth, 2015.

notion that armed groups will help a nonviolent campaign."[19] Still, there
is a paucity of data on this topic, and further research is needed to confirm
or refute Chenoweth and Schock's claim.

Large-Scale, Diverse Participation

In Chenoweth and Stephan's study of movement outcomes, one factor
stands out as having a great impact on the odds of winning: mass participation with a diverse population. They argue, "Over space and time, large
campaigns are much more likely to succeed than small campaigns. . . .
[A]s membership increases, the probability of success also increases."[20]
Of course, mass participation alone will not guarantee success; it must be
coupled with a sound strategy and other factors. Nonetheless, the data are
clear: getting a lot of people to join the struggle can help significantly.

Why does participation matter so much? It makes those dynamics of
nonviolent resistance (discussed in Chapter 5) more effective, especially
when participants come from various gender and age categories, as well as
ethnic, religious, regional, and socioeconomic backgrounds. When the
movement is highly diverse, an opponent cannot easily single out a few
activists for repression. For example, in an economic boycott of common
consumer items, how does one even identify participants, much less sanction them? Or in a demonstration that draws together a million people,
how do you arrest and incarcerate all one million? In these instances, repression becomes more difficult or it forces the opponent to indiscrimi-
nately attack civil resisters. Indiscriminate attacks are much more likely
to backfire, however. In short, mass actions—whether they are marches,
boycotts, or noncooperation—make a repressive response more difficult
and more costly.

Mass participation also enhances a movement's *leverage* or ability to withhold power from an opponent. Take, for example, a labor strike. If only 10 percent of workers in a given industry go on strike, they can be quickly fired or replaced. Strike-breaking coworkers can take on additional shifts to keep the industry functioning. But if 90 percent of the employees in an industry refuse to show up for work, the effect is much greater. Economic boycotts are also more effective with widespread participation. If only a small portion of people refuse to buy a company's goods or services, the company can survive—either by accepting leaner profit margins or raising prices to make up the difference. However, if the majority of their clientele participate in the boycott, the company is likely to face bankruptcy and is therefore more amenable to concessions.

Finally, a diverse movement with mass participation is also more likely to induce defections from political, economic, and military elites. Why? When men and women of all ages, ethnicities, religious backgrounds, and socioeconomic classes participate, then there is a good chance that some of the movement participants will have ties to powerful national players. For instance, military officers may find that their adult children are part of the movement, while military recruits might have friends in the opposition. Political leaders will find their constituents calling for change. If they perceive that the movement has a chance of winning—which may seem likely when hundreds of thousands protest—then they may be concerned about their own political futures and side with the people. Finally, mass participation in economically oriented acts of civil resistance is likely to take a toll on business leaders. In her study of democratic transitions in South Africa and El Salvador, Elisabeth Wood argues that economic elites were deeply affected by the conflicts, facing considerable financial losses. Eventually, this led them to push the state toward negotiations with the opposition, shifting the balance of power in favor of the movements.[21] In short, the broader the participation, the greater is the effect in personal and political spheres.

Internal Unity

Another important factor that shapes the likelihood of success is whether the movement can maintain internal unity and cohesion.[22] As mentioned in Chapter 5, opponents often try to create conflict within movements precisely because it undermines civil resisters' capacity to act collectively. Yet often conflicts erupt, not because of outside interference or counterstrategies, but due to genuine disagreements among movement participants.

What are common issues that create internal movement tensions? One source of conflict is *strategy*. Some civil resisters may wish to push for negotiations and compromise, while others advocate a more confrontational and militant approach, hoping that the system will totally collapse. One faction of a movement may want to combine institutional with noninstitutional methods of resistance, while others may feel that working within the system merely grants legitimacy to it. The growing division between the Black Power movement, represented by Malcolm X, and the U.S. civil rights movement, represented by Martin Luther King, Jr., was a result of such issues. The civil rights movement used nonviolent direct action—including sit-ins, marches, boycotts, and so forth—as well as voter registration campaigns, lobbying, and policy work to achieve its goal of integration. In contrast, Black Power advocates argued that integration should not be the goal; instead, they aimed to strengthen the black community on its own, empowering it financially and politically, instead of working for access to a white-dominated system.[23]

Another source of conflict may stem from *regional, class, ethnic, or religious differences* among civil resisters. For instance, in the 1989 Chinese democracy movement, there were tensions between Beijing students (who had started the resistance and felt they had the right to lead the struggle) and students from outside provinces (who felt they were not given sufficient voice in decision-making processes). There were also tensions between students (who saw themselves as the movement's rightful vanguard) and members of the working class (who felt excluded, even though they played an important role in fundraising and in protest participation). Ethnic and religiously diverse movements may also find that participants have distinct collective identities that may clash at times. In the Central America movement of the 1980s, faith-based participants often wanted to select tactics that reflected a Christian identity (such as commemorative prayer vigils of the slain clergy in El Salvador), while some secular socialist groups did not feel comfortable with such an approach.[24]

Nonviolent movements can also become divided over *leadership*. There may be competing views about what type of leadership system should be in place. Sometimes a charismatic leader naturally emerges, such as Mohandas Gandhi or Martin Luther King, Jr., who commands a significant following and has the ability to unify civil resisters. Yet charismatic leadership has its drawbacks, too: often such leaders become ready targets for repression. If leaders are imprisoned or assassinated, it can cause movements to flounder, since they often have relied heavily on the deceased leader for direction. Indeed, after a leader is gone, there are often internal struggles over who the successor will be; such struggles can derail the entire movement.[25] At other times, movements may choose a radically democratic decision-making/leadership system for their movement. Yet when each civil resister potentially has input into key decisions, this opens more possibilities for participants to disagree with one another about the movement's direction, goals, campaign tactics, and so forth.[26]

Ability to Maintain Nonviolent Discipline

Linked to the issue of internal unity is the ability to maintain nonviolent discipline. If a segment of the civil resistance movement is not convinced that nonviolence is that best strategic approach, those resisters may resort to violence during marches, demonstrations, and other campaign events. When this occurs, the movement's chances for winning tend to decrease for several reasons. First, when violence erupts, it gives the state reason to crack down; they can justify their actions as necessary to prevent harm and to reestablish order and control. Outside observers often do not question such incidents, since it generally assumed that it is the state's responsibility to address any violent activity. Second, when the movement loses its nonviolent discipline, the chance of backfire or "political jiu-jitsu" decreases. Recall that backfire occurs when third parties see the use of force as excessive or unjustified. If some civil resisters become violent, there is a chance that observers will no longer consider the state's use of force as abhorrent; they may well decide it was justified or that troops were merely acting defensively. Third, when violence erupts, it may cause civil resisters to lose credibility. Although some people may applaud it as oppressed people striking back, others might argue that the movement failed to uphold its promise to eschew violence. For all these reasons, the inability to maintain nonviolent discipline can undermine a civil resistance movement.

Wendy Pearlman argues that leadership issues and lack of nonviolent discipline were critical factors shaping the *intifadas* (uprisings) in the Palestinian national movement. In her 2011 book,[27] she uses the technique of process tracing to understand why the Palestinian movement sometimes relied upon nonviolent strategies while at other times it resorted to violence. She argues that the movement's shifting tactics can be explained through her "organizational mediation theory," which holds that nonviolent resistance requires discipline, clear strategic direction, and coordination—something only unified movements can provide through strong leadership and authoritative organizations. She argues that "while the paths to violence are multiple, there is only one prevailing path to nonviolent protest: a path that requires a movement to have or create internal cohesion."[28]

But why is cohesion so important for nonviolent mass mobilization? While terrorist groups can carry out campaigns with only a few individuals, large numbers of participants are necessary for successful boycotts and strikes. Cohesion is also needed to maintain nonviolent discipline. Conversely, internal fragmentation means that a movement's ability to constrain aggression is weakened and subgroups often emerge who pursue a more militant agenda through more militant methods. Tracing the Palestinian national movement's development through five stages, Pearlman notes that each nonviolent stage was preceded by cohesion while each violent stage was preceded by internal fragmentation.

If internal cohesion is critical for successful nonviolence, how is movement cohesion created? Pearlman argues that it comes from several sources. It can come from strong leaders who are able to unify divergent factions. For instance, she discusses how Palestinian leader Yasir Arafat cultivated a "fatherly benefactor" mystique that evoked personal loyalty among activists and helped the movement overcome its internal points of dissension. (Yet this also created a long-term problem when Arafat died and his successor, who did not possess such charisma, was left to find other, less effective means of unifying the movement.) Cohesion also comes from strong, authoritative institutions and a clear collective purpose. Shared goals help to unite a movement, while strong organizations command respect and have the authority to guide the struggle. When these three factors are present, the movement experiences unity and leaders are able to persuade participants to refrain from violence, even in emotionally charged situations.

In my own work on nonviolent revolutions, I found that movements are most likely to maintain nonviolent discipline when they have trained civil resisters in the philosophy, strategy, and techniques of nonviolence. When tense confrontations arise, trained resisters know how to handle the escalating conflict and they understand why it is important not to resort to violence. This was true in the 1986 Philippine "people power" movement. The Filipino Catholic Church had spent months preparing for the revolution by sponsoring workshops on nonviolent resistance.[29] Similarly, in the East German revolution of 1989, pastors at Leipzig's St. Nicholas Church—which had become the center of the movement—had organized workshops on nonviolence, including trainings to identify provocateurs who might try to instigate violence. Because of this training, along with strong institutional sponsorship and leaders who could unite the struggle, these movements were able to remain nonviolent.[30]

In sum, empirical studies propose that several factors enhance a movement's ability to remain nonviolent. These include training and preparation of participants, strong trusted leaders who can reinforce the commitment to nonviolence, internal movement unity, a clear goal, and strong, authoritative institutions.

Security Force Defections

No large sample study to date has systematically tested which nonviolent tactics have the greatest impact or ability to help civil resisters achieve their goals. That is, of the six power sources identified by Sharp and others, we do not yet have empirical evidence about which ones undermine the opponent most effectively when withdrawn. In all likelihood, it probably depends on the movement's goal and target. For movements aiming to overthrow a state regime (either a foreign occupying force or a domestic dictatorship), it appears that withholding the regime's sanctioning power is highly effective.

Two studies have emphasized the importance of defections within the armed forces. In a small sample comparison of six movements, I found that those movements that won over the military—leading to military desertions, refusals to carry out repressive orders, or outright mutiny and defections—were more likely to win. I argue that this factor clearly distinguished the successful from the failed nonviolent revolutionary struggles.[31] Stephan and Chenoweth's large-sample study confirms this finding as well. In fact, their data indicate that nonviolent revolutionary movements were forty-six times more likely to succeed when security forces defected, compared to nonviolent movements where troops remain loyal to the incumbent regime.[32] Why? When police refuse to arrest or attack resisters and when the military refuses to support and defend the regime, even the most authoritarian leaders are left helpless. They have no one to carry out their orders and no one to protect them. Their ability to sanction or punish is gone, as is their power.

Some may think that this is obvious; after all, Leon Trotsky long ago stated that the outcome of any revolutionary struggle is determined by whether the military remains loyal to the state or not. But Stephan and Chenoweth's data indicate that this is only true for nonviolent revolutionary struggles. Security force defections did *not* have any statistically significant effect on whether a violent movement was able to defeat the state.[33] Furthermore, their study indicates that security force defections helped nonviolent movements even more than other factors, such as support for the movement from the international community.[34] Given the importance of this factor, we will return to the question of how and why defections occur in Chapter 7.

International Pressures

Researchers have examined another factor that can influence civil resistance outcomes: international pressures. Yet there is little agreement on whether international involvement is helpful to nonviolent movements. Some argue that international involvement (through sanctions, withdrawal of support, diplomatic pressures, etc.) can help civil resisters by weakening the state. Others argue that such international involvement hurts nonviolent movements. And a third group maintains that there is no discernible effect. We explore each of these positions below.

According to some, international pressures on a regime can help civil resistance movements by weakening the state. Specifically, if foreign nations and global economic institutions withhold aid and loans from a regime, it weakens the state by withdrawing critical financial resources. If allied nations withhold military support or refuse to shore up a failing regime, then this undermines the incumbent state's sanctioning power. If countries cut diplomatic ties, it depletes the state's legitimacy and authority. In short, such international pressures can make a regime vulnerable, thereby giving civil resisters the upper hand.[35]

Others argue that international pressures are largely harmful to civil resistance movements. There is a large literature on sanctions that provides detailed analyses of the various problems that can occur.[36] It is beyond the scope of this book to examine all these issues, but we can summarize the primary concerns. One argument is that economic sanctions often hurt civilian populations more than the regime.[37] For instance, in the struggle against General Manuel Noriega, Panamanians suffered most from the economic sanctions since they did not receive paychecks and had limited ability to purchase food and other basic necessities. Noriega and his supporters, however, were largely immune to these concerns since they had amassed significant personal wealth that enabled them to continue living comfortably. Others argue that sanctions sometimes give too much power to the international community, thereby shifting the locus of power away from the grassroots resisters. In other words, members of the international community—such as leaders of global monetary institutions or political leaders of foreign nations—typically end up deciding what the terms are for a regime to meet in order for the sanctions to be lifted. This can undermine the leadership of local resisters, who are better equipped to determine the terms and conditions needed to improve their country's situation.[38] Others note that sanctions sometimes create new allies for regime leaders through the "rally around the flag effect"; that is, a state can gain new political support through citizens' opposition to foreign involvement. In these instances, then, international pressure has an unintended effect: instead of weakening the regime, it can inadvertently strengthen it, making civil resisters' work more difficult.

Problems can also arise when international groups provide financial and strategic assistance to civil resisters. Foreign support may delegitimize the movement since it may be perceived as a puppet for another nation's agenda.[39] Foreign support can also restrict a civil resistance movement's maneuverability since states often attach conditions to their contributions.[40]

Is there any way to avoid these problems? Cortright and Lopez argue that such problems are most likely to arise from blanket sanctions. Strategically crafted "smart sanctions" that target a regime's pillars of support can effectively undermine a state while leaving the broader population relatively untouched.[41] Another solution is to ensure that civil resisters have direct input in determining which types of sanctions are applied and when they are rescinded. In other words, sanctions should be used only when requested by movement groups representing the subject population.

A third position is that international pressures and support have no discernible effect on the outcome of nonviolent conflicts. This is the view that Stephan and Chenoweth hold.[42] According to their empirical findings, civil resisters' odds of winning do not improve when sanctions are imposed against a regime. Moreover, civil resisters' chances of winning did not improve when the international community provided monetary support for a nonviolent struggle. But financial assistance to armed revolutionary groups does, in fact, significantly increase the likelihood of winning. Why? Civil resistance movements primarily draw their power from the mass participation of local populations. It is mass participation that increases a movement's power and leverage, not its financial base. In other words, what makes a strike or an act of noncooperation effective is widespread involvement, not abundance of money. In contrast, armed groups do need money to buy weapons and support troops who are engaged in warfare on a full-time basis.

How do we make sense of these apparently contradictory findings on international involvement? Obviously, we need more research that closely examines the effects of various types of international pressure and support. It is likely, for instance, that cutting diplomatic ties may generate different effects than economic sanctions do. And do the same issues arise when international groups share strategic knowledge, such as training, instead of money? Are there distinct consequences when civil resisters receive aid from a foreign government versus a nonprofit group? One thing is clear from Stephan and Chenoweth's study: we cannot assume that the literature on sanctions and support for violent movements is applicable to nonviolent ones.

LONGER-TERM OUTCOMES

Numerous studies have shown that civil resistance can destabilize and overturn regimes, particularly autocratic ones. Yet getting rid of a bad political system does not automatically mean that a movement is capable of instituting a new and improved system. In fact, a number of political analysts have expressed doubts about the capacity of nonviolent movements to establish democracies. For instance, Haynes wrote, "[W]hile authoritarian regimes may be overthrown by mass mobilization, this is not likely to result in their replacement by stable liberal democratic regimes."[43]

But what does the empirical evidence show regarding the long-term effects of nonviolent action? Are political transitions that happen through nonviolent means more likely to produce stable democracies? Or does civic disruption lead to a more chaotic political environment that creates new conflicts and tensions? Several recent studies show that, overall, nonviolent movements are more likely than violent movements to secure democratic consolidation, political stability, and economic growth.

Democratic Consolidation

According to several studies, nonviolent movements are more likely than violent revolts to consolidate sustainable democratic systems. Karatnycky and Ackerman conducted one of the first studies, in which they examine sixty-seven political transitions that occurred worldwide since 1972. In forty-seven cases, regime change resulted from nonviolent movements, while twenty were driven by violent uprisings. What they found is that 66 percent of the transitions that occurred nonviolently were able to consolidate democracy, but only 20 percent of the political systems created through violent revolt were able to do so.[44]

Others have confirmed this finding. Chenoweth and Stephan found that "the probability that a country will be a democracy five years after a campaign ends is 57 percent among successful nonviolent campaigns but less than 6 percent for successful violent campaigns."[45] Johnstad found that 82.6 percent of political transitions instigated through nonviolence were able to sustain democracy, compared to 52.6 percent of violent transitions.[46] There are some discrepancies among the exact success rates in these studies, primarily due to variation in the cases included in their samples and the time spans of their studies. Nonetheless, a clear pattern emerges: in each study, democratic transitions through nonviolent means are more stable than those that happen through violent means.[47] This led one author to conclude, "[N]onviolent mass action must be regarded as an effective means not only for tearing down existing autocratic regimes but also for paving the way for durable democracy . . ."[48]

But precisely why are nonviolent means better at establishing durable democracies? Chenoweth and Stephan offer several explanations. First, since nonviolent movements typically require mass participation from citizens, those citizens are likely to remain politically engaged after a democratic system is established. The experience of civil resistance helps individuals develop democratic skills and instills expectations of government accountability. A second possible explanation is that "in a country that has just witnessed the triumph of mass, nonviolent resistance, leaders may attempt to bolster their legitimacy by swearing off violence toward the very civilians that put them in power."[49] In other words, new norms of nonviolent political engagement have been established that will carry through from the resistance phase through the democratic consolidation phase. Third, violent movements have embraced secrecy, coercive force, and military might to achieve their goals. When leaders of these violent groups come to power, they are unlikely to reject these values. They may well use them to achieve new goals, or stop critics, once they hold power— a point that Gandhi raised long ago. In contrast, nonviolent movements are built on values of inclusivity and consent; those values are more compatible with democratic rules of governance.

Less Chance of Recurring Civil Wars

Civil resistance is also likely to promote political stability because it lowers the chance of civil war. In Chenoweth and Stephan's study, only 28 percent of countries that had a nonviolent political transition experienced a civil war within ten years. In contrast, 42 percent of countries that had a violent political transition saw civil war erupt within a decade.[50] In John-stad's study, which has a more limited set of cases that occurred between 1972 and 2005, the results were even starker: in those countries that underwent a nonviolent transition, 95.7 percent were free of civil war, but in those countries that experienced a violent transition, 50 percent had a recurrence of war.[51]

Many conflict scholars have argued that civil wars often create new civil wars—a patterned referred to as "the conflict trap."[52] Why? When violence is used to achieve victory, the divide between opposing sides deepens. Those who are forced to concede defeat have not changed their minds; they were simply overpowered. In fact, there may be greater resentment because of the brutality and humiliation they are likely to have experienced during a civil war. Those tensions can easily erupt again when the defeated group has the chance to reorganize. A second reason for the recurrence of civil war is that it can be difficult after a period of violence to establish social norms of addressing conflict through peaceful, institutional channels. Finally, new political leaders may well be those who led the armed revolt against the state. If they were willing to use violence to achieve their goal of capturing political power, they may be willing to use violence to retain that power when they head the new state.[53] In short, the methods used during a conflict can profoundly shape the long-term outcomes.

Economic Stability

Researchers have also examined whether the mode of political transition affects the economic stability of postrevolutionary societies. Johnstad found that 80.4 percent of societies undergoing a nonviolent transition later experienced moderate to high economic growth. Why? According to Johnstad, "Encouraged by the successful changes they helped bring about on the political level, these people may take with them feelings of empowerment and skills of entrepreneurship to their post-transition lives and therefore be more inclined to start businesses or otherwise contribute to economic growth."[54] Another reason is that nonviolent transitions are much less likely to cause major infrastructural damage; thus, these countries do not need to devote a significant proportion of their resources to reconstruction.

Yet Johnstad also found that 70 percent of countries that underwent a violent transition saw moderate to high economic growth. He argues that it likely reflects reconstruction work being counted as economic growth, which he suggests is "artificial growth" since it is rebuilding that which was destroyed rather than creating a new economy. Moreover, nations with a violent revolutionary history face the challenge of persuading the international community that the country is sufficiently stable for foreign investment and tourism.[55] To summarize, it is easier to build a vibrant economy if the nation's political transformation occurred nonviolently.

CONCLUSION

The empirical data reviewed in this chapter challenge the adage that "the ends justify the means." These studies indicate that the type of resistance used to achieve a goal will, in fact, shape the outcome. Those who chose nonviolent civil resistance will have an easier time consolidating democracy, establishing durable peace, and rebuilding the nation's economy. This is not a guarantee, however, and there are numerous examples—such as Iran, Georgia, Ukraine, and Egypt—where nonviolent methods did not secure democracy, prevent further state violence, or bring about greater levels of citizen satisfaction with the state. Nonetheless, the data do indicate that the chances of creating a thriving, peaceful, democratic nation are greater when resisters choose nonviolence over violence.

CHAPTER 7

༈

Armed Forces, Defections, and Nonviolent Change

"I was trained to deal with enemy soldiers and rebels and I know exactly how to handle them. But when my men and I approached these unarmed, friendly people, I did not know what to do. There were pregnant women and little children there that reminded us of our own families. I knew that if I didn't clear the road and follow orders, I'd be shot. But I also knew that if I did that, I would have to violate my conscience."[1]

Philippine military defector

In an anti-regime struggle, soldiers are often seen as the muscle behind the state, imposing the government's will upon the people, often by force. In many cases, then, security forces are viewed as opponents, the ones who help a ruler maintain political control. Indeed, the armed forces—the police, secret security, and the military—play a pivotal role in civil resistance movements. They may arrest or attack protesters, potentially undercutting the movement's strength or launching the backfire dynamic that can shift the balance of power. They may also refuse orders or even defect, leaving political leaders without any ability to impose sanctions.

Despite their decisive role, scholars and students of nonviolent action have paid little attention to security forces until recently. Several studies have now emphasized the critical role the armed forces play and how defections can give civil resisters a decisive advantage. In fact, as mentioned in Chapter 6, nonviolent movements are forty-six times more likely to win if they can induce defections. Yet what causes security forces to shift sides? What motives, factors, or decision-making processes lead to mutiny? Are defections always good for nonviolent movements or can they sometimes pose new problems? These are the questions we explore in this chapter, using several Arab Spring revolts to illustrate the dynamics of defection and loyalty.

TYPES OF SECURITY FORCE RESPONSES

Security forces are traditionally considered one of the government's "pillars of support." A nonviolent strategy includes campaigns to remove those supports through a variety of mechanisms, thereby weakening the state. In reality, security forces have numerous options during a nonviolent conflict, ranging from full loyalty to partial compliance to mutiny. This spectrum of responses is illustrated in Figure 7.1.

On one end of the spectrum, troops and police may remain *fully loyal*, dutifully carrying out orders and maintaining their allegiance to a regime or ruler. Troops can also engage in everyday resistance known as *shirking*— that is, intentionally doing a poor job, pretending to misunderstand orders and thus carrying them out incorrectly, or covertly disobeying orders to maintain plausible deniability. This enables security forces to give the appearance of remaining loyal and the ability to deny that their actions were intentional, making their lack of cooperation less risky. As one civil resistance organizer has argued, "[Direct] insubordination is easy to punish, but incompetence is not."[2] Hence they are not fully supporting the state but give no outward appearance of being sympathetic to civil resisters' cause.

In the middle of the spectrum, troops may exercise cautionary discretion about when and how they side with the opposition. Security forces may simply become unreliable through *selective compliance* by carrying out some orders while ignoring or refusing others. For instance, in the 1989 East German uprising, some security forces told their commanding

*Loyalty *Shirking *Selective compliance *Desertion *Outright *Mutiny
disobedience

Figure 7.1:
Spectrum of Security Force Responses to Civil Resistance

officers that they would protect property if necessary but would not attack protesters.[3]

We see a more comprehensive withholding of cooperation on the far-right end of the Figure 7.1 spectrum. Security forces may choose to *desert*, leaving their military post without permission and without the intention of returning. Often referred to as being AWOL (absent without leave), this is a relatively common problem in military conflicts, particularly with conscripts. For instance, in the Mexican–American War, many Mexican peasants were forced into service. Underpaid and poorly equipped, these peasants often felt no investment in the battle against the United States, and thus thousands slipped away to return home to their families.[4] Similarly, in the U.S. war in Vietnam, an estimated fifty thousand young men either evaded the draft or deserted from active duty, often seeking asylum in Canada rather than waging a war they did not believe in. With desertions, troops simply refuse to fight. They do not necessarily join the opposition. Still, desertions have a detrimental effect on the state, as political rulers find it difficult to carry out their battles without sufficient armed forces.

Another potential response is *outright disobedience*. This refers to a situation in which security forces refuse orders to repress civil resisters. They do not flee, as in desertions, but rather publicly withdraw from the conflict. In other words, they cut ties to the regime and refuse to cooperate with it, but they do not side with the movement. They simply withhold sanctioning power.

At the far end of the spectrum are defections and mutiny. *Defections* entail a shift of allegiance from one side to another. It means that security forces break ties with the state and cast their support with the opposition. *Mutiny* entails an open challenge to authorities; in other words, the military that once upheld the state now tries to overthrow it. It is more than the withdrawal of support and cooperation (as is the case with desertions); it is the active opposition to the regime.

FACTORS AFFECTING SECURITY FORCE RESPONSES

How do troops decide whether to remain loyal to the state or oppose it during moments of nonviolent conflict? A variety of factors are at play as both sides try to maintain or win the support of security forces. State rulers and civil resisters appeal to armed forces on the basis of personal and political interests as well as ethical and practical considerations. Table 7.1 summarizes these factors.[5]

Table 7.1. FACTORS INFLUENCING SECURITY FORCE DEFECTIONS
AND LOYALTY

Regime Tactics for Maintaining Troop Loyalty

1. Punish (or threaten to punish) troops who are disloyal
2. Offer economic incentives for remaining loyal to the regime (regulated or unregulated patronage)
3. Offer political incentives for remaining loyal to the regime (ethnic or sectarian favoritism)

Civil Resister Tactics for Encouraging Unreliability and Defections

4. Increase the political costs of loyalty
5. Increase the moral costs of loyalty
6. Increase the honor costs of loyalty
7. Lower the personal costs of defecting

Structural/Macro Factors

8. Structural design and historical mission of the military
9. A nation's natural resources and wealth
10. A regime's international ties and alliances

How Regimes Promote Loyalty

Political rulers use various techniques to encourage security forces to remain loyal. Perhaps most commonly, regimes use punishments to deter defections, shirking, or selective compliance. Troops are often closely monitored, and those who show insufficient loyalty can be demoted, fired, imprisoned, or executed. Chilean President and Army General Augusto Pinochet, for instance, routinely monitored his top officers. Those whom he suspected of disloyalty were transferred to foreign posts or forced into early retirement. Purportedly, Pinochet required all officers to sign a letter of resignation, which he kept on file. If the officers questioned his authority, he activated their letters, removing them from the military.[6] In the Middle East, numerous regime leaders have created multiple security force groups—such as the military, police, and secret forces—to monitor each other and report back any breaches of loyalty.[7]

While punishments can deter defections, economic benefits can encourage loyalty. This is called "patronage," which may be regulated or unregulated. Regulated patronage is tantamount to "corporate goodies": increased budgets, pay raises, and new equipment and weaponry.[8] The belief is that enriching the military will increase soldiers' loyalty since they will want to protect the regime that provides such lucrative benefits. Regimes may also offer unregulated patronage, or personal (and often illicit) benefits, in exchange for loyalty. Unregulated patronage is typically offered to high-ranking officers and may take various forms—from cars to private-sector contracts or the right to extort businesses.[9] In Sierra Leone, for instance, troops were given privileged access to the diamond smuggling industry.[10] As long as troops kept the regime in power, they could enrich themselves. If they defected or ousted the regime, their access to the diamond industry would be gone, along with its substantial financial benefits.

Regimes may also reinforce troop loyalty with political benefits, which is known as "coup-proofing." One common coup-proofing practice is "the effective exploitation of family, ethnic, and religious loyalties for coup-critical positions . . ."[11] For example, in countries that are ethnically or religiously divided, a regime controlled by the dominant group may only employ military members from the same social group. This gives officers a stake in maintaining the regime, since a coup could bring to power ethnic or religious minorities, who might implement policies that would take away the dominant group's structural privilege. This practice is evident in numerous Middle Eastern countries: royal family members have influential positions in Saudi Arabia, for instance, and Saddam Hussein appointed members of his tribe and other Sunnis in Iraq.[12]

How Civil Resisters Encourage Security Force Defections

While the state tries to keep troops loyal through a balance of threats and rewards, civil resisters try to undermine this loyalty. The most common techniques they use are raising the political, moral, historical, and personal costs of supporting the regime in the face of a nonviolent challenge.

Activists can undermine troop loyalty by increasing the *political costs* of crackdowns. That is, civil resisters can warn troops that repressive acts will likely yield significant political costs in two ways. First, it will create a legitimacy crisis for the military, both on a domestic and international level. Second, it can result in sanctions. But these political costs will only occur if resisters ensure that the global media captures and airs any repressive event, eliciting international condemnation and punitive actions.

Civil resisters may also erode troop loyalty by highlighting the *moral costs* of supporting the regime. They can accomplish this by emphasizing that regime loyalty requires troops to crush a movement of innocent people who have legitimate grievances. Activists can also underscore the moral dimensions of the conflict by creating "dilemma actions"—that is, actions that force troops to choose between violently repressing those they do not want to harm or conceding political space to resisters. In the Serbian struggle against Milošević, for example, civil resisters often placed women in the forefront of demonstrations. Exploiting Balkan gender beliefs that women should always be protected, the soldiers faced a dilemma: they could violate their moral standards and attack the women or they could refuse orders.[13] Such actions increase the moral costs of remaining loyal and force troops to question the legitimacy of such orders.

Civil resisters may also highlight the *historical or "honor" costs* of supporting the regime. That is, they can emphasize that security forces will go down on the wrong side of history if they attack their own people. During the 1989 Tiananmen Square democracy movement, student resisters appealed to the People's Liberation Army to protect the Chinese people, not the Chinese Communist Party. They emphasized the historical costs of attacking the resisters: "If you dare to raise your hands against the people . . . history will forsake you. . . . You will remain condemned through the ages."[14]

Personal costs are also part of the calculations that security force members make as they contemplate whether to defect. If troops are poorly paid and work in substandard conditions, civil resisters may point out that troops gain very little from the state. They may promise that a new regime would compensate them fairly and improve their social status. Of course, this approach will only work if security forces are excluded from financial and political opportunities; otherwise troops will be immune to such appeals. Civil resisters can also lower the personal risks for defectors by offering assistance. In the 1979 Iranian revolution, civil resisters helped defectors evade prosecution by offering them civilian clothing and providing them with the money needed to go into exile or return to their families.[15] Such actions lower (but do not eliminate) the risks of defection, making it a more viable option for security forces.

Structural and Contextual Factors Affecting Defections

Although soldiers calculate the costs and benefits of defecting, structural factors shape their decision-making process as well. For instance, the organizational, historical, and constitutional design of the military may make a difference. If the military has had a historical mission of only protecting a nation's borders from attacks, they may be less inclined to get involved in the internal political machinations of the state. Similarly, if the military is largely composed of conscripts, their commitment to the regime may be more vulnerable since conscripts are forced to serve, sometimes against their will. Moreover, conscripts typically reflect the general population and thus may share civil resisters' concerns and goals, making them potentially sympathetic to the movement. Also, if there are constitutional principles or legal premises that secure a military's resources and power regardless of who is in power, then troops may be more willing to shift their allegiance to the opposition since there is little to be lost, one way or another, for the institution as a whole.[16]

A nation's natural resources may also affect the likelihood of defections. Michael Ross has argued that countries with significant natural resource wealth, particularly oil, are better positioned to keep their troops loyal.[17] This is because the significant revenue that the nation gets from oil (and other valuable resources) allows political leaders to heavily invest in their militaries without placing burdensome taxes on the population. Troops who are well funded and highly compensated tend to be more loyal, even when given orders to repress civil resisters.

International ties constitute yet another structural factor that can shape the chance of defections. For instance, if an allied country is willing to intervene militarily on the regime's behalf, then the state appears more durable. If soldiers believe that the opposition movement will lose and the state will win, they are unlikely to rebel.[18] However, international relations can shift suddenly, leaving a regime without outside military support. For instance, Mikhail Gorbachev announced in 1989 that the Soviet Union would no longer militarily intervene in the domestic affairs of allied Eastern Europe countries. While the Soviet Union had once readily ordered its troops to nations such as East Germany and Czechoslovakia, this had changed. Hence, when civilian uprisings occurred in these nations, their governments were vulnerable without Kremlin reinforcements. This likely contributed to troop unreliability, since security forces' decisions to defect are heavily shaped by their perception of the regime's strength or fragility.[19]

In short, there are roughly ten factors, summarized in Table 7.1, that influence the likelihood of security force defections. But is it just a matter of troops choosing the path that maximizes their gains and minimizes their costs? No. Political conditions can shift rapidly in a revolutionary context, and rank-and-file soldiers may not have accurate or complete information about the degree of the regime's strength or vulnerability. In other words, soldiers must make decisions in a short time frame with limited information. Under these conditions, troops' reactions may be instinctive and visceral rather than coolly calculated.

They may choose a path based on what they feel is the most ethical course, not what is most advantageous to them personally, politically, and institutionally.[20]

Security forces also try to gauge the likelihood that their colleagues will defect. There is an implicit gamble involved: if one soldier defects, he or she will be punished. However, if many defect, it will be difficult for the regime to sanction everyone, and therefore the risks are significantly lower. But how does a soldier know what his or her colleagues will do? How do soldiers get some level of assurance that they will not be the only defectors?[21] In some cases, entire units may discuss it and collectively decide to defect.[22] In other situations, a few brave individuals may take a stance, inspiring others to follow their example.[23] As more troops shift their allegiance to the opposition, the number of defections can cascade, creating a "revolutionary bandwagon effect."[24]

Obviously, defection decisions are complex. Nonetheless, some have argued that two of the factors listed in Table 7.1 have greater influence than others: (1) whether troops receive any financial or political benefits from the regime and (2) troops' perceptions of the regime's strength.[25] Yet for some security forces, moral considerations may trump all other concerns. To illustrate how these factors play out in real struggles, I will examine several cases in the 2011 Arab Spring uprisings. In some nations, such as Tunisia and Egypt, security forces sided with civil resisters. In other countries, such as Bahrain, the military loyally defended the state. And in Libya and Syria, the military was divided, with some troops remaining loyal and others defecting.

THE ROLE OF SECURITY FORCES IN ARAB SPRING REVOLTS

To many observers, it appeared that the Arab Spring revolts erupted unexpectedly, but in fact, citizens in this region had been suffering for some time and conditions were ripe for a nonviolent uprising. Specifically, there were widespread grievances against the state. Although the economies in these countries had grown, few citizens had seen any personal financial improvements. Instead, a wealthy minority had grown richer while the average person grew poorer. For instance, former Egyptian president Hosni Mubarak had amassed a family fortune estimated between $40 billion and $70 billion, while thirty-nine of his allied business leaders and officials established fortunes estimated at $1 billion each.[26] In contrast, the typical Middle Easterner suffered from high unemployment and inflation rates. Food prices in the region were up 32 percent in 2010. And, even though the population in the Middle East and North Africa had increased its overall level of education due to various modernization policies, there were persistent unemployment problems. Young adults faced an unemployment rate of 38 percent in Bahrain and Tunisia; the rate in Yemen stood at 50 percent. In Egypt, those with a college degree were ten times as likely to be unemployed as someone with only an elementary school education.[27] Moreover, political liberties were highly restricted in this region. These financial and political problems affected people of various socioeconomic backgrounds, bringing together a cross-class group who wanted change.

Those grievances erupted into protests after a "trigger event" galvanized public outrage. This event happened on December 17, 2010, in a small town in Tunisia's interior. On that day, a young man named Mohamed Bouazizi set himself on fire. He had a college degree but could not find a job, so he worked as a street vendor. When his cart was confiscated for operating a business without the proper license, Bouazizi went to the provincial headquarters to pay his fine and retrieve his produce cart. He was unable to get a hearing at the headquarters, so he left. He returned an hour later, doused himself with a flammable liquid, and immolated himself to protest the lack of economic and political opportunities in the country. Bouazizi was transferred to a hospital near Tunis and died a short while later.

Bouazizi's action ignited the entire country and indeed the whole region. Within weeks, millions were calling for an end to autocracies and a new era of democracy. But the militaries in these nations responded in different ways. Some sided with civil resisters, some opposed them, and some were divided over how to handle the nonviolent revolutionary movements.

When the Military Sides with Civil Resisters: Tunisia and Egypt 2011

After Bouazizi's immolation, other Tunisians committed protest suicides. In response, thousands poured into the streets, demanding comprehensive political changes, not just economic reforms. The police responded with violence, injuring numerous demonstrators. Although the police claimed to be acting in self-defense, most Tunisians did not believe it. Instead, the repression led to greater mobilization. By early January, almost all of the nation's lawyers went on strike. Then, teachers joined in.[28] Shortly thereafter, resisters engaged in civil disobedience, refusing to comply with state-imposed curfews. The demonstrations continued, with tens of thousands of Tunisians gathering in the capitol city of Tunis, demanding a new government. In response, a few political leaders resigned from office.[29]

Tunisian President Ben Ali tried numerous counterstrategies to stop the rising tide of resistance. He attempted to tarnish the image of protesters, calling them extremists and mercenaries. He negated news accounts, accusing a foreign media agency of "exaggeration, fabrication and fallacy in its coverage of social protests."[30] He used intimidation tactics and closed all schools and universities.[31] When those approaches yielded little effect, he made some concessions, firing several cabinet members and promising to create new jobs.[32] He also announced that he would not alter the constitution so he could remain president indefinitely. But nothing curbed the protests.

On January 12, 2011, Ben Ali called upon the military to act, authorizing them to use live ammunition against civil resisters. But the army's chief of staff, General Rachid Ammar, refused. Ben Ali tried to arrest the general, but the military officers would not cooperate; instead, there were reports that soldiers actually defended the protesters from the police. Then, on January 13, the military withdrew completely from Tunis—a clear message to Ben Ali that they would not support him. When Ben Ali saw that the military had abandoned him, he realized that he had lost control of the nation. Civil resisters refused to back down, strikes were crippling business, and security forces would not carry out his orders. He had little choice: on January 14, he fled to Saudi Arabia.[33]

Tunisia's successful revolution inspired Egyptian citizens, who had also grown weary of economic hardship, political repression, and police brutality. Egyptian organizers called for a demonstration in Cairo's Tahrir Square on January 25, 2011. The event coincided with the National Police Day and was designed to protest police abuses and corruption.[34] Supported by various civil society organizations, an unanticipated twenty thousand heeded the call. Building on this momentum, organizers announced new demonstrations on January 28, which they named the "Day of Rage." Hundreds of thousands of Egyptians turned out that day.

Like Ben Ali before him, Egyptian President Hosni Mubarak responded with both repression and concessions. Mubarak pledged to make government reforms and to not seek re-election. But he also established a curfew and sent out the military to disperse protesters. However, instead of a crackdown, the soldiers reportedly protected protesters from the aggressive actions of the Egyptian police and security forces.[35]

Then, on January 29, the military openly declared that it would not shoot at demonstrators.[36] Civil resisters were empowered. They would not accept Mubarak's concessions and go home. They would not stop until they removed Mubarak from office and set up a new state. With widespread support, the movement expanded to an estimated 1.5 million protesters on February 7. Just four days later, Mubarak fled the country.[37]

Why did the militaries side with civil resisters in these two cases? One reason is that neither the Tunisian nor the Egyptian military would benefit if the incumbent regimes retained power. Indeed, the regimes were a threat to both militaries' organizational interests, and thus they had no real incentive to protect the ailing rulers. A second reason deals with the nature of the militaries' relationship to civil resisters, which generated sympathy among troops for the cause.

In Tunisia, President Ben Ali had intentionally kept the military small to minimize its ability to stage a coup. The entire military was less than thirty-six thousand—the majority of whom were conscripts. This is miniscule compared to the police and security forces, estimated to be between 120,000 and 200,000. Also, the military was poorly funded and its equipment was largely out of date. Its budget was roughly 1.4 percent of the country's gross domestic product, which placed it as 109th in the global ranking of best-funded armed forces.[38] This policy was put in place to limit the military's ability to overthrow Ben Ali, but it also meant that the military had little stake in maintaining the regime. This led one analyst to conclude that if Ben Ali had provided "corporate goodies" to the Tunisian military, then "General Ammar and his fellow officer may have thought twice about tossing their sugar daddy overboard."[39]

Another factor is that Tunisian soldiers did not receive opportunities for political influence or personal enrichment. Tunisia is highly homogenous: nearly all Tunisians are Sunni Muslims and tribal identities are quite weak. This meant that there was no real capacity to use ethnic or sectarian favoritism. Moreover, Ben Ali did not offer any sort of patronage. In short, the Tunisian military had nothing to lose if the regime were ousted.

The historical mission of the military also played a role in the decision to side with civil resisters. Ben Ali had kept the military out of politics, relying upon the police and secret service to control the population. The military was mostly stationed in rural areas, and its responsibilities were in disaster relief, humanitarian assistance, infrastructure development, and border control. This meant that the general population did not view the military negatively. Moreover, it meant that military's purpose was never about preserving the Ben Ali regime but rather defending and aiding the Tunisian people. One analyst noted:

> One important byproduct of the marginalization of the military and its rele-
> gation to the periphery of the regime is that it effectively granted the military
> some degree of organizational autonomy. In part as a result, the military was
> able to sustain a corporate ethos that prioritized mission and duty and regard
> for the military as an institution. . . . The division of labor also may have had
> an important implication in January 2011: when the regime crisis occurred,
> the military was not identified by Tunisians as being part of the coercive appa-
> ratus in the same was as were police and other security forces. This created an
> opening for the military to capitalize on these sentiments and to enhance its
> social position and prestige by not using armed force . . ."[40]

Since the military had not gained much politically or economically from the regime, it had little reason to protect Ben Ali in the face of grow-ing opposition—especially when loyalty would have harmed their reputa-tion and prestige. But there was another important factor: the military's sympathetic connection to civil resisters. Although we do not have much information on how Tunisian protesters fostered these ties, there are nu-merous reports that troops fraternized with demonstrators. Since the Tu-nisian army is composed of conscripts, mostly drawn from the nation's rural and economically depressed regions, it is likely that they shared civil resisters' concerns and identified with them. The solidarity was strong enough that demonstrators sought shelter behind military tanks and ve-hicles when the police attacked.[41]

The Egyptian military's decision to side with civil resisters was also driven, in part, by the costs of protecting the incumbent regime. In con-trast to Tunisia, however, it was financial and political concerns that played the largest role. Specifically, the Egyptian military was on the verge of losing major assets if Mubarak retained power and handed power to his son, Gamal, his appointed successor. Over the decades, Mubarak had per-mitted the military to amass a conglomeration of businesses from manu-factured goods, such as cars and appliances, to restaurants, agribusinesses, and a variety of services.[42] By several estimates, the military controlled between 20 and 40 percent of the national economy. Military officers also received patronage, such as homes in exclusive communities and access to a wide range of goods and services that were unavailable to the general population. Also, officers often used their positions to purchase busi-nesses or win government contracts.[43] Individual officers and the military as an institution had grown wealthy under the Mubarak regime.

Mubarak had developed these policies to keep the military loyal. Yet, in the winter of 2011, the military knew that if Gamal Mubarak took office, he would likely implement privatization policies that could harm their business interests. Therefore, when civil resisters began demanding an end to Hosni Mubarak's rule, the military saw it as an opportunity to stop the handover of power from father to son.

The Egyptian military was also concerned about losing its funding from the United States. If Mubarak ordered a crackdown and the military complied, officers feared that President Obama would cut the $1.3 billion in aid that they received each year.[44] Moreover, officers did not want to jeopardize "its arms relationship with the United States, which has provided the Egyptian armed forces with some of the most sophisticated weaponry in the world."[45] Hence loyalty to Mubarak would have potentially yielded additional material costs.

However, the military's decision to side with the opposition was not based purely on a cost/benefit analysis. Similar to the Tunisian case, civil resisters made personal appeals to the troops. They shared food and water with soldiers. They initiated conversations about the country's troubles and the need for political change. Demonstrators chanted, "The people and the army are one!" Perhaps because Egypt's military is largely a conscript force drawn from the middle to lower classes, many troops were sympathetic. Several military officers even joined the demonstrations in Tahrir Square, proclaiming that the protesters' demands were legitimate. Eventually, there were reports of soldiers shaking hands with protesters and inviting them to climb onto the tanks. After several days, the military announced that that it would "not use force against the Egyptian people."[46] Therefore, even though the military had economic and political reasons for wanting Mubarak out, this connection to civil resisters added another element: there would be high moral costs for attacking unarmed citizens who had valid grievances.

When the Military Remains Loyal: Bahrain

The movements in Tunisia and Egypt inspired Bahraini citizens to demand political, social, and economic change. Once a British protectorate, Bahrain was granted independence in 1971 and political control was given to the royal Khalifa family. As the British withdrew their armed forces, the United States saw an opportunity to gain a military foothold in the region. It seized the opportunity, establishing the U.S. Naval Central Command Center and Fifth Fleet in southern Bahrain. In 1973, the ruling family instituted a constitutional monarchy that preserved the Khalifas' political dominance but allowed citizen input through a national assembly. Yet tensions quickly erupted along sectarian lines. The Khalifas, who are Sunni Muslims, dominated the country's political and military offices while the nation's largest religious group, Shi'ite Muslims (roughly 70 percent of the population), suffered from discrimination in housing, education, and employment. Shi'ites felt the government ignored their concerns, and thus protests periodically erupted. The police quickly quashed any resistance, preserving Sunni dominance. The state did not hesitate to use repression, leading to a deteriorating human rights record.[47]

Hoping to replicate the success of nonviolent movements in Tunisia and Egypt, Bahraini citizens took to the streets of the capitol city, Manama, on February 14, 2011. They demanded a new constitution, free elections and a representative council, an end to torture and political repression, and good-faith dialogue with opposition groups. They also called for an end to the "political naturalization" of Sunni immigrants, whom the Khalifa monarchy had recruited to join Bahrain's military. Approximately 50 percent of the nation's defensive armed forces are composed of Sunni foreigners, largely from Pakistan, Yemen, Syria, and Jordan.[48] The percentage of foreign Sunnis is even higher in the country's internal security units: they make up roughly 75 percent of the National Security Agency members and nearly 90 percent of the paramilitary Special Security Forces.[49] In exchange for their service, these immigrants are granted citizenship and various financial benefits. Not surprisingly, these security force members are largely disconnected from the local population; indeed, many do not even speak the local dialect, thereby obstructing civil resisters' ability to build rapport and trust.

The demonstrations in Manama swiftly turned into an encampment, with tens of thousands occupying the city's "Pearl Roundabout"—a monument in homage to the country's once-thriving pearl industry. But within a few days, Bahrain's King Hamad ibn Is al Khalifa ordered troops to disperse the crowd. The troops attacked during the night, injuring hundreds and killing four, including a two-year-old child.[50] Bahraini officials tried to minimize any backlash by claiming that they found weapons and flags from the militant Lebanese group Hezbollah, whom the state argued was responsible for the violence. Few believed this claim, holding the Khalifa monarchy responsible. Even in the face of such repression, civil resisters managed to maintain their nonviolent discipline. As they gathered to protest or hold vigils where the wounded civil resisters were hospitalized, they held their hands up high to the security forces, showing that they were unarmed, and shouting "Peaceful! Peaceful!" But the security forces continued to attack, wounding more resisters, journalists, and medical personnel.[51]

It did not take long for backlash to erupt. As the state cracked down, more Bahrainis joined the protests. One analyst estimated that the movement expanded to two hundred thousand people—roughly 40 percent of the indigenous Bahraini population.[52] Moreover, the movement became more radical: civil resisters began calling for a revolution that would transform the monarchy into a representative democracy.[53] With this radicalization came new tactics of resistance: protesters engaged in nonviolent disruption, blockading state television networks and parliament.

King Hamad promptly implemented a multifaceted counterstrategy. First, he requested security reinforcements from the Gulf Cooperation Council. Saudi Arabia responded by sending a thousand soldiers, while the United Arab Emirates deployed five hundred police to Bahrain. Second, King Hamad declared martial law and a state of emergency. Third, he escalated the level of repression. Troops destroyed the Pearl Roundabout and ejected all protesters. The police also raided Shi'ite neighborhoods at night, arresting thousands. Shi'ite citizens were subjected to various forms of intimidation, including checkpoint beatings and the withholding of medical care.[54] Although the movement persisted through the violence, it has not been able to achieve its goals.

One of the reasons that the movement has faltered is because Bahraini civil resisters have not been able to win over the security forces. In fact, members of the military, police, and secret service have remained overwhelmingly loyal to the Khalifa regime. Why? The sectarian tensions between Sunnis and Shi'ites have given the predominantly Sunni security forces clear reasons to support the monarchy. If the royal family were ousted, there is a good chance that the mainly Shi'ite population would rebuild the state in a manner that would end Sunni privilege. Moreover, the Sunni immigrants who were recruited to Bahrain's military have personal reasons for remaining loyal. Given the highly controversial "political naturalization" policy, security forces may fear that their citizenship would be revoked if a new regime were put in place. For personal and political reasons, then, the security forces have loyally supported the state.[55]

Another likely explanation for the security forces' loyalty is their perception of regime strength. Even if there is a great deal to gain through defections, soldiers are unlikely to rebel if it appears that the state will be victorious over civil resisters.[56] And in the Bahraini context, it appeared that the monarchy was quite durable. This perception was grounded in a couple of factors. First, the international community did not loudly condemn the crackdown in Bahrain; in fact, it has been largely silent on this matter. The Obama administration has not wanted to strain its relationship with the Khalifa family, largely due to concerns about maintaining the U.S. Naval Command Center and Fifth Fleet in Bahrain. Furthermore, the presence of Saudi troops in support of the monarchy complicates the situation. Dependent on Saudi oil and strategic friendly relations in the region, the United States has not wanted to damage this critical relationship by siding with civil resisters. In short, the movement has not been able to win international allies who could weaken the regime, but the Khalifa family has retained important allies (Saudi Arabia and the United Arab Emirates), who have intervened in support of the monarchy. To the average security force member, the state appears stable and strong, even in the face of massive protests.

Finally, the Sunni-dominated Bahraini security forces have a tenuous connection to the local Shi'ite population, thereby minimizing any inherent sympathy for the movement. The longstanding sectarian division meant that there is a degree of distrust between troops and civil resisters, in contrast to the Egypt and Tunisia cases, where conscripts reflected the broader population's demographics. Moreover, the presence of foreigners in the security forces created another barrier as civil resisters found it difficult to establish rapport with troops who do not share the same national origin, religious sect, or in some cases language. Given the structure of the military, the moral and personal appeals of civil resisters were less effective.

When the Military Splits: Civil War in Libya and Syria

In some nonviolent conflicts, the military will shift allegiance to the movement and abandon the state. In others, the military remains loyal to the regime, dutifully defending it. But there is also a third scenario: some troops defect while others remain loyal. This has occurred in two Arab Spring cases: Libya and Syria. In both instances, defectors chose to take up weapons against the state, bringing these nations to civil war. Let us take a closer look at the conditions that can lead to a divided military.

Beginning in February 2011, thousands of Libyans took action to end the ruthless practices of the state and Muammar Qaddafi, but their grievances had been developing for decades. In 1969, Qaddafi and a number of Arab Nationalist officers overthrew King Idris I in a "bloodless coup." Once Qaddafi seized political control, he implemented various policies that improved the population's health and increased literacy. He also implemented a system of direct democracy whereby various committees contributed to overall governance.

After an initial period of support for Qaddafi, many Libyans grew frustrated. The democracy they hoped for did not materialize since Qaddafi was a master manipulator, controlling the various political committees that made up the Libyan state. He had appointed trusted family members to key political and military positions, ensuring that they would carry out his will. In addition, many citizens saw their financial situations deteriorate even though Libya had grown wealthy as a result of its oil exports. There was growing evidence that political leaders were using oil revenues for their own purposes and for Qaddafi's personal enrichment. Moreover, citizens were weary of state surveillance and internal spying as well as severe restrictions on liberties, including the death penalty for political dissent.

By 2011, many Libyans were deeply frustrated with the state. Hence many responded to an Internet-based call for mass demonstrations in late January. The individual who put forth the call was arrested, as were other opposition figures. This generated further outrage, causing protests to erupt throughout the country. These actions culminated on February 17, 2011, during the "Day of Rage" demonstration where protesters attacked police stations and government buildings. The next day, police and military officers withdrew from the city of Benghazi, unprepared for the level of resistance. Some of these security force members deserted, unwilling to repress protesters. Many of the deserters joined the opposition, bringing their weapons with them. On February 24, the first attack by armed rebels occurred, with defectors taking control of the town of Misrata.

Naturally, the Libyan government used a variety of moves to stop the uprising. It tried to discredit the protesters by claiming they were dupes of Osama bin Laden or lackeys of Western interests. They tried to tarnish resisters' reputations by claiming that the armed defectors were terrorizing children and civilians. Furthermore, Qaddafi cut off the Internet to prevent further organizing and to block resisters' access to international media agencies. Finally, the Libyan regime resorted to violence. Government snipers shot at demonstrators and medics who helped the injured. The military also used heavy artillery and cluster bombs. But some soldiers refused to attack civil resisters. According to an Amnesty International report, many of those soldiers were promptly executed.

Qaddafi's repressive actions backfired, causing some elites to cut ties to the regime. The Justice Minister and the Interior Minister joined the movement while others, such as the Oil Minister and Foreign Minister, fled the country. And within the first week of resistance, several high-ranking military leaders defected, along with an entire elite battalion known as the Thunderbolt unit. The defections within the fifty-thousand-person military continued steadily after that. By some estimates, six thousand troops (or 12 percent of the total armed forces) defected within the first week. By the end of May 2011, roughly forty thousand (80 percent) had defected.[57]

By the summer of 2011, the nation was in a full-fledged civil war, with rebel forces gaining numbers daily. By August, the rebel army had captured major cities, including the capitol of Tripoli. Qaddafi and his family went into hiding, but NATO aircraft fired upon his convoy of vehicles. Qaddafi, his family, and his bodyguards were killed in October 2011.[58]

In the Libyan case, the civil war began when defectors turned their weapons against the regime. This begs the question: Why did some troops defect while others did not? And was there a pattern to these defections? The simple answer is that soldiers who were part of Qaddafi's tribe were most likely to remain loyal. Qaddafi had used ethnic favoritism, appointing family and tribal members to high-ranking positions. This meant that they had a vested interest in keeping the regime in power since Qaddafi's enduring influence ensured their tribal dominance. Moreover, since the tribal-affiliated segment of the military had received a fair amount of financial patronage, they also had economic incentives to remain loyal. But the other segments of the Libyan military, who had no ethnic ties to Qaddafi and received no patronage, began defecting.

A similar dynamic was at play in the Syrian conflict. Like other Middle Easterners, Syrians had suffered from human rights abuses, high unemployment rates, and deteriorating standards of living. They had lived under emergency rule for nearly fifty years and endured the repressive measures of the Alawite-dominated Ba'ath Party. To understand how Alawites, a religious minority who make up 12 percent of the population, had gained control of the country, we need to look back to the conclusion of World War I, when the French gained control of Syria. The French had used the standard "divide and conquer" technique to maintain control, favoring the country's religious minorities over the majority Sunni Muslims. When Syrians won independence from France in 1946, Sunnis gained political ascendancy. This led to decades of political instability as coups and counter-coups intensified the country's sectarian divide.[59]

By 1966, the Alawite minority had gained political control of the state, under the umbrella of the Ba'ath Party, headed by Hafez al-Assad. Hafez al-Assad maintained dominance through severe repression and a reliance on the Soviet Union. He purged Sunnis and other sectarian groups from the highest military positions, making this the nearly exclusive domain of Alawites, who filled over 90 percent of key posts.[60] Similar to Qaddafi, al-Assad used patronage and sectarian favoritism to keep these Alawite officers loyal. In terms of regulated patronage, he devoted a significant portion of the GDP toward the military and received the latest weaponry from the Soviets and later Russia. There was plenty of unregulated patronage, too: Alawite officers controlled lucrative businesses and were permitted to engage in smuggling, looting, and drug trafficking in Lebanon, up until they were ousted in the 2005 "cedar revolution." Hence officers had both political and personal reasons to keep al-Assad in power.[61]

When Hafez al-Assad passed away in 2000, his son, Bashar, took over. Initially, Syrians were hopeful as he implemented economic and political reforms.[62] But those hopes were short-lived as their new political leader opposed any significant change. Frustrated by the entrenched status quo, a Syrian citizen set himself on fire on January 26, 2011, imitating the immolation that sparked Tunisia's revolt. Small demonstrations took place, mostly in remote regions, but they were quickly quashed by the Syrian military. The real event that ignited the Syrian uprising occurred in Dara'a on March 6, 2011, when a dozen youths were arrested and tortured for painting the slogan "The People Want the Regime to Fall" on walls throughout the city.[63] Within weeks of this incident, tens of thousands were protesting throughout the country. The military responded with snipers and tanks, killing numerous civilians.

By the summer of 2011, the conflict triggered security force defections. Most defectors were Sunni recruits, who were highly averse to killing protesters (who were mostly Sunnis) to protect an oppressive Alawite-dominated state. By the spring of 2012, an estimated one fifth of the military had defected.[64] Some of these defectors sought asylum abroad. Others were publicly executed. Another group formed the Free Syrian Army, which launched an armed struggle against the Assad regime, pushing the country into civil war.

Why did some Syrian troops defect while others faithfully defended the state? Sectarian identities play a role. Alawites make up roughly 12 percent of the Syrian population yet they control the vast majority of influential military, political, and economic positions. This was part of the Assad family's "coup-proofing" plan: Alawite military officers would defend the state because their fate is tied to the regime's survival.[65] In contrast, the lower ranks of Syria's military are filled with Sunni conscripts, who had no political benefits at stake. Moreover, when the Alawite-dominated state issued orders to harm civil resisters, the conscripts were faced with a moral quandary: loyalty to the regime would require them to attack their own people. As one journalist summarized, "The [defectors] say they were forced to detain people and to shoot people. These were their brothers, they say; they couldn't stay in this army and do this to their brothers."[66] For many, the moral costs were too high, so they deserted or turned their weapons against the regime.

The Arab Spring cases reveal that the military can significantly influence the course of a nonviolent struggle. However, winning over security forces is not a simple task. Although there are things that civil resisters can do—such as raising the political and moral costs of a crackdown and limiting the personal risks of defection—a number of structural factors are also at play. On the one hand, undermining troop loyalty is more difficult in nations that have a history of sectarian or ethnic divides. This is particularly true if political leaders have exploited these divisions, filling the military with individuals who wish to preserve their group's dominance and control. In this situation, troops' interests are pitted against civil resisters' interests, eroding any sympathy that security forces may feel for the opposition movement. Civil resisters' appeals are also less likely to be effective if security force officers receive monetary benefits from the regime and wish to see those benefits continue. While carefully framed moral and personal appeals may still work, reaching the conscience of individual soldiers, those appeals are weighed against the advantages of the current system. On the other hand, civil resisters may find themselves in an advantageous position if security force members are conscripts who come from similar socioeconomic, religious, and ethnic backgrounds. Such conscripts may readily identify with activists and their goals, especially when civil resisters are friendly rather than hostile. In short, while all nonviolent movements should find ways to undermine this key pillar of state support, civil resisters should be aware of the military's structural design and how that might facilitate or obstruct their efforts. Some movements will have a harder time inducing defections than others, depending on their country's historical and demographic conditions as well as any previous coup-proofing actions.

THE RISKS OF MILITARY DEFECTIONS IN NONVIOLENT STRUGGLES

Overall, empirical evidence shows that defections do increase the likelihood that a nonviolent movement will attain its goal of regime change.[67] Yet is it always desirable to win over the security forces? The Arab Spring cases examined here reveal that sometimes defections bring new challenges and risks.

One of the main risks with defections is the possibility that the nonviolent conflict will be transformed into a violent one. In other words, there is a considerable chance that defectors will take their weapons, regroup, and launch an armed struggle against the state. This can shift the situation from civil resistance to civil war, as happened in Libya and Syria. When this occurs, a whole host of consequences are possible. The nonviolent movement may be lost in the escalating violence, seen by the broader public as irrelevant in an armed conflict. The chances of achieving a durable, lasting democracy may decrease (as described in Chapter 6), while the likelihood of human, infrastructural, and environmental devastation increases. In short, once defectors turn to armed revolt, it may be extremely difficult for civil resistance leaders to control the struggle.

A second problem is that the military may seize more political power once it cuts ties from the state. When the armed forces side with the opposition movement, officers may usurp the movement's power and impose their own agenda, which may not be consistent with civil resisters' goals. In Egypt, for example, the military initially held power after President Hosni Mubarak was deposed. Yet instead of immediately holding multiparty elections, it retained control. After a period of civilian pressure, the military eventually conceded and Mohammed Morsi of the Muslim Brotherhood was elected president. Civil resisters quickly became disenchanted with Morsi, who expanded his presidential authority and granted himself unlimited powers without any judicial oversight. Hence they started a new civil resistance struggle, known as the Tamarod campaign, which attracted millions of participants. After just a year in office, it appeared that civil resisters had won again: the military backed the movement and Morsi was forced out of office in July 2013.

But was the Tamarod campaign really a success for civil resisters? Several analysts have noted that the military and the movement may have worked too closely. Some even suggest that the military used the movement for its own purposes. Chenoweth wrote:

> During Egypt's recent turmoil . . . one could argue that there was too much collusion between nonviolent people power and security forces. After several days of demonstrations and protests by the well-organized, millions-strong Tamarod campaign, the Egyptian military declared that it had no choice but to remove Mohammed Morsi from power. Yet there are indications that Tamarod organizers and military elites had coordinated their plan for months. As early as February of 2013, some senior Egyptian army officers were in private talks

with liberal opposition groups, asking them whether they would approve of the military ousting Morsi. Such accounts indicate that this was less of a process of protest-induced defections than of a popularly backed coup, with uncertain implications for human rights, democratic transition, economic wellbeing and civil stability.[68]

How can movements avoid these problems? That is, how can civil resisters retain control over the movement as defections occur? More research is needed to fully answer this question but some suggestions have emerged. One is that civil resisters must facilitate defectors' integration into the movement. It is not enough to get soldiers to refuse orders or cut ties with the regime; they must be convinced to leave their weapons behind and join the nonviolent effort as the most promising way to enact political change. This would reduce the chance of civil war.

Others, such as Chenoweth, have recommended that civil resisters encourage the military to take a stance of outright disobedience.[69] This, she argues, is preferable to desertions or defections. With desertions, former soldiers can regroup and start an armed struggle. With defections, the military withdraws its support from the regime and turns against it, joining with civil resisters to oust incumbent rulers. Yet as the military sides with the opposition, there is the potential for the armed forces to take over, pursuing their own interests, not the people's interests. Outright disobedience is what happened in Tunisia, where military leaders publicly stated that they would not carry out Ben Ali's orders to repress civil resisters. They simply refused to cooperate with the regime and then withdrew. They did not join the movement, nor did they push Ben Ali out through force. In essence, the military removed itself from the struggle, allowing civil resisters to continue their fight. This, Chenoweth argues, is the best possible scenario because it undercuts the state's sanctioning power while permitting civil resisters to maintain independence and control of the movement and thus its nonviolent character.

While considerably more research is needed on this topic, one thing is clear: the security forces cannot be ignored in nonviolent conflicts. Their actions can make a difference, for better or worse, and affect the outcome and consequences of the struggle.

CHAPTER 8

ᴑᴑ

The Global Diffusion of Nonviolence

At certain moments in history, waves of civil resistance erupt and spread rapidly through a region. Through the global media, potential activists can observe and gain inspiration from movements in neighboring nations, adopting similar strategies to achieve their own goals. This creates a cascading effect as nonviolent techniques spill across national borders. This was evident at the start of the twenty-first century. First came the challenge to President Slobodan Milošević in 2000, when Serbs ousted their longstanding autocrat. Flush off their success, Serbian organizers shared their expertise with civil resisters in Georgia (2003), Ukraine (2004), and Egypt (2011). One leader in the Serbian movement acknowledged how this information was refined along the way. He observed, "It took Gandhi 30 years to walk across India and spread the spirit of *satyagraha*, the Serbs 10 years to remove Milošević, the Georgians and Ukrainians two to three years to win, the Tunisians a month and a half, and the Egyptians 19 days—a real nonviolence blitzkrieg!"[1]

Since waves of civil resistance often spread quickly, many believe that these movements are spontaneous. Yet while activists may be inspired by nonviolent techniques developed overseas, local resisters typically engage in careful discussion, planning, and experimentation before fully adopting such methods. This chapter offers insights into the global diffusion of nonviolence. It also offers an in-depth look at one important case of diffusion: the spread of Gandhian nonviolence to the U.S. civil rights movement.

UNDERSTANDING DIFFUSION ACROSS MOVEMENTS

Social movement scholars have, for some time, been analyzing how "repertoires of contention"[2] (or specific types of tactics) spread from one movement to another. One explanation of this process is called the *transmission model*. This model begins with activists in one location who implement innovative tactics to attain their goals. These actions can be inspiring and novel, capturing the attention of the media. As stories are reported about the movement—through televised broadcasts, newspaper accounts, or online videos—people in distant locations may be inspired to try the same methods. The activists who create these distinctive repertoires are called "innovators." Distant groups who adopt their techniques are called "emulators."[3]

But precisely how does the information and "know how" spread from the innovators to the emulators?[4] As illustrated in Figure 8.1, the transmission of information across borders can happen through three channels. It can happen through direct *relational ties*—that is, personal connections between activists in one location who share their experiences and knowledge with activists in another place. Information can also be transmitted through indirect or *nonrelational ties*. Typically, emulators learn about a movement through news reports, documentary films, or websites. Finally, transmission can occur through *mediated ties*, in which a neutral third party promotes connections between groups. For instance, some international nongovernmental organizations devoted to nonviolence have facilitated the global flow of information about civil resistance from innovators to new movement groups.[5] Once contact has been made, informational know how can be shared, allowing the technique to be adopted in a new struggle.

The transmission model has been critiqued, however, for a couple of reasons. First, it tends to downplay the importance of human agency and

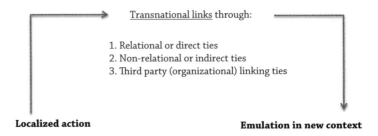

Figure 8.1:
Transmission Model of Social Movement Tactical Diffusion

efforts, assuming that the mere presence of information is enough for diffusion to occur.[6] In reality, there is often a great deal of work put into creating contacts between groups and explaining these ideas. The transmission model cannot capture such in-depth interactions. Second, diffusion doesn't typically happen in the tidy, linear fashion suggested by this model. Often, transmission only happens after significant debate, experimentation, and reinvention.[7]

On the basis of these critiques, Sean Chabot has proposed an alternative called the *collective learning model* of nonviolent diffusion.[8] Chabot defines collective learning as the ability of groups to understand, communicate, reinvent, and apply the repertoire of nonviolent resistance in a new location and movement.[9] In this approach, there are several stages involved in the adoption of a nonviolent repertoire, shown in Table 8.1.

In the first step, potential activists in one location *gain knowledge* about a movement in another location. This typically happens through any of the three mechanisms described in the transmission model: through media accounts (nonrelational ties), personal contact with the movement (relational ties), or a linking organization. At this stage, the potential adopters are in dialogue with the innovators. Chabot emphasizes that a reciprocal exchange between innovators and emulators is more effective than a monologue whereby hierarchical authorities dictate information to passive recipients.[10]

In the second step, would-be emulators discuss these ideas among themselves. Some may perceive "hyper-differences" in the respective settings and struggles. Others fall into a perception of "over-likeness" in which they erase or overlook the unique circumstances of both cases. Gradually, through debate and dialogue, emulators come to understand the distinctions and commonalities between the two movements.

Table 8.1. STAGES IN THE COLLECTIVE LEARNING MODEL
OF NONVIOLENT DIFFUSION

---

1. *Knowledge and dialogue*: Learning through conversations between innovators and emulators
2. *Discussion*: Discussing the ideas and tactics of nonviolence and its relevance for adopters' own situation
3. *Translation and dislocation*: Explaining concepts in terms that make sense to local populations and encouraging people to imagine the techniques in their own context
4. *Experimentation*: Engaging in small-scale campaigns and a trial-and-error process
5. *Implementation*: Full-scale use of culturally adapted nonviolence

---

At this point, they begin the third step of *translation and dislocation*. This requires emulators to describe nonviolence in terms that make sense culturally and socially to their supporters. They also encourage their supporters to imagine what nonviolent resistance would look like in their own context. Activists may debate the writings and practices of nonviolence teachers. For instance, Matthew Eddy describes how activists in Palestine debate whether the practice of stone throwing is consistent with Gandhi's teachings on *satyagraha*. As he notes, activists often disagree about how to properly translate these ideas.[11]

The fourth step is *experimentation and relocation*, whereby activists begin undertaking small-scale, local actions. They engage in trial-and-error experimentation, gaining practical knowledge about what does or doesn't work. Eventually, the emulators sufficiently adapt the nonviolent repertoire to the new context so that they are ready for the fifth step: *full implementation*.

The collective learning process can be challenging since it often entails failures, twist and turns, and revisions. It rarely proceeds in an orderly, sequential fashion. For example, activists may engage in small-scale experimentation (stage 4) only to find themselves returning to the words and texts of the innovators (stage 2), trying to make sense of them. This process can also be time consuming. In the contemporary world, with instantaneous communication technologies, the transmission model has an implicit assumption that this process can happen quickly. Yet the ability to translate ideas, persuade people of their utility in a new context, and adapt them to new struggles can be a lengthy process. When done well, the collective learning process can give a movement new vitality and energy. When done poorly, however, activists can find themselves embroiled in arguments and giving up after failures.

In reality, these two diffusion models are not contradictory but complementary. The transmission model explains how channels of information link nonviolent innovators and emulators. The collective learning model emphasizes how that information is absorbed by the local population, is transformed to suit a different struggle, and takes root in a new context. To illustrate these dynamics, we take a closer look at how the Gandhian repertoire diffused from India to the U.S. civil rights struggle.

FROM INDIA TO THE UNITED STATES

Many have documented the influence of Gandhi's movement on the African-American struggle for civil rights. Martin Luther King, Jr. himself claims that after studying Gandhi, he became convinced that nonviolence could work in the African-American struggle. In his own words,

> Gandhi was probably the first person in history to lift the love ethic of Jesus above mere interaction between individuals to a powerful and effective social force on a large scale. Love, for Gandhi, was a potent instrument for social and collective transformation. It was in this Gandhian emphasis on love and non-violence that I discovered the method for social reform that I had been seeking for many months.[12]

Indeed, the "Gandhian repertoire" was indelibly present in the U.S. civil rights movement, but African-American leaders modified it. Precisely how did Gandhi's ideas and tactics travel from India to the United States? The transmission and collective learning models offer insight into the global dissemination of the Gandhian repertoire.

Transmission Channels and Initial Knowledge

Initial information about Gandhi spread across national borders through nonrelational ties, namely media accounts of the Indian independence movement. Although Gandhi began experimenting with his distinctive form of civil resistance in South Africa at the end of the nineteenth century, U.S. citizens did not learn much about him until the 1920s as newspaper journalists covered key events in the Indian struggle such as the salt march. Yet the news coverage was mixed.[13] Some conservative periodicals portrayed Indians as fanatically and irrationally worshipping Gandhi, incapable of governing themselves. Liberal and progressive periodicals gave more favorable accounts but still drew upon stereotypes of Gandhi as the Eastern mystic who captured the hearts of Indians through his spiritual powers. For instance, one Westerner wrote in *The Nation*, "The Indians listen to [Gandhi's teachings]. They like it immensely because they have always been hero-worshippers. And here is a saint and a revolutionary one."[14] Regardless of the biased depictions, there was widespread coverage of Gandhi, reaching a broad North American audience. Indeed, Gandhi became a household name in the United States after *Time* magazine selected him as their "Man of the Year" in 1931.[15]

As more information about Gandhi and his movement became available, this unique form of nonviolence piqued the interest of U.S. religious pacifists, many of whom were affiliated with the Fellowship of Reconciliation

(FOR), the largest faith-based pacifist organization in the United States at the time. FOR members were distancing themselves from earlier isolationist pacifist positions and were moving toward the use of nonviolent action to challenge injustices, including racial segregation and discrimination.[16] Thus Gandhi's distinctive form of nonviolence was particularly intriguing, and several FOR leaders traveled to India to learn more on a first-hand basis. When they returned, they gave lectures and wrote about Gandhi for American audiences. Hence knowledge of the "Gandhian repertoire" also came through relational ties.

Indian nationalists living in the United States constituted a second set of relational ties, linking Gandhian activists in India to would-be activists in the United States.[17] Most of these individuals were highly educated and living in major urban areas throughout the United States. They spread information about the Indian independence movement to garner U.S. support for the cause, which they felt would place further pressure on the British to withdraw from India.[18] Perhaps the most influential Indian nationalist was Krishnalal Shridharani, who had participated in the 1930 salt march with Gandhi.[19] After coming to the United States, Shridharani wrote *War Without Violence: A Study of Gandhi's Method and its Accomplishments*, which promoted Gandhian philosophy and techniques.[20]

Discussion

As knowledge about Gandhi and the Indian independence movement became available in the United States, African-American leaders discussed its relevance to their own cause. One of these leaders was W. E. B. Du Bois, who had been following the events in India since the start of the twentieth century. Du Bois, a board member for the National Association for the Advancement of Colored People (NAACP), immediately saw similarities between the plight of Indians and African Americans. He wrote:

> The problem of the Negroes . . . remain[s] part of a worldwide clash of color. So, too, the problem of Indians can never be simply a problem of autonomy in the British commonwealth of nations. They must always stand as representatives of the colored races—as the yellow and black peoples as well as the brown—of the majority of mankind, and together with the Negroes they must face the insistent problem of the assumption of the white peoples of Europe that they have a right to dominate the world and especially so to organize it politically and industrially so as to make most men slaves and servants.[21]

As the editor of the NAACP's newsletter, Du Bois used this forum to write about Gandhi, further educating African Americans about civil resistance. Yet Du Bois and many NAACP readers were not convinced that these techniques would work in the U.S. civil rights struggle. In fact, after elaborate discussions, many concluded that these methods would provoke massive repression of African Americans.

They came to this view because African Americans' discussions of Gandhi and India often focused on "hyper-differences."[22] Chabot defines "hyper-difference" as the exaggeration of differences between Self and Other, between the innovators and the potential emulators.[23] In this case, it was the accentuation of differences between Indians and African Americans. Gandhi was seen as primarily a Hindu spiritual leader, not a Western political leader. Moreover, the national contexts were perceived as dramatically different: Indians were fighting for autonomy and independence from a colonial power while African Americans were fighting for integration into a democracy. In India, civil resisters constituted a majority against the minority ruling British. In the United States, African Americans constituted only a small percentage of the population. On this basis, many concluded that Gandhi's methods would not work in the United States. NAACP member William Pickens wrote:

> If the Negro of Mississippi starts a boycott against working for and trading with white people, or against buying or employing any of the facilities owned and controlled by whites, the Negro race would be the very first to freeze and starve. White Mississippi would be crippled, but black Mississippi would be utterly ruined. Also, Gandhi's people may practice civil disobedience with at least some temporary and partial success—such as not paying taxes, refusal to hold office, to vote or to obey the ordinary laws of the British-controlled government. Suppose the Negroes of America should try not paying taxes, not voting and declining to hold office, resigning as policemen, firemen, clerks—how beautifully they would deliver themselves into the hands of their worst enemies! Inside of twelve months, all their property would be seized for taxes and all the leaders of their small minority would be in jail.[24]

Another common aspect of these discussions is the tendency to exaggerate similarities between the two movements and minimize important differences. Such "Western over-likeness" was evident as religious pacifists emphasized how Gandhi was comparable to Jesus Christ. For example, Kirby Page met with Gandhi in India. When he returned to the United States, he wrote a pamphlet entitled, *Is Mahatma Gandhi the*

Greatest Man of the Age? In it, he directly states the similarities between Gandhi and Christ:

> The Great Soul of India has many faults . . . but his supreme devotion to the poor, his utter reliance upon love in the conflict with evil, his courageous and sacrificial spirit, his unshaken trust in God are much nearer to the religion of Jesus than are the lives of most persons who call themselves Christians. Not everyone saith Lord, Lord! But he that doeth! More than any man of the age, the Spinner of Sabarmati reminds me of the Carpenter of Nazareth.[25]

Others made similar comparisons, emphasizing the compatibility of Gandhi and the West.

Translation and Dislocation

Over time, African-American thinkers came to a synthesis of these views and began translating Gandhi's ideas into Western terms. As Chabot writes:

> Gradually some (but certainly not all) African Americans and their allies moved beyond hyper-difference and over-likeness . . . as they engaged in the translation of the Gandhian repertoire into language that their audiences understood. Translation was not a mechanical process of converting the author's fixed set of words and texts into the exact same set of words and texts for readers. At best, translators served as creative mediators between authors (Gandhi and Gandhian activists in India) and readers (African Americans and allies in the United States), who were able to express the original meanings and implications of the Gandhian repertoire in equivalent and accessible terms. By traveling to India, meeting with Gandhi and associates, encountering cultural similarities and differences, and discussing new insights at home, they encouraged American audiences to imagine *dislocation* of the Gandhian repertoire beyond Indian soil.[26]

There were numerous individuals who translated Gandhian thought to U.S. audiences. For white religious pacifists, the key translator was Richard Gregg. During the 1920s, Gregg lived in India for several years, spending some of his time in Gandhi's *ashram* or commune. They had a close, symbiotic relationship: Gregg shared his knowledge of science and education while Gandhi shared his ideas about nonviolence. After returning to the United States, Gregg continued to correspond with Gandhi until his death in 1948.[27] Based on this experience, Gregg wrote a book, *The Power of Nonviolence*,[28] which had the explicit purpose of expressing Gandhian ideas in familiar Western concepts. Gregg wrote:

> It is difficult for one trained in modern Western modes of thought and action to understand this idea [of nonviolence] or believe that its practice can be cogent. Even Gandhi's explanations of it fail to carry weight with most of us. His explanations come out of a background of thought, feeling and attitude to life very different from ours. . . . Therefore I have felt it desirable to restate and explain this method in modern Western concepts and terminology.[29]

For African-American audiences, the key translators were black theologians, pastors, and intellectuals. This included a number of prominent figures at Howard University, the leading black university in the United States during the 1930s. The university's president, Mordecai Johnson, was an early advocate of Gandhian ideas, encouraging faculty and the student body to study them. Several faculty members carried out this mission, including Howard Thurman, who was chapel dean, and Benjamin Mays, who was the dean of the School of Religion. Thurman and Mays traveled to India and spoke with Gandhi about the utility of nonviolent resistance in the U.S. civil rights struggle. Gandhi reassured them that "a minority can do much more in the way of non-violence than a majority. . . . I had less diffidence in handling my minority in South Africa than I had here [in India] handling a majority. . . . With right, which is on their side, and the choice of non-violence as their only weapon, if they will make it such, a bright future is assured."[30] When Thurman and Mays returned home, they embarked on a series of national lectures, published writings, and did radio spotlights to help African Americans understand the relevance of Gandhian ideas in the U.S. civil rights struggle.[31] Chabot stated, "[Johnson, Thurman, and Mays] were among the first to recognize the practical and political potential of the Gandhian repertoire for African Americans."[32]

Experimentation

Once activists could envision Gandhi's ideas in the U.S. civil rights struggle, then they began experimenting with them. Yet immediately, movement leaders recognized that they could not merely duplicate Gandhi's actions. James Farmer wrote:

> Certain societal and cultural differences between the United States and India, and certain basic differences between the problems to be dealt with in the two countries, militate strongly against an uncritical duplication of the Gandhian steps in organization and execution. . . . Using Gandhism as a base, our approach must be creative to be effectual.[33]

Working with the Congress for Racial Equality (CORE), Farmer began this stage of Gandhian experimentation in 1942, when he launched a campaign to desegregate Jack Spratt Coffee House in Chicago. Following Gandhi's steps, he tried to negotiate with the coffee house owners, who refused to make any changes. Hence CORE launched a sit-in with a group of twenty-eight whites and African Americans. The waitresses were dumbfounded. When they served the white customers, they promptly passed their food on to their African-American companions. Next, the waitresses announced that they would serve all black customers if they would move to the basement. They refused. Finally, the servers called the police and asked them to arrest the activists for disturbing the peace. The police arrived and announced that no arrests would be made since it was a completely peaceful situation. Eventually, the wait staff served all the customers. CORE activists replayed the action every few weeks to ensure that the policy change was, in fact, permanent.[34]

Farmer's success in Chicago led to new chapters of CORE in Denver, Seattle, New York, and Philadelphia. Inspired by the growing number of participants, CORE decided to hold a conference in 1943. The goal of the conference was to plan a nationally coordinated nonviolent campaign against segregation. Their guest speaker was Indian nationalist Shridharani, who decided to give conference participants some concrete experience in civil resistance. Shridharani led participants in a sit-in at a local restaurant, where the restaurant owner reluctantly agreed to desegregate. Flush off this success, CORE activists were eager to try out these techniques in their own communities. Throughout the 1940s, they experimented with Gandhian methods, desegregating restaurants as well as swimming pools, movie theaters, barbershops, and public housing.[35]

For a period of time, these Gandhian experiments flourished. But the momentum slowed in the late 1940s and early 1950s when Senator McCarthy's anticommunist efforts resulted in significant repression of progressive movements. The escalating Cold War and growing anticommunist sentiments made it increasingly difficult for civil rights leaders. As a result, the incipient movement worked to simply keep the ideas of nonviolent direct action alive. Various pacifist organizations helped with this goal, including the Fellowship of Reconciliation, the War Resisters League, and Myles Horton's Highlander Folk School. These groups maintained the ideas and practices of nonviolence so that they could be rapidly implemented when conditions shifted, permitting a full-scale civil rights movement that would use the Gandhian repertoire.[36]

Full Implementation

All the dialogue, translation, and experimentation with the Gandhian repertoire during the 1930s and 1940s laid important groundwork. By 1955, when Rosa Parks refused to give up her seat on the bus to a white customer, numerous U.S. movement organizations were familiar with Gandhian-style civil resistance and ready to put it into action. Rosa Parks herself had recently spent time at one of these organizations, the Highlander Folk School, learning about nonviolence. So on that fateful day when she was arrested, she provided the opportunity to fully implement Gandhian techniques in the civil rights struggle.[37]

Upon Parks' arrest, several local African-American leaders decided to call for a boycott of the bus company on Monday, December 5, 1955. To get the word out, they printed fliers and passed them out to high school students as they left classes, while local black ministers announced it from their pulpits and printed it in their church bulletins.[38] Their efforts paid off: roughly 90 percent of black customers refused to ride the buses that day. Inspired by the level of participation, local leaders decide to continue the boycott. To provide direction to the movement, they formed the Montgomery Improvement Association, which coordinated carpools, issued press releases, engaged in negotiations with the bus company, and organized rallies to sustain motivation. When the boycott culminated in success, as bus companies conceded to the movement's demands, the nation had proof that Gandhian nonviolence could be effective in the struggle against racial segregation.[39]

The success in Montgomery led to further implementation of the Gandhian repertoire. Leaders from the Montgomery Improvement Association founded a new organization in 1957, the Southern Christian Leadership Conference (SCLC), with the goal of expanding the use of nonviolent action against various forms of segregation. In this process, Martin Luther King, Jr., as president of the SCLC, became one of the most articulate translators of Gandhian ideas to U.S. audiences. As a minister, King was able to explain nonviolence in terms that resonated with his audience, many of whom were patriotic Christians. For instance, in his famous "Letter from Birmingham Jail," King underscored how the tactic of civil disobedience—that is, intentionally breaking a law—is a familiar part of Judeo-Christian and democratic traditions. He wrote:

> You express a great deal of anxiety over our willingness to break laws. This is certainly a legitimate concern. Since we so diligently urge people to obey the Supreme Court's decision of 1954 outlawing segregation in the public schools, at first glance it may seem rather paradoxical for us consciously to break laws. One may well ask: "How can you advocate breaking some laws and obeying others?" The answer lies in the fact that there are two types of laws: just and unjust. One has not only a legal but a moral responsibility to obey just laws. Conversely, one has a moral responsibility to disobey unjust laws. . . . Of course, there is nothing new about this kind of civil disobedience. It was evidenced sublimely in the refusal of Shadrach, Meshach and Abednego to obey the laws of Nebuchadnessar, on the ground that a higher moral law was at stake. It was practiced superbly by the early Christians, who were willing to face hungry lions and the excruciating pain of chopping blocks rather than submit to certain unjust laws of the Roman Empire. . . . In our own nation, the Boston Tea Party represented a massive act of civil disobedience. We should never forget that everything Adolf Hitler did in Germany was "legal" and everything the Hungarian freedom fighters did was "illegal." It was "illegal" to aid and comfort a Jew in Hitler's Germany. Even so, I am sure that, had I lived in Germany at the time, I would have aided and comforted my Jewish brothers. If today I lived in a Communist country where certain principles dear to the Christian faith are suppressed, I would openly advocate disobeying that country's antireligious laws.[40]

Although King was still seen as a controversial radical, more and more Americans became convinced that nonviolent ideas and actions were, in fact, compatible with their values.

By the late 1950s, civil rights activists began to focus their efforts on lunch counters. In Nashville, the campaign to desegregate lunch counters was organized by the local SCLC affiliate and spearheaded by James Lawson, a young pacifist African American. As a result of his pacifism, Lawson refused conscription during the Korean War and was sent to federal prison. Upon his release in the early 1950s, he moved to India for several years, where he studied Gandhian ideas. He returned to the United States in 1955 and met Martin Luther King, Jr., who encouraged Lawson to move south to help in the civil rights struggle. Lawson agreed and landed in Nashville, where he enrolled in Vanderbilt Divinity School and began working with the local SCLC group, headed by Kelly Miller Smith. Starting in 1959, Lawson and Smith offered workshops on nonviolence, sharing Gandhi's ideas with students from Nashville's black colleges.[41]

Before the Nashville students took action, Lawson wanted to ensure that they truly understood the spirit and ideals of nonviolence and that they had experimented with it on a smaller scale. Hence they engaged in roleplaying, with students taking on the roles of both resisters and antagonists. This also gave students a chance to develop the discipline to not strike back. Next, the students went to downtown restaurants to conduct small-scale "test sits." They were not to get arrested but merely see how people reacted and then to return to the workshops to debrief. Such actions were designed to prepare and train students, but it was also part of students' process of dislocating Gandhi's ideas and envisioning them within the context of the Nashville civil rights struggle. One Nashville workshop participant described his initial reluctance about Gandhian nonviolence:

> But the first meeting as I recall, I think there were 7 or 8 of us students there and Jim [Lawson] started talking about this Mahatma Gandhi and this philosophy of nonviolence. And I'm thinking that's whacked; somebody hits me, I'm creaming them. Nonviolence? No. That's not even logical. I'm sitting there listening but I'm thinking this doesn't make sense. But obviously it's something he said that stuck with me and . . . enough to get me to come back to the next meeting. Then the more I thought about it, I said let's do a little research, that's when I started to see there's some merit there. . . . [T]he more I went to the meetings, the more I began to learn from Jim and my readings, I realized that it took a much braver person to practice nonviolence than one to strike back. . . . I began to see [nonviolence] as a very practical tool.[42]

The training, discussion, dislocation, and experimentation culminated in a full-scale sit-in movement. Within months, the students succeeded in desegregating six downtown lunch counters. Martin Luther King, Jr. proclaimed Nashville's students an inspiration for the entire civil rights movement.[43]

The lunch counter sit-ins spread rapidly to dozens of cities throughout the South.[44] Within a few years, civil rights activists used nonviolent direct action in the Freedom Rides, which challenged segregation on interstate bus travel. Then there was Freedom Summer, designed to resist the obstacles to black voter registration in Mississippi. The Gandhian repertoire was finally being fully implemented, decades after the ideas were introduced to African Americans. And the tactical knowledge spread further as activists in the peace movement and women's movements also adopted these practices.[45]

CONCLUSION

Information about the Gandhian repertoire spread from India to the U.S. civil rights struggle through a couple of channels. First, U.S. citizens learned about Gandhi through the nonrelational ties of media coverage. Second, relational ties facilitated the spread of knowledge about Gandhi. These person-to-person contacts came from Indian nationalists living in North America and preaching Gandhi's message. Contact also was forged as a number of African-American intellectuals and U.S. religious pacifists traveled to India to learn more about this distinct form of nonviolence. Through these ties, U.S. citizens first encountered the ideas of the "Mahatma."

Yet the simple act of receiving information about Gandhian nonviolence did not automatically lead to its implementation in the African-American civil rights struggle. Instead, for years, activists discussed and debated whether this repertoire would work in the U.S. context. Some emphasized the differences between the Indian circumstances and the African-American ones. Others exaggerated the similarity of Gandhi's ideas and practices to Western religious ideals. Eventually, though, a handful of leaders were able to find a balance, translating the ideas to an American audience and helping them to envision how this form of nonviolence could be practiced in the fight against racial segregation. They convinced enough people that this was worth pursuing that they began, on a small scale, to experiment with nonviolent direct action. As early as the 1940s, groups such as the Congress of Racial Equality engaged in local sit-ins. By the mid-1950s, Montgomery citizens were boycotting, withholding material resources from a company practicing discrimination. After the Montgomery bus boycott, African Americans fully implemented the Gandhian repertoire, and nonviolent direct action because the heart of their strategy for well over a decade. Although it had a distinctively American flavor to it, Gandhi's techniques were successfully emulated in the civil rights struggle, yielding numerous victories.

Of course, the Gandhian repertoire is not the only form of civil resistance that has spread. The nonviolent strategy of electoral revolutions has also spilled from country to country, most notably in the so-called color revolutions at the turn of the twenty-first century. The color revolutions have occurred in Eastern Europe, the Balkans, and Soviet successor states. In fact, the diffusion of this nonviolent strategy has had a considerable impact in the region: roughly 40 percent of former communist states have instigated political changes using these techniques.[46] The transmission model and the collective learning model provide us with the theoretical framework to understand how such waves of nonviolent action occur, spreading across national boundaries. Undoubtedly, the dissemination of nonviolence will continue as new forms and practices are invented and actors throughout the world seek to emulate those practices in their own movements.

CHAPTER 9

✑

Future Directions in Nonviolence and Civil Resistance Research

These are exciting times for civil resistance studies. Beginning in the mid-twentieth century, the field mostly consisted of Gandhian-focused work—a trend that continued for decades. In the latter part of the twentieth century, Sharp's pragmatic nonviolence took center stage and subsequent publications were devoted to persuading the wider public that nonviolence does, in fact, work. But at the start of the twenty-first century, we have an expanding number of publications that address a range of theoretical and analytical questions. The field has also become increasingly empirical in nature, drawing upon comparative case studies as well as large-sample statistical databases.[1] While most of this book offers an overview of this field, summarizing its key findings and concepts, this final chapter points out gaps in our knowledge. Hence this chapter is not a conclusion but rather a survey of areas where further scholarly inquiry and development is needed. It will, I hope, spur on more research so that the field of nonviolence or civil resistance studies continues to grow.

STUDYING DIVERSE REGIME CONTEXTS

To date, researchers have primarily focused on civil resistance movements in four types of political contexts. The majority of studies focus on movements that operate in authoritarian regimes. This includes uprisings against personal dictatorships (such as the Philippine's 1986 "People Power" movement) as well as nonviolent resistance against fascist regimes (such as Hitler's Third Reich) and military dictatorships (such as those in

Chile, Panama, Burma, and so forth).[2] A smaller number have focused on nonviolent liberation movements against colonial powers.[3] Some explore reform-oriented movements within democracies.[4] Finally, a few scholars have examined nonviolent movements in hybrid regimes—such as Ukraine, Georgia, Serbia, and other former communist regions—where elections are either unfair or only for certain symbolic positions while the real power is still concentrated in the hands of an autocratic ruler.[5]

What we have learned from studies in these four contexts is that nonviolent strategies may vary depending on the political system. For instance, many civil resistance movements in postcommunist autocracies have operated through an electoral strategy, whereby resisters mobilize a mass movement to expose election fraud. The hope is that exposure will reveal the regime's corruption and set the stage for legal action that culminates in new elections where genuinely democratic processes can occur under the watchful eye of the international community. In contrast, movements challenging authoritarian regimes cannot take such an approach since elections are generally not held. Thus civil resisters living in dictatorships may be forced to choose other tactical approaches, such as boycotts and strikes, since the domains where they can resist are in their purchasing power and their ability to cooperate.

What about nonviolent movements in other political contexts? Do nonviolent dynamics differ, for instance, when civil resisters challenge a monarchy? What new insights can we gain by studying nonviolent struggles against theocracies? And how do nonviolent movements operate in "fragmented tyrannies" or areas controlled by narco-traffickers, warlords, or terrorist groups?[6] Studies of civil resistance in these types of political settings are relatively rare, and thus merit further investigation.

STUDYING MOVEMENTS WITH DIVERSE GOALS

In addition to studying nonviolent conflict in diverse political settings, we also need to examine how the odds of success vary based on different movement goals. Chenoweth and Stephan have demonstrated that nonviolent struggle is not equally successful with all types of political goals.[7] In their study, they found that civil resistance was more successful in revolutionary movements against authoritarian regimes (59 percent) but less successful in movements seeking to oust foreign occupying forces (35 percent). Furthermore, they found that none of the secessionist movements in their database were able to achieve their goals through nonviolent means, although they only had a total of four such cases in their study, which limits the generalizability of their findings. Nonetheless, their study suggests that civil resistance is more effective in anti-regime struggles than anti-occupation or secessionist movements. Why? We don't fully know. More research is needed to tease out these dynamics and to develop models of nonviolent resistance based on types of goals as well as regime type.

STUDYING DIVERSE TARGETS

We also need to examine nonviolent movements that challenge targets beyond the state, since activists resist a variety of organizations and practices.[8] For example, the Occupy Wall Street movement challenged corporate practices, particularly the financial services sector.[9] The U.S. Plowshares movement has pushed Catholic leaders to reconsider the church's just war position in favor of nonviolence.[10] Other groups are addressing organized crime and police corruption. Shaazke Beyerle has studied such movements,[11] including a citizen initiative in Sicily, Italy, to end the Mafia practice of *pizzo*, or extortion payments from local business owners in exchange for protection. After concerted efforts to organize resistance, eventually 100 percent of business owners in the city of Palermo refused to pay. Although the Mafia retaliated, their attacks and acts of vandalism backfired, strengthening the community's resolve. Eventually the Mafia gave up, ending their extortion practice.

Nonviolent movements have also challenged structural violence.[12] This term refers to institutional and social relations that systematically limit the life chances and opportunities of particular social groups. It refers to any obstacle, imposition, or restraint that keeps humans from meeting their basic needs or developing their full potential.[13] Hence structural violence may include systems of economic exploitation or discrimination based on race, ethnicity, sex, religion, socioeconomic status, or sexual orientation. Since much of the literature is focused on movements challenging an authoritarian government, where oppressive practices are highly visible and explicit, we do not know if the same model is applicable to structural violence, where such oppression may be implicit. Critics have raised this concern, arguing that Sharp's pragmatic nonviolence model is not easily applicable, for instance, for those challenging racism, which has multiple sites of power and is manifested in many forms.[14] The U.S. civil rights movement fought structural violence by challenging the South's racial segregation policies. Yet Martin Luther King, Jr. found it more difficult to mobilize a nonviolent campaign in the Northern United States, where racism was often embedded in covert cultural attitudes and practices rather than overt policies. Future researchers ought to document how civil resistance movements against structural injustice may be similar to or different from anti-regime movements.

As we explore these varied types of nonviolent movements, we need to continually update our theories. It is likely that organized criminal groups or corrupt police forces, for example, have different vulnerabilities, pillars of support, and interests than a dictatorial regime. We cannot simply assume that the factors shaping nonviolent revolutions against political rulers are the same as the factors that shape nonviolent struggles against businesses or religious organizations or patriarchal systems.

EXPANDING THEORIES OF NONVIOLENT POWER

Another area for development is in the refinement of our theories of nonviolent power. In the West, the dominant theory comes from Gene Sharp, who focused on the role of consent and cooperation. While Sharp's theoretical model has been extremely useful for practitioners and researchers alike, several people have pointed out its limitations. The primary limitation is that Sharp's theory portrays the decision to cooperate and consent as individualistic and voluntary, obscuring the complexity of political life. His theory gives the impression that each person can withhold consent as easily as one can turn off a switch.[15] Several critics have argued that this does not sufficiently account for the structural roots of power. Specifically, when a group gains dominance, it structures social institutions and cultural norms to perpetuate that power over time. For instance, patriarchy is not as simple as individual men holding power over individual women. Rather, patriarchy is reproduced through a division of labor in the marketplace that systematically puts women, as a whole, in a more vulnerable economic position. Many religious institutions are structured so that men possess the leadership and policymaking roles. The mass media can perpetuate sexist norms and attitudes. Hence Sharp's ruler/subject dichotomy does not adequately capture the multiple sites of patriarchal power. Consequently, a woman cannot just withdraw her personal consent and expect patriarchy to collapse.

Sharp's theory has advanced our thinking significantly but we need alternative theories of nonviolent power. There have been a couple of efforts toward that goal. For example, Souad Dajani argues that we ought to shift the question from "why do people obey?" to "why do power relations persist?" This latter question points us to the location of unjust power within social structures and patterns. Once the sources of oppression are identified, then it can be unmasked and challenged through nonviolent resistance.[16]

Stellan Vinthagen has proposed another theory. Based on his conviction (like Dajani's) that power is grounded in a multidimensional social process, he turns to Jürgen Habermas' theory that distinguishes among (1) goal rationality in the material world; (2) normative rationality in the social world; (3) expressive rationality in one's individual, psychological life; and (4) communicative rationality in the "life world" of mutual understanding. Vinthagen believes that these rationalities correspond to four realms of nonviolent action: power breaking, moral action, utopian enactment, and dialogue facilitation. While Sharp has advocated nonviolent "power breaking," Vinthagen claims that the other three types of rational action are also necessary.[17]

Finally, Chabot argues that Sharp's model has been invaluable at articulating the abstract principles of nonviolent power (*episteme*) and the technical know-how of civil resistance (*techne*). Yet he has not left sufficient room for the practical and moral wisdom (*phrenosis*) that civil resisters develop through experience. Some knowledge, Chabot argues, can be derived from theories and practical advice. Yet as in any field—whether it is teaching, athletics, or civil resistance—there is some knowledge that can be derived only from experience. [18] He writes:

> Sharp's theoretical framework reflects a positivist approach to knowledge that favors universal truths, fixed binaries, and instrumentalist assumptions about actors, goals, choices, and outcomes. The basic arguments of his *episteme* are clear, simple, law-like, and general. It all starts with a society in which a freedom-seeking population faces an oppressive regime. If the population can overcome its fear and obedience, it is capable of undermining the regime's pillars of domination through courageous nonviolent action. . . . Cultural differences, human spontaneity, moral visions, everyday life, and subtle forms of oppression play only a minor part in Sharp's model—mostly as indicators of given social conditions or factors obstructing expediency and efficiency.[19]

Phrenosis is the instinctive, creative knowledge that cannot be captured in a rulebook for civil resisters. It is how nonviolent activists come up with novel tactics, generate trust within the movement, build a sense of community, and promote constructive political communication.

Dajani, Vinthagen, and Chabot have encouraged us to think beyond the traditional (and limited) model put forth by Sharp. They have added new dimensions to our understanding of how nonviolent power and action works. Yet their models refine and challenge Sharp's ideas rather than offer real alternatives. We need others to develop new theories or paradigms of nonviolent power.

STUDYING SHIFTS

Nonviolent struggle is a constantly evolving process, yet academic studies are only beginning to capture this fluidity and change over time. For instance, Chapter 4 presented different types of nonviolent resistance, ranging from hidden forms of "everyday resistance" to overt struggles to overthrow the state. One set of questions that we should explore is: How, why, and under which conditions do those who engage in covert resistance shift to overt resistance? Or vice versa? Existing studies have focused nearly exclusively on overt forms of nonviolence. Obviously, it is more difficult to study hidden resistance. Yet when we only study overt resistance, this occludes our view of nonviolence by narrowly defining its parameters. Moreover, it may prevent us from seeing how movements persist but change over time. It is a longstanding assertion within the social movements literature that protest often occurs in waves. Yet a movement doesn't necessarily end when the wave subsides; rather, activists may simply shift to other forms of resistance or engage in covert activities until conditions change.[20] Hence, if we give more attention to hidden forms of resistance, we will expand our knowledge of when and why actors operate covertly, and it may also give us a better picture of a movement's course over time and the various factors that shape tactical choices.

Even when nonviolent movements are in their overt phases, we need a better understanding of why they sometimes shift to violence. Some civil resistance movements start out with a nonviolent strategy but, when faced with repression, fight back violently. Sometimes this happens unintentionally, resulting from lack of discipline or clear leadership.[21] Yet there are instances where groups intentionally abandon civil resistance in favor of armed struggle. Much of the revolutions literature simply asserts this point with little or no empirical backing, assuming that violence is selected as the method of last resort when resisters see "no other way out."[22]

We need to empirically analyze why such shifts occur. Gregory Maney has pointed us in this direction with his study of the civil rights movement in Northern Ireland. He claims that Catholic activists adopted the armed struggle of the Irish Republican Army because of a "paradox of reform."[23] In other words, the nonviolent struggle sufficiently pushed the British-controlled state to make concessions, but the slow implementation of those reforms actually made resisters frustrated with the pace of change. Moreover, some civil rights activists believed that the state was not serious about making any real changes, only modest reforms. This is also consistent with a study by Santoro and Fitzpatrick, who argue that some U.S. civil rights advocates began to shift away from nonviolence in the late 1960s because they felt it could only bring limited reforms.[24] This led them to conclude (albeit incorrectly) that nonviolence did not have revolutionary potential. Thus, ironically, smaller successes with nonviolence led to a shift toward violence in these two cases, which activists felt would yield larger successes.

Shellman, Levey, and Young argue that other factors can instigate shifts from nonviolence to violence.[25] In their study of Sri Lanka's Tamil Tigers and the Philippines' Moro Islamic Liberation Front, they highlight the influence of government repression on tactical choice. When state repression is low, a movement is more likely to use violent methods; when repression is high, resisters turn to nonviolent techniques. This may seem counterintuitive, but this pattern does indeed make sense. For example, when police attack demonstrators with billy clubs, dogs, and rubber bullets, protesters may instinctively fight back, throwing rocks or Molotov cocktails. However, as repression escalates to abductions and torture or indiscriminate shootings, people may use nonviolent methods, such as boycotts, that make it difficult for the state to target them.

A small body of research focuses on the opposite trend, studying the reasons why violent groups sometimes lay down their weapons and shift toward nonviolence. Surprisingly, this research suggests that civil resistance—not armed struggle—may be the method of last resort. That is, violent groups sometimes realize that they are not achieving their goals, so they shift toward unarmed struggle. Dudouet delineates numerous factors that may explain this type of strategy shift.[26] First, she focuses on internal factors within a movement and its support base. For example, the following can occur: (1) leaders may determine that violent tactics have not been successful and thus they are willing to try a new approach; (2) leaders may try to win new supporters and realize that this is most likely to occur through nonviolent forms of fighting; or (3) the existing support base may ask for the strategic shift since it is often civilian supporters who bear the brunt of state crackdowns on revolutionary activities. Second, Dudouet highlights external factors that may lead to strategy shifts. This includes the influence of outside groups, who may withhold support unless the conflict is waged nonviolently. It can also include changing political circumstances that make violent struggle more difficult. More research is needed to explore and test Dudouet's claims and document the factors that have the greatest influence in the shift from violence to nonviolence.

CO-PRESENCE OF VIOLENT AND NONVIOLENT METHODS

Sometimes armed movements strategically shift to nonviolence. In other circumstances, they maintain their violent struggle but act in consort with a nonviolent movement. They remain separate movements but work simultaneously toward similar goals using different means. What effect does the presence of an armed movement have on civil resistance campaigns? As discussed in Chapter 6, Chenoweth and Schock's research on the "radical (violent) flank effect" suggests that the presence of an armed group does not help or strengthen the bargaining position and power of a nonviolent group. Yet other scholars have come to the opposite conclusion.[27] More research is needed to confirm or refute this finding. Moreover, our research ought to take into account the various tactical mixes that often occur in such conflicts, measuring this in a more nuanced manner than strict, simplified violence/nonviolence binaries.[28] For instance, future researchers could create a quantitative index that measures the approximate ratio of violent and nonviolent actions in a struggle, indicating if there is a tipping point at which a radical flank effect occurs or if there is a point at which a nonviolent movement loses its credibility because the proportion of violent episodes has increased beyond the level of acceptability.

OTHER FACTORS SHAPING OUTCOMES
OF NONVIOLENT STRUGGLES

Although nonviolent movement outcomes have been studied perhaps more than anything else in the field, there are still a number of questions that have not been asked or sufficiently explored. There are at least four areas that could extend our knowledge of both the short- and long-term effects of nonviolent movements.

Mechanisms of Change

Several studies have examined the long-term effects of violent versus nonviolent transitions to democracy. There is strong empirical evidence that nonviolent methods increase the chance of democratic stabilization and decrease the likelihood of civil war. There is also some evidence that civil resistance might have economic benefits in the post-conflict stage. Yet one might also ask whether the "mechanisms of change," as described by Sharp, have any long-term consequences. In other words, Sharp argues that nonviolent change can occur through persuasion (in which the opponents are convinced that it is the right thing to do), accommodation (where they make concessions for practical reasons but without any fundamental change of heart), coercion (where they are forced to change against their will), and disintegration (where the system simply implodes). We can empirically compare whether there are differences in long-term outcomes when movements win their goals through these various processes. This may also enable us to examine whether there are real distinctions in the long run between principled nonviolent movements (aiming for conversion) and pragmatic nonviolent movements (aiming for accommodation or coercion). In general, there has been virtually no empirical analysis that compares the outcomes of principled versus pragmatic civil resistance, leaving this an area wide open for exploration.

Religious Defections

Another understudied factor is the role of religious institutions in nonviolent struggles. While we have examined the effects of political and economic elites cutting ties to a regime, little attention has been given to the role that religious elites can play. Social movement scholars have noted that religious groups can offer a wide array of resources, ranging from financial contributions to recruitment networks to theologies that justify resistance.[29] But few civil resistance scholars have looked at this. One exception is my own study of nonviolent revolutions,[30] where I document how it can be beneficial to a movement to have religious leaders on its side. This may grant civil resisters the ability to operate and strategize in religious places, which are difficult (although not impossible) to attack or destroy without provoking outrage for the violation of sacred spaces. Religious leaders who support nonviolent struggles also grant civil resisters a degree of moral credibility, making it difficult to dismiss them as a lunatic fringe.[31] Religious institutions can frequently gain moral support and material help from their affiliated faith communities overseas. Finally, as Ron Pagnucco's study shows, religious movement groups have traditionally been better than their secular counterparts at persisting over time and sustaining their struggles through changing (and often hostile) political climates.[32]

Of course, religious leaders can go either way: they may support civil resisters or they may publicly oppose a nonviolent movement. But what are the factors that make it likely that religious leaders will remain loyal to a state or side with opposition groups? And does their "defection" make any difference in movement outcomes? More research is needed to answer these questions.

Security Forces

We have strong empirical research to substantiate the claim that security force defections increase the likelihood that civil resisters will win. However, researchers have overwhelmingly focused on the military's role in nonviolent conflicts. In reality, "security forces" are generally composed of multiple units: the military (generally including air force, navy, and army branches), police, and paramilitary or secret police. When we take into account all security forces, we get a new set of questions. For instance, what happens when the military defects but the police and paramilitary groups remain loyal? Or vice versa? And what happens if the army sides with civil resisters, for example, but the air force and navy do not? Do military defections have a greater (or lesser) impact on the conflict's outcome than police defections? There is plenty of room for more research that investigates these issues.

We also need to employ various research methodologies to explore this topic. To date, most research on defections has relied upon newspaper data or historical documents. Although it is difficult to do, qualitative work is needed to understand the factors that shape troops' decisions. In an ideal scenario, ethnographers could collect data while nonviolent struggles develop. Researchers ought to interview soldiers about their thoughts before, during, and after decisions to defect or remain loyal. Since people tend to reconstruct their narratives after the fact, ethnographers could compare their observational notes with the accounts given during in-depth interviews. That would give us better data about the decision-making processes that occur as nonviolent conflicts unfold.

International Influences

As mentioned in Chapter 6, civil resistance scholars hold conflicting views about whether international involvement helps or hurts nonviolent struggles. Some scholars argue that international pressure and assistance can strengthen civil resisters' odds of victory by providing financial, technical, and strategic support, by pressuring repressive regimes, and by boosting civil resisters' morale by demonstrating that the world cares.[33] Cortright and Lopez, for instance, propose that the international community can help civil resisters by implementing "smart sanctions"—that is, sanctions that are tailored to impose costs on the targeted oppressive regime, including individual government and military leaders, while minimizing the civilian population's suffering.[34] In contrast to comprehensive bans on aid or trade, smart sanctions include weapons embargos, targeted asset freezes, and travel bans. The belief is that such actions weaken the state's key leaders and their ability to repress opposition activists, thereby giving civil resisters a greater chance of winning.[35]

Daniel Ritter also maintains that international pressures can help civil resisters.[36] Instead of focusing on the impact of sanctions, Ritter examines the role of diplomatic pressures in international relations. Through an analysis of Iran's 1979 nonviolent revolution and the 2011 Tunisian and Egyptian uprisings, he argues that the success of these civil resistance movements is linked to these nations' close ties to Western democracies. He argues,

> [T]he success of nonviolent revolutionary movements can be traced to a set of contradictions and compatibilities inherent in democracy-autocracy relations. I contend that amicable, high-profile relations between a democratic state and an autocratic regime based on mutually beneficial economic and geopolitical considerations threaten to constrain both governments by holding them hostage to the liberal rhetoric on which their relationship must by necessity rest. Within a discursive context officially governed by norms and values such as democracy, human rights, individual freedom and the rule of law, civil resistance becomes highly potent due to its compatibility with these Western core principles. Conversely, any attempt to overtly suppress or forbid nonviolent protest is a severe contradiction of the rhetoric the democratic state and its authoritarian patron rely on to justify the relationship, thus making repression politically very costly. In short, the liberal discourse that surround democracy-autocracy relationships makes nonviolent protest an indisputable right and its repression an inexcusable violation.[37]

To summarize, when a repressive regime is closely linked to a major Western power with a commitment to human rights and democratic liberties, authoritarian rulers will find themselves in a dilemma. If they crack down on civil resisters, they risk their standing with key Western allies, jeopardizing various forms of assistance. Yet if they permit civil resisters to organize, this creates new opportunities for a movement to launch campaigns, increase its leverage, and undercut the pillars of state support. Hence this special relationship effectively ties the hands of rulers, thereby enhancing civil resisters' power.

Other scholars are less optimistic about international involvement in nonviolent conflicts. Some have argued that actions taken by the international community can be harmful if they generate new allies for authoritarian leaders, who may tout this as another case of foreign imperialism.[38] Given the historic role of Western interventions, sometimes driven by self-serving economic and political interests, such sanctions may indeed generate backlash. Moreover, any support from Western nations may lead to unfair accusations that local civil resisters are part of foreign conspiracies.[39] Also, when outsiders decide when international sanctions are applied and rescinded, without the input from civil resisters, this can shift the locus of power from local civil resisters to international actors, with detrimental consequences.

Other critics of international involvement have pointed out the problems of smart sanctions. In examining the empirical evidence, it appears that smart sanctions have had limited effect; in fact, one analyst went so far as to call them "a noble failure."[40] Why? Smart sanctions often end up harming the local population even though they are narrowly targeted at state actors. An arms embargo, for instance, may make it more difficult for the military to repress demonstrators. Yet it can also increase a regime's costs for procuring weapons, thereby inadvertently leading to budget shifts that increase military spending and decrease domestic spending on social programs that benefit citizens. Similarly, travel sanctions can inhibit the ability of opposition leaders to get their message out globally and it can obstruct the delivery of food and medical supplies. In short, civil resisters can be harmed, even when the sanctions are smartly targeting their opponents.

Finally, there is a third position on international involvement in nonviolent conflict. This position is evident in Chenoweth and Stephan's work, where they find that international involvement has no discernible effect on nonviolent movement outcomes.[41]

Given these divergent views, further investigation is warranted. As scholars take a closer, systematic look at the effects of international pressures, they need to distinguish between various types of sanctions and different sanctioning agents. For instance, economic sanctions—in the form of cutting aid, relinquishing trade agreements, or refusing loan applications—may have distinct effects compared to political sanctions, such as the cutting of diplomatic ties or the refusal to admit a nation into an international alliance. We should also explore the effects of informally withdrawing support versus imposing sanctions. For instance, in the 2011 struggle in Egypt, U.S. President Obama never cut aid from Egyptian President Hosni Mubarak. However, he did encourage him to step down, indicating that he could no longer count on U.S. backing. This type of informal but highly public withdrawal of support may be much more powerful than cutting a trade agreement, for example, since it might embolden resisters and discourage other nations from coming to a regime's aid.

Another area to explore is the effect of direct aid from foreign agencies to civil resisters. Certainly, an influx of money can help a nonviolent movement defray the costs of campaigns. It can enable some people to work full time for the cause. It can cover rent for offices or other movement materials—such as pamphlets, flyers, and the construction of websites. However, taking foreign contributions can also be problematic. Gandhi, for instance, was reluctant to include foreign support—primarily because he wanted Indians to know that they could liberate themselves, thereby defying any psychological colonialism. The other potential problem is that foreign assistance makes civil resisters vulnerable to charges that they are puppets acting on behalf of foreign interests.[42] On a related note, few empirical studies have analyzed the effects of sharing strategic knowledge or technical support. Not all aid needs to have a financial component, and thus our studies ought to look at non-material support.

A similar issue that merits further investigation is the effect of international accompaniment groups in a nonviolent conflict. As discussed in Chapter 4, this refers to individual solidarity activists—many of whom are from Europe and North America[43]—traveling to conflict zones to offer a nonviolent presence. They may accompany local activists who, because of their work, are at high risk for being attacked or assassinated. Their presence often deters such attacks because the international companion will release the information to global media groups. These activists may also live in war zones to deter attacks since armed groups may not want to generate international condemnation by killing citizens of powerful nations. While such groups have helped movements, they may have also created new problems. For instance, local groups may feel that international activists are exerting too much influence on the movement's direction. Others feel that the privilege and protection afforded to these generally middle-class Northerners merely reinforces an unjust global power structure. Hence empirical research is needed to see whether such movements do more harm than good or whether they are, in fact, essential in drawing global attention to a conflict situation.

In short, we need more research on the effects of international involvement in civil resistance struggles. Future researchers ought to take a more nuanced approach to this issue, disentangling the effects of different types of support (financial, technical, communications/media, strategic, protective intervention, and monitoring) as well as sanctions (economic, social, diplomatic).

CONCLUSION

We have more information about nonviolent resistance than ever before. Yet, as we have seen, there are still many unanswered questions. While many practitioners, analysts, and scholars are hopeful that effective civil resistance can reduce the amount of violent conflict in the world, it is clear that we need more research. This chapter points out some of these areas that merit further investigation. It is up to current researchers, together with a new generation of scholars and practitioners, to continue building our knowledge about nonviolent action.

Appendix: Discussion Questions

CHAPTER 1

1. What is the difference between pacifism and nonviolence?
2. Why do many people assume that violence is more effective than non-violence when the evidence shows the opposite? Where do such misconceptions originate?
3. When civil resisters willingly suffer for their cause without striking back, what effects can this have?
4. This chapter summarizes the main differences between principled and pragmatic nonviolence. How might these differences be evident in movement praxis and action?

CHAPTER 2

1. Across religious traditions, what are the general conditions under which war has been justified?
2. How do religions try to ensure fairness in combat? What problems might arise in applying these rules?
3. How can the same religious scriptures be used for contradictory purposes—for example, waging wars versus waging nonviolent resistance? What might explain such divergent interpretations?
4. What are the main values at the heart of nonviolence, whether it is motivated by religious or secular beliefs?

CHAPTER 3

1. Why do so many citizens subscribe to the monolithic view of political power? Why do they seldom recognize the forms of power they possess?
2. Why did Gandhi believe it was important to engage in not only civil resistance but also the "constructive program"?
3. What is meant by the "Gandhian dialectic"? How does this differ from compromise?
4. Are there significant differences in the strategies of principled versus pragmatic nonviolence?

CHAPTER 4

1. Why do some people engage in everyday and covert resistance rather than launch a large-scale, overt nonviolent movement?
2. Why might symbolic moral action be useful, even if it rarely achieves any concrete political goals?
3. What is transitional justice? What are its potential strengths and weaknesses?
4. What are the key distinctions among negotiated revolutions, people power revolutions, and electoral revolutions?

CHAPTER 5

1. Why is it important for civil resistance movements to build a diverse, cross-class coalition?
2. How do movements increase their leverage?
3. Why is tactical diversity important?
4. What facilitates backlash following a repressive act?

CHAPTER 6

1. What is a radical flank and how can it affect nonviolent movements?
2. Why does the size of participation make such a difference in civil resistance campaign outcomes?
3. Is there a particular form of leadership that is most beneficial for a nonviolent movement?

4. Why is it the case that when regime change occurs through nonviolent means, it is more likely to lead to stable democracies and economies? What challenges do nation-states face when regime change occurs violently?

CHAPTER 7

1. What is the difference between military desertion and defection?
2. How do regimes keep troops loyal?
3. What are some strategies that civil resisters can use to encourage defections?
4. What are the primary factors that influence whether a military will remain loyal, side with the opposition, or divide internally?
5. What problems might arise when troops defect?

CHAPTER 8

1. How did African-American civil rights leaders learn about the "Gandhian repertoire"? What were some of their initial concerns?
2. How did Martin Luther King, Jr. and other civil rights leaders make Gandhi's ideas and tactics compatible with U.S. culture and traditions?
3. What steps do local activists take when they seek to adopt the tactics of a foreign movement?

CHAPTER 9

1. Why has most research historically focused on nonviolent resistance against authoritarian rulers rather than other targets? How might a nonviolent strategy look different in a struggle against organized crime or religious leaders, for example?
2. What are some of the reasons that armed groups shift their tactics, adopting unarmed methods of resistance? Why do some continue with armed struggle, even when they see little to no progress?
3. What other topics might nonviolence and civil resistance researchers pursue?

NOTES

PRELIMS

1. Exodus 1:15–18.
2. Howes, Dustin Ells. Forthcoming in 2015. "Defending Freedom with Civil Resistance in the Early Roman Empire." Chapter 8 in Kurt Schock (Ed.). *Comparative Perspectives on Civil Resistance*. Minneapolis: University of Minnesota Press.
3. Sharp, Gene. 2012. *Sharp's Dictionary of Power and Struggle: Language of Civil Resistance in Conflicts*. New York: Oxford University Press.
4. Case, Clarence Marsh. 1923. *Non-Violent Coercion: A Study in the Methods of Social Pressure*. New York: Century.
5. Gregg, Richard B. 1935. *The Power of Non-violence*. London: Routledge.
6. Shridharani, Krishnalal. 1939. *War Without Violence: A Study of Gandhi's Method and its Accomplishments*. London: Gollancz.
7. King, Jr., Martin Luther. 2010 [1958]. *Stride Toward Freedom: The Montgomery Story*. New York: Beacon Press, pp. 77–95.
8. Bondurant, Joan. 1958. *Conquest of Violence: The Gandhian Philosophy of Conflict*. Princeton, NJ: Princeton University Press.
9. Sharp, Gene. 1973. *The Politics of Nonviolent Action*. Boston: Porter Sargent.
10. For more on Sharp's transformation from a Gandhian position to this strategic emphasis, see Weber, Thomas. 2003. "Nonviolence is Who? Gene Sharp and Gandhi." *Peace & Change* 28(2): 250–270.
11. Chabot, Sean, and Majid Sharifi. 2013. "The Violence of Nonviolence: Problematizing Nonviolent Resistance in Iran and Egypt." *Sociologists Without Borders* 8: 218.
12. For a comprehensive overview of this literature, see Carter, April, Howard Clark, and Michael Randle. 2006. *People Power and Protest Since 1945: A Bibliography of Nonviolent Action*. London: Housmans Bookshop; McCarthy, Ronald M., and Gene Sharp. 1997. *Nonviolent Action: A Research Guide*. New York: Garland; Powers, Roger S., William B. Vogele, Douglas Bond, and Christopher Kruegler (Eds.). 1997. *Protest, Power, and Change: An Encyclopedia of Nonviolent Action from ACT-UP to Women's Suffrage*. New York: Garland.
13. Ackerman, Peter, and Christopher Kruegler. 1994. *Strategic Nonviolent Conflict: The Dynamics of People Power in the Twentieth Century*. Westport, CT: Praeger.
14. Schock, Kurt. 2005. *Unarmed Insurrections: People Power Movements in Nondemocracies*. Minneapolis: University of Minnesota Press.
15. Nepstad, Sharon Erickson. 2011. *Nonviolent Revolutions: Civil Resistance in the Late 20th Century*. New York: Oxford University Press.

16. Chenoweth, Erica, and Maria Stephan. 2011. *Why Civil Resistance Works: The Strategic Logic of Nonviolent Conflict*. New York: Columbia University Press.

17. Duduoet, Véronique (Ed.). *Civil Resistance and Conflict Transformation: Transitions from Armed to Nonviolent Struggle*. New York: Routledge.

18. A number of articles on these topics were published in two recent special issues on nonviolent civil resistance: Volume 34 of *Research in Social Movements, Conflict, and Change* (guest edited by Sharon Erickson Nepstad and Lester Kurtz in 2012) and Volume 50, Issue 3 in the *Journal of Peace Research* (guest edited by Erica Chenoweth and Kathleen Cunningham in 2013).

CHAPTER 1

1. My definitions are slightly different from others that are used in the literature. For instance, Theodore Koontz and Dustin Ells Howes argue that pacifism is the belief that killing is wrong under any circumstances. As I argue in this chapter, such views are quite rare. Pacifists are opposed to war but some accept violence in self-defense. For further discussion of these terms, see: Howes, Dustin. 2013. "The Failure of Pacifism and the Success of Nonviolence." *Perspectives on Politics* 11(2): 427–446; Koontz, Theodore J. 2008. "Christian Nonviolence: An Interpretation." In *Christian Political Ethics*, edited by John Aloysius Coleman. Princeton, NJ: Princeton University Press; Teichman, Jenny. 1986. *Pacifism and the Just War: A Study in Applied Philosophy*. Oxford: Basil Blackwell.

2. This definition is similar to one offered by Cynthia Boaz in her article, "Must We Change Our Hearts Before Throwing Off Our Chains?" published in *Waging Nonviolence* on July 9, 2012. In this article, Boaz defines nonviolence as "organized, collective action in pursuit of a clear and achievable objective, carried out with nonviolent weapons."

3. There are many different ways to categorize pacifism. John Howard Yoder, for instance, identifies twenty-two variations of pacifism in his 1992 [1971] book, *Nevertheless: Varieties of Religious Pacifism*. Scottdale, PA: Herald Press. Others, such as Douglas Lackey, have made distinctions between private and universal pacifists, denoting those who justify the use of violence to protect oneself on the individual versus societal level. (See Lackey, Douglas P. 1989. *The Ethics of War and Peace*. Upper Saddle River: Prentice Hall.)

4. Cady, Duane. 1989. *From Warism to Pacifism: A Moral Continuum*. Philadelphia: Temple University Press, pp. 61–62.

5. Cortright, David. 2008. *Peace: A History of Movements and Ideas*. New York: Cambridge University Press, p. 334.

6. As quoted in Merton, Thomas (Ed.). 1965. *Gandhi on Nonviolence: A Selection from the Writings of Mahatma Gandhi*. New York: A New Directions Book.

7. Ford, John C. "The Morality of Obliteration Bombing." In Richard Wasserstrom (Ed.). 1970. *War and Morality*. Belmont, CA: Wadsworth, p. 15.

8. Harwell, M. A. 1984. *Nuclear Winter: The Human and Environmental Consequences of Nuclear War*. New York: Springer-Verlag.

9. Cady, 1989, *From Warism to Pacifism*, p. 64.

10. See the Global Nonviolent Action Database at: http://nvdatabase.swarthmore.edu.

11. For a summary of the evidence that supports this claim, see Howes, 2013, "The Failure of Pacifism and the Success of Nonviolence," pp. 431–432.

12. King, Martin Luther, Jr. 2010 [1958]. *Stride Toward Freedom: The Montgomery Story*. Boston: Beacon Press.

13. Although "strategic nonviolence" is the most commonly used term, I prefer "pragmatic nonviolence" since both types of nonviolence have strategies for winning. "Pragmatic" implies that nonviolence is chosen because it works, which accurately captures that category of nonviolence.
14. Stiehm, Judith. 1968. "Nonviolence Is Two." *Sociological Inquiry* 38: 23–30.
15. Weber, Thomas. 2003. "Nonviolence is Who? Gene Sharp and Gandhi." *Peace & Change* 28(2): 250–270.
16. For example, most believe that Gandhi, as the key figure of principled nonviolence, was driven by a religiously based ethical imperative. For further information, see Erikson, Erik. 1970. *Gandhi's Truth: On the Origins of Militant Nonviolence.* New York: Norton and Company.
17. Wood, Houston. 2015. *Invitation to Peace Studies.* New York: Oxford University Press.
18. Sharp, Gene. 1979. "Nonviolence: Moral Principle or Political Technique? Clues From Gandhi's Thought and Experience." In Gene Sharp (Ed.). *Gandhi as a Political Strategist: With Essays on Ethics and Politics.* Boston: Porter Sargent, pp. 273–309.
19. Majmudar, Uma. 2005. *Gandhi's Pilgrimage of Faith: From Darkness to Light.* Albany, NY: SUNY Press.
20. Bondurant, Joan. 1988. *Conquest of Violence,* Princeton, NJ: Princeton University Press, pp. 18–19, 25.
21. Nagler, Michael. 2004. *The Search for a Nonviolent Future: A Promise of Peace for Ourselves, Our Families, and Our World.* Novato, CA: New World Library.
22. King, Jr., Martin Luther. 1991. "An Experiment in Love." In James M. Washington (Ed.). *Testament of Hope: The Essential Writings and Speeches of Martin Luther King, Jr.* New York: Harper Collins, pp. 16–20.
23. For more information about the concept of "the beloved community," see King, Martin Luther, Jr. [1958] 1987. *Stride Toward Freedom: The Montgomery Story.* New York: Harper Collins.
24. Burrowes, Robert J. 1996. *The Strategy of Nonviolent Defense.* Albany: SUNY Press.
25. Nikolayenko, Olena. 2011. *Citizens in the Making in Post-Soviet States.* New York: Routledge.
26. Burrowes, *Strategy of Nonviolent Defense.*
27. Bondurant, *Conquest of Violence,* p. 33.
28. Quoted in Weber, Thomas. 2001. "Gandhian Philosophy, Conflict Resolution Theory and the Practical Approaches to Negotiation." *Journal of Peace Research* 38(4): 495.
29. Dalton, Dennis. 1993. *Mahatma Gandhi: Nonviolent Power in Action.* New York: Columbia University Press, p. 43.
30. Dalton, *Mahatma Gandhi,* p. 45.
31. Bondurant, *Conquest of Violence,* p. 229.
32. Gregg, Richard. 1935. *The Power of Nonviolence.* London: George Routledge.
33. The validity of this concept has been questioned. For instance, Thomas Weber (1993) argues that there is no empirical evidence to back up Gregg's claim that suffering throws an opponent off balance.
34. For further elaboration of this strategic approach, see Sharp's (1973) landmark three-volume work, *The Politics of Nonviolent Action,* Boston: Porter Sargent.
35. Sharp, Gene. 1990. *Civilian-Based Defense: A Post-Military Weapons System.* Princeton, NJ: Princeton University Press.

36. Sharp, Gene. 1990. *The Role of Power in Nonviolent Struggle*. Cambridge, MA: The Albert Einstein Institute.
37. Sharp, *Role of Power in Nonviolent Struggle*, p. 15.
38. Burrowes, *Strategy of Nonviolent Defense*, p. 99.
39. Schock, Kurt. 2003. "Nonviolence and Its Misconceptions: Insights for Social Scientists." *PS: Political Science and Politics* 36: 705–712.
40. Ackerman, Peter, and Christopher Kruegler. 1994. *Strategic Nonviolent Conflict: The Dynamics of People Power in the Twentieth Century*. Westport, CT: Praeger.
41. For instance, see Nagler, *The Search for a Nonviolent Future*.
42. Van Hook, Stephanie. 2012. "How to Sustain a Revolution." Retrieved September 28, 2012, at http://truthout.org/index.php?option=com_k2&view=item&id=5895:how-to-sustain-a-revolution.
43. For more detailed explanation of these problems, see Chabot, Sean, and Majid Sharifi. 2013. "The Violence of Nonviolence: Problematizing Nonviolent Resistance in Iran and Egypt." *Sociologists Without Borders* 8: 205–232.
44. Richards, Jerald. 1991. "Gene Sharp's Pragmatic Defense of Nonviolence." *International Journal of Applied Philosophy* 6(1): 59–63.
45. Sharp, Gene. 1980. *Social Power and Political Freedom*. Boston: Porter Sargent, p. 396.
46. Weber, "Nonviolence is Who?"
47. Boaz, "Must We Change Our Hearts?"
48. For elaboration of this point, see Satha-Anand, Chaiwat. 2015. "Overcoming Illusory Division Between Nonviolence as a Pragmatic Strategy and as a Way of Life." In Kurt Schock (Ed.). *Comparative Perspectives on Civil Resistance*. Minneapolis: University of Minnesota Press.
49. Boaz, "Must We Change Our Hearts?"
50. Quoted in Sharp, *Gandhi as a Political Strategist*, p. 278.
51. Quoted in Sharp, *Gandhi as a Political Strategist*, p. 278.
52. Colaiaco, James A. 1993. *Martin Luther King, Jr.: Apostle of Militant Nonviolence*. New York: St. Martin's Press.
53. Sharp, *Politics of Nonviolent Action* (Part III), pp. 633–634.
54. I thank Brian Martin for highlighting this point.
55. For an overview of the advantage of strategic nonviolence over violence, see Martin, Brian. 2008. "How Nonviolence is Misrepresented." *Gandhi Marg* (July–September): 235–257.
56. Bob, Clifford. 2005. *The Marketing of Rebellion*. New York: Cambridge University Press. Chenoweth, Erica, and Maria Stephan. 2011. *Why Civil Resistance Works: The Strategic Logic of Nonviolent Conflict*. New York: Columbia University Press.
57. As quoted in Merton, *Gandhi on Nonviolence*, p. 29.
58. Chenoweth and Stephan, *Why Civil Resistance Works*, pp. 34–35.
59. Burrowes, *Strategy of Nonviolent Defense*, p. 239.
60. For empirical evidence to support this assertion, see Abrahms, Max. 2006. "Why Terrorism Does Not Work." *International Security* 31(2): 42–78. Of course others, such as Robert Pape (2003), have claimed that terrorism does work. Yet Pape's methods and theoretical analysis have been critiqued, casting doubts on the veracity of his claim. For more information on these critiques, see Ashworth, Scott, Joshua D. Clinton, Adam Meirowitz, and Kristopher W. Ramsey. 2008. "Design, Inference, and the Strategic Logic of Suicide Terrorism." *American Political Science Review* 102(2): 269–273.

61. For a strong overview of these misconceptions and others, see Schock, "Nonviolent Action and Its Misconceptions."

62. Sharp defines nonviolent resistance as actions that extend beyond the bounds of conventional political action. Thus drafting, signing, and submitting a petition in an authoritarian regime may be considered nonviolent action but the same act would not be in a democratic nation that respects civil liberties. I thank Brian Martin for drawing my attention to this distinction.

63. King, Martin Luther, Jr. 1964. *Why We Can't Wait*. New York: Mentor Books, p. 78.

64. Ackerman, Peter, and Jack DuVall. 2000. *A Force More Powerful: A Century of Nonviolent Action*. New York: Palgrave; Chenoweth, Erica, and Maria Stephan. 2011. *Why Civil Resistance Works*; Nepstad, Sharon Erickson. 2011. *Nonviolent Revolutions: Civil Resistance in the Late 20th Century*. New York: Oxford University Press; Roberts, Adam, and Timothy Garton Ash (Eds.). 2009. *Civil Resistance and Power Politics: Non-Violent Action from Gandhi to the Present*. Oxford: Oxford University Press. Schock, Kurt. 2005. *Unarmed Insurrections: People Power in Nondemocracies*. Minneapolis: University of Minnesota Press.

65. Corr, Anders. 1999. *No Trespassing: Squatting, Rent Strikes, and Land Struggle Worldwide*. Cambridge, MA: South End Press.

66. Deming, Barbara. 1971. *Revolution and Equilibrium*. New York: Grossman Publishers. McAllister, Pam. 1982. *Reweaving the Web of Life: Feminism and Nonviolence*. Philadelphia: New Society Publishers.

67. Schock, "Nonviolence and Its Misconceptions," p. 706.

68. Zunes, Stephen. 1994. "Unarmed Insurrections Against Authoritarian Governments in the Third World: A New Kind of Revolution?" *Third World Quarterly* 15: 403–426.

69. Bunce, Valerie, and Sharon Wolchik. 2011. *Defeating Authoritarian Leaders in Post-Communist Societies*. New York: Cambridge University Press. Nikolayenko, Olena. 2012. "Tactical Interactions Between Youth Movements and Incumbent Governments in Post-Communist States." *Research in Social Movements, Conflict, and Change* 34: 27–61.

70. Johnstad, Petter Grahl. 2010. "Nonviolent Democratization: A Sensitivity Analysis of How Transition Mode and Violence Impact the Durability of Democracy." *Peace and Change* 35(3): 464–482. Sharp, *Civilian-Based Defense*.

71. For elaboration of these dynamics, see Bob, Clifford, and Sharon Erickson Nepstad. 2007. "Kill a Leader, Murder a Movement?: Leadership and Assassination in Social Movements." *American Behavioral Scientist* 50(10): 1370–1394.

72. Corr, *No Trespassing*. McCarthy, Ronald, and Christopher Kruegler. 1993. *Toward Research and Theory Building in the Study of Nonviolent Action*. Boston, MA: The Albert Einstein Institution.

73. Chabot, Sean. 2011. *Transnational Roots of the Civil Rights Movement: African American Explorations of the Gandhian Repertoire*. Lanham, MD: Lexington Books.

74. Brown, Judith M. 1972. *Gandhi's Rise to Power*. Cambridge, UK: Cambridge University Press. Brown, Judith M. 1977. *Gandhi and Civil Disobedience*. Cambridge, UK: Cambridge University Press. Dalton, *Mahatma Gandhi*.

75. Parkman, Patricia. 1988. *Nonviolent Insurrection in El Salvador: The Fall of Maximiliano Hernández Martínez*. Tucson: University of Arizona Press.

76. Chabot, Sean, and Stellan Vinthagen. 2007. "Rethinking Nonviolent Action and Contentious Politics: Political Cultures of Nonviolent Opposition in the Indian Independence Movement and Brazil's Landless Workers Movement." *Research*

in Social Movements, Conflicts, and Change 27: 91–121. Schock, Kurt. 2012. "Land Struggles in the Global South: Strategic Innovations in Brazil and India." In Gregory Maney, Rachel Kutz-Flamenbaum, Deana Rohlinger, and Jeff Goodwin (Eds.). *Strategies for Social Change*. Minneapolis: University of Minnesota Press, pp. 221–244.

77. Shepherd, Mark. 2001. *Mahatma Gandhi and His Myths*. Los Angeles: Simple Productions.
78. Chenoweth and Stephan, *Why Civil Resistance Works*.
79. Schock, "Nonviolence and Its Misconceptions."
80. Chenoweth and Stephan, *Why Civil Resistance Works*. See also Stephan, Maria, and Erica Chenoweth. 2008. "Why Civil Resistance Works: The Strategic Logic of Nonviolent Conflict." *International Security* 33(1): 22.
81. Chenoweth and Stephan, *Why Civil Resistance Works*. Johnstad, "Nonviolent Democratization." Karatnycky, Adrian, and Peter Ackerman. 2005. " How Freedom is Won: From Civil Resistance to Durable Democracy." Washington, D.C.: Freedom House Report.
82. Churchill, Ward. 1998. *Pacifism as Pathology*. Winnipeg: Arbeiter Ring.
83. Gelderloos, Peter. 2007. *How Nonviolence Protects the State*. Cambridge, MA: South End Press.
84. Gelderloos, *How Nonviolence Protects the State*, pp. 10–11.
85. Gelderloos, *How Nonviolence Protects the State*, p. 99.
86. Gelderloos, *How Nonviolence Protects the State*, p. 7.
87. For a full review of the double standards in Gelderloos' book, see Martin, Brian. 2008. "How Nonviolence is Misrepresented." *Gandhi Marg* 30(2): 235–257.
88. Indeed, this is one of the primary criticisms of Chabot and Sharifi (2013).
89. Martin, "How Nonviolence is Misrepresented," p. 243.
90. The one exception that Chenoweth and Stephan note is that nonviolence has been less successful in secessionist movements. Yet in these cases, violent struggle also has very low rates of success.
91. Biddle, Stephen D. 2004. *Military Power: Explaining Victory and Defeat in Modern Battle*. Princeton, NJ: Princeton University Press.
92. Springer, Kimberly. 2006. "Black Feminists Respond to Black Power Masculinism." In Peniel E. Joseph (Ed.). *The Black Power Movement: Rethinking the Civil Rights-Black Power Era*. New York: Routledge, pp. 105–118.
93. Gelderloos, *How Nonviolence Protects the State*, p. 100.
94. Zunes, Stephen. 2008. "Nonviolent Action and Pro-Democracy Struggles." *Foreign Policy in Focus*, January 28.
95. For further debate on this topic, see Bunce, Valerie, and Sharon Wolchik's forthcoming book, *Defeating Authoritarian Leaders in Mixed Regimes: U.S. Democracy Assistance, International Diffusion, and Local Electoral Strategies*. New York: Cambridge University Press. Also see Wilson, Andrew. 2005. *Ukraine's Orange Revolution*. New Haven, CT: Yale University Press, pp. 183–189.
96. Gelderloos, *How Nonviolence Protects the State*, p. 67.
97. Gelderloos, *How Nonviolence Protects the State*, pp. 50–51.

CHAPTER 2

1. For a thorough analysis of religiously inspired war and terrorism, see Juergensmeyer, Mark. 2001. *Terror in the Mind of God: The Global Rise of Religious Violence*. Berkeley: University of California Press.
2. Deuteronomy 19:21 (New Living Translation).

3. For elaboration of this distinction, see Gregg, Heather Selma. 2004. "The Causes of Religious Wars: Holy Nations, Sacred Spaces, and Religious Revolutions." PhD Dissertation, Department of Political Science, Massachusetts Institute of Technology. To understand the ways in which religion and violence can get entangled, see Chuman, Joseph. 2006. "Does Religion Cause Violence?" In Karikottuchira K. Kuriakose (Ed.). *Religion, Terrorism, and Globalization*. New York: Nova Science Publishers, pp. 15–30.

4. The traits are derived from Steffen, Lloyd. 2007. *Holy War, Just War: Exploring the Moral Meaning of Religious Violence*. Lanham, MD: Rowman & Littlefield; and Victoria, Brian A. 2007. "Holy War: Toward a Holistic Understanding." *Journal of Religion, Conflict, and Peace* 1(1) [online].

5. For elaboration of the just war criteria, historical development, and key debates, see O'Donovan, Oliver. 2003. *The Just War Revisited*. Cambridge, UK: Cambridge University Press; Steinhoff, Uwe. 2007. *On the Ethics of War and Terrorism*. New York: Oxford University Press; and Walzer, Michael. 1977. *Just and Unjust Wars: A Moral Argument with Historical Illustrations*. New York: Basic Books.

6. These principles are derived from the just war tradition within Christianity.

7. For more on this topic, see Bass, Gary J. 2004. "Jus Post Bellum." *Philosophy and Public Affairs* 32(4): 384–412; and Orend, Brian. 2007. "*Jus Post Bellum*: The Perspective of a Just War Theorist." *Leiden Journal of International Law*. 20: 571–591.

8. Wink, Walter. 1996. "Beyond Just War and Pacifism." In J. Patout Burns (Ed.). *War and Its Discontents: Pacifism and Quietism in the Abrahamic Traditions*. Washington, DC: Georgetown University Press, p. 115.

9. Oxtoby, Willard (Ed.). 2002. *World Religions: Eastern Traditions*. New York: Oxford University Press.

10. Shastri, Sunanda Y., and Yajneshwar S. Shastri. 2007. "Ahimsa and the Unity of All Things: A Hindu View of Nonviolence." In Daniel L. Smith-Christopher (Ed.). *Subverting Hatred: The Challenge of Nonviolence in Religious Traditions*. Maryknoll, NY: Orbis, pp. 57–75 (esp. pp. 61–62).

11. Narayahan, Vasudha. 2002. " The Hindu Tradition." In Willard G. Oxtoby (Ed.). *World Religions: Eastern Traditions*. Don Mill, Ontario: Oxford University Press Canada, pp. 13–125.

12. Bondurant, Joan. 1988 [1958]. *Conquest of Violence: The Gandhian Philosophy of Conflict*. Princeton, NJ: Princeton University Press, p. 111.

13. Shastri and Shastri, "Ahimsa."

14. Also see Chapter 2 in Jahanbegloo, Ramin. 2014. *Introduction to Nonviolence*. New York: Palgrave Macmillan.

15. Hunter, Doris. 1990. "On the Baghavad-Gita." In Robert L. Holmes (Ed.). *Nonviolence in Theory and Practice*. Belmont, CA: Wadsworth Publishing Company, pp. 16–19.

16. Gandhi, Mohandas K. *Gita the Mother*. Lahore, India: Free India Publications, pp. 155, 160.

17. Shastri and Shastri, "Ahimsa," p. 63.

18. BCE = "before the Common Era." This reference system has been adopted by many scholars so that Christianity is not given a privileged position in historical references.

19. Chappel, Christopher Key. 2007. "Jainism and Nonviolence." In Daniel L. Smith-Christopher (Ed.). *Subverting Hatred: The Challenge of Nonviolence in Religious Traditions*. Maryknoll, NY: Orbis Books, pp. 1–13.

20. Dundas, Paul. 1992. *The Jains*. London: Routledge.
21. The phrase "*Ahimsā paramo dharmah*" is actually found in the Hindu *Mahab-harata* before it enters the Jain tradition.
22. Narayahan, Vasudha. 2002. "The Jain Tradition." In Willard G. Oxtoby (Ed.). *World Religions: Eastern Traditions*. Don Mills, Ontario: Oxford University Press Canada, pp. 161–197.
23. Babb, Lawrence A. 1994. *Absent Lord: Ascetics and Kings in a Jain Ritual Culture*. Berkeley: University of California Press.
24. Chappel, "Jainism and Nonviolence," pp. 10–11.
25. Gethin, Rupert. 1998. *Foundations of Buddhism*. Oxford, UK: Oxford University Press; Harvey, Peter. 1990. *Introduction to Buddhism: Teachings, History and Practices*. Cambridge, UK: Cambridge University Press; Walpola, Rahula. 1974 [1959]. *What the Buddha Taught*. New York: Grove Press.
26. Amore, Roy C., and Julia Ching. 2002. "The Buddhist Tradition." In Willard G. Oxtoby (Ed.) *World Religions: Eastern Traditions*. Don Mills, Ontario: Oxford University Press Canada, pp. 198–315.
27. Kraft, Kenneth (Ed.). 1992. *Inner Peace, World Peace: Essays on Buddhism and Nonviolence*. Albany: SUNY Press.
28. Queen, Christopher S. 2007. "The Peace Wheel: Nonviolent Action in the Buddhist Tradition." In Daniel L. Smith-Christopher (Ed.). *Subverting Hatred: The Challenge of Nonviolence in Religious Traditions*. Maryknoll, NY: Orbis, pp. 14–37.
29. Hanh, Thich Nhat. 1987. *Being Peace*. Berkeley: Parallax Press, pp. 61–62.
30. Loy, David. 2008. *Money, Sex, War, Karma: Notes on a Buddhist Revolution*. Somerville, MA: Wisdom Publications.
31. For further information about Engaged Buddhism, see Hanh, Thich Nhat. 1987. *Interbeing: 14 Guidelines for Engaged Buddhism*. Berkeley, CA: Parallax Press; Hanh, Thich Nhat. 1987. *Being Peace*. Berkeley, CA: Parallax Press.
32. King, Sallie B. 2005. *Being Benevolence: The Social Ethics of Engaged Buddhism*. Honolulu: University of Hawaii Press.
33. For an overview of cases in which Buddhists have waged war, see Jerryson, Michael, and Mark Juergensmeyer (Eds.). 2010. *Buddhist Warfare*. New York: Oxford University Press.
34. Amore and Ching, "The Buddhist Tradition."
35. Broyde, Michael J. 1996. "Fighting the War and the Peace: Battlefield Ethics, Peace Talks, Treaties, and Pacifism in the Jewish Tradition." In J. Patout Burns (Ed.). *War and Its Discontents: Pacifism and Quietism in the Abrahamic Traditions*. Washington, DC: Georgetown University Press, pp. 1–30.
36. Maimonides, *Laws of Kings* 6:1.
37. Mirsky, Yehuda. 1998. "The Political Morality of Pacifism and Nonviolence: One Jewish View." In J. Patout Burns (Ed.). *War and Its Discontents: Pacifism and Quietism in the Abrahamic Traditions*. Washington, DC: Georgetown University Press, pp. 47–66 (see p. 51).
38. Jewish ethics of warfare are heavily influenced by the writings of medieval Jewish philosopher and Torah scholar Moses Maimonides (or RaMBaM in Hebrew).
39. Gendler, Everett E. 1981. "Therefore Choose Life." In Allan Solomonow (Ed.). *Roots of Jewish Nonviolence*. Nyack, NY: Jewish Peace Fellowship, pp. 7–16.
40. Bleich, Rabbi J. David. 1991. "Nuclear War." In Daniel Landes (Ed.). *Confronting Omnicide: Jewish Reflections on Weapons of Mass Destruction*. Northvale, NJ: Jason Aronson.

41. Broyde, "Fighting the War and the Peace," pp. 7, 10.

42. Broyde, "Fighting the War and the Peace," p. 17.

43. Gendler, Rabbi Everett. 1996. "The Pursuit of Peace: A Singular Commandment." In J. Patout Burns (Ed.). *War and Its Discontents: Pacifism and Quietism in the Abrahamic Traditions.* Washington, DC: Georgetown University Press, pp. 31–46.

44. For more on this historical act of Jewish civil resistance, see Crossan, John Dominic. 1992. *The Historical Jesus: The Life of a Mediterranean Jewish Peasant.* New York: HarperCollins; Horsely, Richard A. 1987. *Jesus and the Spiral of Violence: Popular Jewish Resistance in Roman Palestine.* San Francisco: Harper & Row.

45. *Antiquities* 18.8.3, quoted in Akers, Keith. 2000. *The Lost Religion of Jesus: Simple Living and Nonviolence in Early Christianity.* New York: Lantern Books.

46. Konvitz, Milton R. 1994. "Conscience and Civil Disobedience in the Jewish Tradition." In Murray Polner and Naomi Goodman (Eds.). *The Challenge of Shalom: The Jewish Tradition of Peace and Justice.* Philadelphia: New Society Publishers, pp. 174–185. This same argument is articulated by Martin Luther King, Jr. as he justified civil disobedience in "Letter from a Birmingham Jail" in *Why We Can't Wait* (1964, Mentor Books).

47. Schwarzschild, Steven S. 1981. "Shalom." In Murray Polner and Naomi Goodman (Eds.). *The Challenge of Shalom: The Jewish Tradition of Peace and Justice.* Philadelphia: New Society Publishers, pp. 16–25.

48. Goodman, Naomi. 1996. "Pacifism and Nonviolence: Another Jewish View." In J. Patout Burns (Eds.). *War and Its Discontents: Pacifism and Quietism in the Abrahamic Traditions.* Washington, DC: Georgetown University Press, pp. 67–73.

49. For more information, see Brock, Peter. 1999. *Varieties of Pacifism: A Survey From Antiquity to the Outset of the Twentieth Century.* Syracuse, NY: Syracuse University Press; Hershberger, Guy F. 1944. *War, Peace, and Nonresistance.* Scottdale, PA: Herald Press; Hornus, Jean Michel. 1980. *It is Not Lawful for Me to Fight: Early Christian Attitudes toward War, Violence, and the State.* Scottdale, PA: Herald Press; Nuttall, Geoffrey. 1971. *Christian Pacifism in History.* Berkeley, CA: World Without War Council; Oxford: Blackwell.

50. Akers, Keith. 2000. *The Lost Religion of Jesus: Simple Living and Nonviolence in Early Christianity.* New York: Lantern Books.

51. Cadoux, C. John. 1919. *The Early Christian Attitude Toward War.* London: Headley Bros.

52. Bainton, Roland. 1960 [1923]. *Christian Attitudes Toward War and Peace: A Historical Survey and Critical Reevaluation.* New York: Abingdon Press.

53. Matthew 5:38–41, 43–44. See also Luke 6:29–30.

54. For more on this point, see Myers, Ched. 1988. *Binding the Strong Man: A Political Reading of Mark's Story of Jesus.* Maryknoll, NY: Orbis.

55. Wink, Walter. 1987. *Violence and Nonviolence in South Africa: Jesus' Third Way.* Philadelphia: New Society Publishers, p. 13.

56. Wink, Walter. 1987. *Violence and Nonviolence in South Africa: Jesus' Third Way.* Philadelphia: New Society Publishers, p. 15.

57. Wink, *Violence and Nonviolence in South Africa*, pp. 18–19.

58. Wink, *Violence and Nonviolence in South Africa.*

59. Chernus, Ira. 2004. *American Nonviolence: The History of an Idea.* Maryknoll, NY: Orbis Books.

60. Abu-Nimer, Mohammed. 2003. *Nonviolence and Peace Building in Islam: Theory and Practice.* Gainsville: University of Florida Press, p. 29; Afsaruddin,

Asma. 2010. "Recovering the Early Semantic Purview of Jihad and Martyrdom: Challenging Statist-Military Perspectives." In Qamar-ul Huda (Ed.). *Crescent and Dove: Peace and Conflict Resolution in Islam*. Washington, DC: United States Institute of Peace Press, pp. 39–62.

61. For elaboration of the conditions that legitimate war within the Islamic tradition, see the work of Sohail Hashmi (1996) and Abdul Aziz Sachedina (1996).

62. Donner, Fred. 1991. "The Sources of Islamic Conceptions of War." In John Kelsay and James Turner Johnson (Eds.). *Just War and Jihad: Historical and Theoretical Perspectives on War and Peace in Western and Islamic Traditions*. New York: Greenwood Press, pp. 31–69; Kalin, Ibrahim. 2010. "Islam and Peace: A Survey of the Sources of Peace in the Islamic Tradition." In Qamar-ul Huda (Ed.). *Crescent and Dove: Peace and Conflict Resolution in Islam*. Washington, DC: United States Institute of Peace Press, pp. 3–37.

63. Tibi, Bassam. 1995. "War and Peace in Islam." In Terry Nardin (Ed.). *The Ethics of War and Peace: Religious and Secular Perspectives*. Princeton, NJ: Princeton University Press, pp. 128–145.

64. Sachedina, Abdul Aziz. *The Islamic Roots of Democratic Pluralism*. New York: Oxford University Press, p. 121.

65. Kelsay, John. 1993. *Islam and War: A Study in Comparative Ethics*. Louisville, KY: Westminster/John Knox Press.

66. Engineer, Ashgar. 1994. "Sources of Nonviolence in Islam." In Mahendra Kumar (Ed.). *Nonviolence: Contemporary Issues and Challenges*. New Delhi: Gandhi Peace Foundation.

67. This includes Abu-Nimer (1996a, b; 2000); Easwaran (1984); Kishtainy (1990); and Satha-Anand (1993).

68. Ahmad, Razi. 1993. "Islam, Nonviolence, and Global Transformation." In Glenn Paige, Chaiwat Satha-Anand, and Sarah Gilliatt (Eds.). *Islam and Nonviolence*. Honolulu: Center for Global Nonviolence Planning Project, Matsunaga Institute for Peace, University of Hawaii, pp. 27–53.

69. Halverson, Jeffrey R. 2012. *Searching for a King: Muslim Nonviolence and the Future of Islam*. Washington, DC: Potomac Books.

70. Hashmi, Sohail H. 1996. "Interpreting the Islamic Ethics of War and Peace." In Terry Nardin (Ed.). *The Ethics of War and Peace: Religious and Secular Perspectives*. Princeton, NJ: Princeton University Press, pp. 144–166.

71. Johansen, Robert C. 1997. "Radical Islam and Nonviolence: A Case Study of Religious Empowerment and Constraint among Pashtuns." *Journal of Peace Research* 34(1): 53–71; and Raqib, Mohammad. 2009. "The Muslim Pashtun Movement of the North-West Frontier of India, 1930–1934." In *Civilian Jihad: Nonviolent Struggle, Democratization, and Governance in the Middle East*. New York: Palgrave Macmillan, pp. 107–118.

72. For more on some of these early nonviolent organizations, see Cortright, David. 2008. *Peace: A History of Movements and Ideas*. New York: Cambridge University Press.

73. Howes, Dustin Ells. 2013. "The Failure of Pacifism and the Success of Nonviolence." *Perspectives on Politics* 11(2): 429.

74. Alonso, Harriet Hyman. 1993. *Peace as a Women's Issue: A History of the U.S. Movement for World Peace and Women's Rights*. Syracuse, NY: Syracuse University Press; Foster, Catherine. 1989. *Women for All Seasons: The Story of the Women's International League for Peace and Freedom*. Athens: University of Georgia Press.

75. For instance, see pp. 3–46 in Moskos, Charles, and John W. Chambers II. 1993. *The New Conscientious Objection: From Sacred to Secular.* New York: Oxford University Press.

76. WRL was a branch of War Resisters International, which was founded in 1921.

77. Bennett, Scott H. 2001. "Radical Pacifism and the General Strike Against War: Jessie Wallace Hughan, the Founding of the War Resisters League, and the Socialist Origins of Secular Radical Pacifism in America." *Peace and Change* 26(3): 361.

78. Bennett, Scott H. 2004. *Radical Pacifism: The War Resisters League and Gandhian Nonviolence in America, 1915–1963.* Syracuse, NY: Syracuse University Press.

79. Deming, Barbara. 1982. *Two Essays/New Men New Women: Some Thoughts on Nonviolence.* Philadelphia: New Society Publishers.

80. Lynd, Staughton, and Alice Lynd (Eds.). 1995. *Nonviolence in America*, 2nd edition. Maryknoll, NY: Orbis Books, p. 415.

CHAPTER 3

1. Mills, C. Wright. 2000 [1956]. *The Power Elite.* New York and Oxford: Oxford University Press.

2. For more on the overrepresentation of business leaders and the upper class in the U.S. Senate, see Domhoff, G. William. 1967. *Who Rules America?* Englewood Cliffs, NJ: Prentice Hall.

3. Ganz, Marshall. 2010. *Why David Sometimes Wins: Leadership, Organization, and Strategy in the California Farm Worker Movement.* New York: Oxford University Press.

4. Shaw, Randy. 2008. *Beyond the Fields: Cesar Chavez, the UFW, and the Struggle for Justice in the 21st Century.* Berkeley and Los Angeles: University of California Press, p. 43.

5. Shaw, *Beyond the Fields*, p. 43.

6. Gene Sharp (and others such as the group CANVAS) use the phrase "pluralist theory." However, this can be confused with the "pluralist theory" promoted by social scientists such as Robert Dahl and Seymour Martin Lipset, which emphasizes that most political decision making occurs within state systems but that other nongovernmental groups, such as social movements, have the ability to influence legislation. Dahl and Lipset argue that this is what ensures democracy, since state power can be balanced by other groups. In the nonviolence literature, the pluralist theory refers to the forms of power that citizens possess that can be used to undermine the state in nondemocratic conditions. To avoid confusion, I refer to the theory of "citizen-based power."

7. Boétie, Etienne. 1975 [1552–53]. *The Politics of Obedience: The Discourse of Voluntary Servitude.* Translated by Harry Kurz. New York: Free Life Editions, p. 46.

8. Boétie, *The Politics of Obedience*, pp. 52–53.

9. Thoreau, Henry David. 2008 [1849]. *On The Duty of Civil Disobedience.* Radford, VA: Wilder.

10. Naess, Arne. 1958. "A Systemization of Gandhian Ethics of Conflict Resolution." *Journal of Conflict Resolution* 2(4): 140–155.

11. The nine steps described in this section are derived from Bondurant, *Conquest of Violence*, p. 40.

12. Weber, Thomas. 2001. "Gandhian Philosophy, Conflict Resolution Theory and Practical Approaches to Negotiation." *Journal of Peace Research* 38(4): 493–513.

13. See Chabot, Sean. 2011. *Transnational Roots of the U.S. Civil Rights Movement: African American Explorations of the Gandhian Repertoire.* Lanham, MD: Lexington Books; Cortright, David. 2006. *Gandhi and Beyond: Nonviolence in an Age of Terrorism.* Boulder, CO: Paradigm Publishers; Scalmer, Sean. 2011. *Gandhi in the West: The Mahatma and the Rise of Radical Protest.* Cambridge and New York: Cambridge University Press.

14. Bondurant, *Conquest of Violence*, pp. 38–41.

15. Naess, Arne. 1974. *Gandhi and Group Conflict. An Exploration of Satyagraha. Theoretical Background.* Oslo: Universitetsforlaget.

16. Gandhi did, however, encourage civil resisters to compromise on nonessentials.

17. Wehr, Paul. 1979. *Conflict Regulation.* Boulder, CO: Westview Press, pp. 55–68.

18. Bondurant, Joan. 1988 [1958]. *Conquest of Violence: The Gandhian Philosophy of Conflict.* Princeton, NJ: Princeton University Press, pp. 180–181.

19. This account of the Gandhian movement is derived from Brown, Judith. 2008. *Gandhi and Civil Disobedience: The Mahatma in Indian Politics, 1928–1934.* Cambridge, UK: Cambridge University Press; and Brown, Judith. 1989, *Gandhi: Prisoner of Hope.* New Haven, CT: Yale University Press.

20. Information about the Quit India campaign is drawn from: Hutchins, Francis. G. 1973. *India's Revolution: Gandhi and the Quit India Movement.* Cambridge, MA: Harvard University Press; Wolpert, Stanley. 2006. *A Shameful Flight: The Last Years of the British Empire in India.* Oxford, UK: Oxford University Press.

21. From: www.trueweb.50webs.com/quitindiamovement.html.

22. Read, Anthony, and David Fisher. 1998. *The Proudest Day: India's Long Road to Independence.* New York: W.W. Norton, p. 329.

23. Sharp elaborates on these in numerous publications. For a succinct summary, see Sharp, Gene. 1990. *The Role of Power in Nonviolent Struggle.* Cambridge, MA: The Albert Einstein Institution.

24. Sharp refers to this as "human resources." To avoid confusion with the business use of the term, I simply refer to it as obedience and cooperation.

25. For further information, see Hallie, Philip P. 1994. *Lest Innocent Blood Be Shed: The Story of the Village of Le Chambon and How Goodness Happened There.* New York: Harper Perennial; Semelin, Jacques. 1993. *Unarmed Against Hitler: Civilian Resistance in Europe, 1939–1943.* Westport, CT: Praeger.

26. Sharp, *The Role of Power in Nonviolent Struggle*, p. 9.

27. Sharp, Gene. 2005. *Waging Nonviolent Struggle: 20th Century Practice and 21st Century Potential.* Boston: Porter Sargent.

28. See, for instance, Nepstad's (2011b) discussion of religious groups' roles in nonviolent uprisings in East Germany, Chile, the Philippines, Kenya, and Panama.

29. For a summary of studies that emphasize the importance of elite support, see Goldstone, Jack. 2001. "Toward a Fourth Generation of Revolutionary Theory." *Annual Review of Political Science* 4: 139–187.

30. Popovic et al., CANVAS, p. 68.

31. Popovic, Srdja, Slobodan Djinovic, Andrej Milivojevic, Hardy Merriman, and Ivan Marovic. 2007. *CANVAS Core Curriculum: A Guide to Effective Nonviolent Struggle.* Serbia: Canvas Publications.

32. Sharp, Gene. 1973. *The Politics of Nonviolent Action, Volume II: The Methods of Nonviolent Action.* Boston: Porter-Sargent.

33. Information about Otpor and the nonviolent resistance against Slobodan Milošević is drawn from the following sources: Cevallos, Albert. 2001. *Whither the Bulldozer?: Nonviolent Revolution and the Transition to Democracy in Serbia.*

Washington, DC: United States Institute of Peace Special Report; Nikolayenko, Olena. 2011. *Citizens in the Making in Post-Soviet States*, Routledge; Vejvoda, Ivan. 2009. "Civil Society versus Slobodan Milosevic: Serbia, 1991–2000." In Adam Roberts and Timothy Garton Ash (Eds.). *Civil Resistance and Power Politics: The Experience of Nonviolent Action from Gandhi to the Present*. Oxford: Oxford University Press.

34. For more on Otpor's use of humor, see Sombutpoonsiri, Janjira. 2012. *The Use of Humour as a Vehicle for Nonviolent Struggle: Serbia's 1996–7 Protests and the OTPOR (Resistance) Movement*. PhD Thesis, School of Politics and International Relations, La Trobe University.

35. Sørensen, Majken Jul. 2008. "Humor as a Serious Strategy of Nonviolent Resistance to Oppression." *Peace & Change* 33(2): 167–190.

36. Cevallos, *Whither the Bulldozer?* p. 10.

CHAPTER 4

1. For a quick overview of different locations where civil resistance has been used, see the Global Nonviolent Action Data base at http://nvdatabase.swarthmore.edu. Also see Roberts, Adam, and Timothy Garton Ash. 2009. *Civil Resistance and Power Politics: The Experience of Nonviolent Action from Gandhi to the Present*. Oxford, UK: Oxford University Press; Zunes, Stephen, Lester R. Kurtz, and Sarah Beth Asher (Eds.). 1999. *Nonviolent Social Movements: A Geographical Perspective*. Malden, MA: Blackwell Publishing.

2. This definition is derived from James C. Scott's 1985 book, *Weapons of the Weak: Everyday Forms of Peasant Resistance*. New Haven, CT: Yale University Press.

3. Camp, Stephanie. 2004. *Closer to Freedom: Enslaved Women and Everyday Resistance in the Plantation South*. Chapel Hill: University of North Carolina Press; White, Deborah Gray. 2000. " Let My People Go: 1804–1860." In Robin D. G. Kelley and Earl Lewis (Eds.). *To Make Our World Anew: A History of African Americans*. New York: Oxford University Press, pp. 169–226.

4. This account of Le Chambon's resistance is drawn from the following accounts: Halie, Philip P. 1979. *Lest Innocent Blood Be Shed: The Story of the Village of Le Chambon and How Goodness Happened There*. New York: Harper and Row Publishers; Unsworth, Richard P. 2012. *A Portrait of Pacifists: Chambon, the Holocaust, and the Lives of André and Magda Trocmé*. Syracuse, NY: Syracuse University Press.

5. This definition is derived from Margalit, Avishai. 2002. *The Ethics of Memory*. Cambridge, MA: Harvard University Press, p. 147. Although Margalit is referring to people who have themselves experienced this evil and lived to tell others about it, here we refer simply to civil resisters whose actions reflect these experiences and expose the suffering that is caused by a social injustice.

6. Winter, Jay. 2007. "The Moral Witness and the Two World Wars." *Ethnologie française* 37(3): 467.

7. Simmen, Edward R., and Richard F. Bauerle. "Chicano: Origin and Meaning." *American Speech* 44.3 (Autumn 1969): 225–230.

8. Nepstad, Sharon Erickson. 2008. *Religion and War Resistance in the Plowshares Movement*. New York: Cambridge University Press, p. 30.

9. For more information on the Catholic Left draft board raids, see McNeal, Patricia. 1992. *Harder Than War: Catholic Peacemaking in Twentieth Century America*. New Brunswick: Rutgers University Press; Meconis, Charles A. 1979. *With Clumsy Grace: The American Catholic Left, 1961–1975*. New York: Seabury Press;

Polner, Murray, and Jim O'Grady. 1997. *Disarmed and Dangerous: The Radical Lives and Times of Daniel and Philip Berrigan*. New York: Basic Books.

10. Quotation from Berrigan, Daniel. 1987. "Swords Into Plowshares." In *Swords Into Plowshares: Nonviolent Direct Action for Disarmament*. San Francisco: Harper & Row, pp. 55, 65.

11. Nepstad, *Religion and War Resistance*, p. 33.

12. Quote from Nepstad, *Religion and War Resistance*, p. 62.

13. It should be noted that the civil rights movement targeted a number of social institutions, not just the state. Activists targeted businesses with segregation practices. They also targeted cultural attitudes of prejudice.

14. In 2013, the Boy Scouts did change their policy to admit gay youth, but they still refuse to allow gay adults in leadership roles.

15. For more information on this movement, see Bruce, Tricia. 2011. *Faithful Revolution: How Voice of the Faithful is Changing the Church*. New York: Oxford University Press.

16. For more information about the nonviolent strategy of the UFW, see Chapter 4 ("Gandhi in the Fields") in Cortright, David. 2006. *Gandhi and Beyond: Nonviolence for an Age of Terrorism*. Boulder, CO: Paradigm Publishers; Merriman, Hardy. 2005. "California Grape Workers' Strike and Boycott, 1965–1970." In Gene Sharp (Ed.). *Waging Nonviolent Struggle: 20th Century Practice and 21st Century Potential*. Boston: Extending Horizons Books, pp. 173–188.

17. For in-depth information about the UFW's strategy, see Ganz, Marshall. 2010. *Why David Sometimes Wins: Leadership, Organization, and Strategy in the California Farm Worker Movement*. New York: Oxford University Press.

18. From Lawson, George. 2005. "Negotiated Revolutions: The Prospect of Radical Change in Contemporary World Politics." *Review of International Studies* 31(3): 473–493. Quotation from p. 479.

19. Lawson, "Negotiated Revolutions," p. 487.

20. For elaboration on the democratic transition in South Africa, see Wood, Elisabeth Jean. 2000. *Forging Democracy From Below: Insurgent Transitions in South Africa and El Salvador*. New York: Cambridge University Press.

21. Frankel, Philip H. 2001. *An Ordinary Atrocity: Sharpeville and Its Massacre*. New Haven, CT: Yale University Press.

22. Schock, Kurt. 2005. *Unarmed Insurrections: People Power Movements in Nondemocracies*. Minneapolis: University of Minnesota Press, p. 64.

23. Zunes, Stephen. 2015. "South Africa: The Townships Rise Up." In Véronique Duduoet (Ed.). *Civil Resistance and Conflict Transformation: Transitions from Armed to Nonviolent Struggle*. New York: Routledge.

24. Lodge, Tom. 1988. "State of Exile: The African National Congress of South Africa, 1976–1986." In Philip Frankel, Noam Pines, and Mark Swilling (Eds.). *State, Resistance, and Change in South Africa*. London: Croom Helm, pp. 229–258.

25. Price, Robert M. 1991. *The Apartheid State in Crisis: Political Transformation in South Africa, 1975–1990*. Oxford, UK: Oxford University Press.

26. For details of the secret meetings and transition process, see Sparks, Allistair. 1995. *Tomorrow is Another Country: The Inside Story of South Africa's Road To Change*. Chicago: University of Chicago Press.

27. Tutu, Desmond. 2000. *No Future Without Forgiveness*. New York: Doubleday.

28. Sharp, Gene. 2002. *From Dictatorship to Democracy: Conceptual Framework for Liberation*. Cambridge, MA: The Albert Einstein Institute.

29. Burton, Sandra. 1989. *Impossible Dream: The Marcoses, the Aquinos, and the Unfinished Revolution.* New York: Warner, p. 291.

30. Lee, Terence. 2009. "The Armed Forces and Transitions from Authoritarian Rule: Explaining the Role of the Military in 1986 Philippines and 1998 Indonesia." *Comparative Political Studies* 42: 640–669.

31. Bunce, Valerie, and Sharon Wolchik. 2006. "Favorable Conditions and Electoral Revolutions." *Journal of Democracy* 17(4): 5–18.

32. Wolchik, Sharon L. 2012. "Putinism Under Siege: Can There Be a Color Revolution?" *Journal of Democracy* 23(3): 63–70 (quotation is on p. 64).

33. Wolchik, "Putinism Under Seige," p. 64.

34. The color revolutions include the following: Serbia's bulldozer revolution (2000), Georgia's rose revolution (2003), Ukraine's orange revolution (2004), Kyrgyzstan's tulip revolution (2005), Lebanon's cedar revolution (2005), Belarus' jeans revolution (2006), Myanmar/Burma's saffron revolution (2007), and Iran's green revolution (2009).

35. The account of the orange revolution is drawn from Wilson, Andrew. 2006. *Ukraine's Orange Revolution.* New Haven, CT: Yale University Press; Aslund, Anders, and Michael McFaul (Eds.). 2006. *Revolution in Orange: The Origins of Ukraine's Democratic Breakthrough.* Washington, DC: Carnegie Endowment for International Peace.

36. Karatnycky, Adrian. 2005. "Ukraine's Orange Revolution." *Foreign Affairs* (March/April): 1–2.

37. For elaboration of this category of nonviolent action, see: Sharp, Gene, and Bruce Jenkins. 2003. *The Anti-Coup.* Boston: The Albert Einstein Institution.

38. Sharp and Jenkins, *The Anti-Coup*, p. 9.

39. Sharp and Jenkins, *The Anti-Coup*, p. 26.

40. Brysk, Alison. 1994. *The Politics of Human Rights in Argentina: Protest, Change, and Democratization.* Stanford, CA: Stanford University Press, p. 35.

41. Arditti, Rita. 1999. *Searching for Life: The Grandmothers of the Plaza del Mayo and the Disappeared Children of Argentina.* Los Angeles and Berkeley: University of California Press; Taylor, Diana. 1997. *Disappearing Acts: Spectacles of Gender and Nationalism in Argentina's Dirty War.* Durham, NC: Duke University Press.

42. Rigby, Andrew. 2001. *Justice and Reconciliation: After the Violence.* Boulder, CO: Lynne Reinner Publishers, pp. 72–73.

43. Boothe, Ivan, and Lee A. Smithey. 2007. "Privilege, Empowerment and Nonviolent Intervention." *Peace and Change* 32(1): 39–61.

44. These four categories of nonviolent intervention are elaborated in Boothe and Smithey, "Privilege, Empowerment and Nonviolent Intervention," pp. 42–43.

45. Coy, Patrick. 2011. "The Privilege Problematic in International Nonviolent Accompaniment's Early Decades." *Journal of Religion, Conflict, and Peace* 4(2) [online].

46. For more information on these techniques and the problems of privilege associated with them, see Coy, Patrick. 2001. "Shared Risks and Ethical Dilemmas on a Peace Brigades International Team in Sri Lanka." *Journal of Contemporary Ethnography* 30(5): 575–606.

47. Dudouet, Véronique. Forthcoming in 2015. "Sources, Functions, and Dilemmas of External Assistance to Civil Resistance Movements." In Kurt Schock (Ed.). *Comparative Perspectives on Civil Resistance.* Minneapolis: University of Minnesota Press.

48. More detailed information on Witness for Peace can be found in the following books: Griffin-Nolan, Ed. 1991. *Witness for Peace.* Louisville, KY: Westminster/

John Knox; Nepstad, Sharon Erickson. 2004. *Convictions of the Soul: Religion, Culture, and Agency in the Central America Solidarity Movement*. New York: Oxford University Press; Peace, Roger. 2012. *Call to Conscience: The Anti-Contra War Campaign*. Amherst and Boston: University of Massachusetts Press; Smith, Christian. 1996. *Resisting Reagan: The U.S.-Central America Peace Movement*. Chicago: University of Chicago Press.

49. Nepstad, 2004, *Convictions of the Soul*; Smith, 1996, *Resisting Reagan*.
50. Coy, Patrick. 1997. *Protecting Human Rights: The Dynamics of International Nonviolent Accompaniment by Peace Brigades International in Sri Lanka*. Dissertation, Syracuse University.
51. Coy, *Protecting Human Rights*, p. 282.
52. For an excellent overview of the problems of nonviolent interventionism, as well as constructive ideas about how to address these issues, see Boothe and Smithey, "Privilege, Empowerment and Nonviolent Intervention."
53. Martin, Brian. 2009. "Dilemmas in Promoting Nonviolence." *Gandhi Marg* 31(3): 429–453; Zunes, Stephen. 2008. "Nonviolent Action and Pro-Democracy Struggles." *Foreign Policy in Focus*, 24 January [online].

CHAPTER 5

1. It is important to mention that Rosa Parks' act was not spontaneous. She was a long-time member of the NAACP and had recently returned to Montgomery after receiving activist training at the Highlander Folk School. While spontaneous action may play a role in movements, galvanizing people into action, some degree of organizing is generally needed to sustain it over time.
2. For more on free spaces, see Futrell, Robert, and Pete Simi. 2004. "Free Spaces, Collective Identity, and the Persistence of U.S. White Power Activism." *Social Problems* 51(1): 16–42; Polletta, Francesca. 1999. "'Free Spaces' in Collective Action." *Theory and Society* 28: 1–38.
3. Foran, John, and Jean-Pierre Reed. 2002. "Political Cultures of Opposition: Exploring Idioms, Ideologies, and Revolutionary Agency in the Case of Nicaragua." *Critical Sociology* 28(3): 335–370.
4. Jasper, James. 1997. *The Art of Moral Protest*. Chicago: University of Chicago Press.
5. Brook, Timothy. 1992. *Quelling the People: The Military Suppression of the Beijing Democracy Movement*. New York: Oxford University Press, p. 21.
6. Smith, Christian. 1996. *Resisting Reagan: The U.S.-Central America Peace Movement*. Chicago: University of Chicago Press.
7. For more on negotiations with security forces, see Binnendijk, Anika Locke, and Ivan Marovic. 2006. "Power and Persuasion: Nonviolent Strategies to Influence State Security Forces in Serbia (2000) and Ukraine (2004)." *Communist and Post-Communist Studies* 39(3): 411–429.
8. This figure is taken from Popovic, Srdja, Slobodan Djinovic, Andrej Milivojevic, Hardy Merrimand, and Ivan Marovic. 2007. *CANVAS Core Curriculum: A Guide to Effective Nonviolent Struggle*. Serbia: Canvas Publications, p. 32.
9. Schock, Kurt. 2013. "The Practice and Study of Civil Resistance." *Journal of Peace Research* 50(3): 283. Also see Summy, Ralph. 1994. "Nonviolence and the Case of the Extremely Ruthless Opponent." *Pacifica Review* 6(1): 1–29.
10. Kempe, Frederick. 1990. *Divorcing the Dictator: America's Bungled Affair with Noriega*. New York: G. P. Putnam's Sons, p. 214.

11. Ackerman, Peter, and Jack DuVall. 2000. *A Force More Powerful: A Century of Nonviolent Conflict*. New York: Palgrave.

12. This point is also underscored in Ackerman, Peter, and Christopher Kruegler. 1994. *Strategic Nonviolent Conflict: The Dynamics of People Power in the Twentieth Century*. Westport, CT: Praeger.

13. McAdam, Doug. 1983. "Tactical Innovation and the Pace of Insurgency." *American Sociological Review* 48: 735–754.

14. Alinsky, Saul. 1989 [1971]. *Rules for Radicals*. New York: Vintage Books, p. 128.

15. Burrowes, Robert J. 1996. *The Strategy of Nonviolent Defense: A Gandhian Approach*. Albany: State University of New York Press, pp. 224–225.

16. Schock, Kurt. 2005. *Unarmed Insurrections: People Power Movements in Nondemocracies*. Minneapolis: University of Minnesota Press.

17. Chenoweth, Erica, and Maria Stephan. 2011. *Why Civil Resistance Works: The Strategic Logic of Nonviolent Conflict*. New York: Columbia University Press.

18. For evidence and an expanded discussion on the importance of participation, see Chenoweth and Stephan, *Why Civil Resistance Works*, pp. 39–61.

19. Schock, "The Practice and Study of Civil Resistance," p. 283.

20. Chenoweth and Stephan, *Why Civil Resistance Works*, p. 40.

21. For a comprehensive overview of the various ways that movements are repressed, see Earl, Jennifer. 2003. "Tanks, Tear Gas and Taxes: Toward a Theory of Movement Repression." *Sociological Theory* 21: 44–68.

22. Garrow, David. 1981. *The FBI and Martin Luther King, Jr.: From Solo to Memphis*. New York: W.W. Norton & Company.

23. Gould, John, and Edward Moe. 2012. "Beyond Rational Choice: Ideational Assault and the Strategic Use of Frames in Nonviolent Civil Resistance." *Research in Social Movements, Conflict, and Change* 34: 123–151.

24. Marx, Gary T. 1979. "External Efforts to Damage or Facilitate Social Movements: Some Patterns, Explanations, Outcomes, and Complications." In Mayer Zald and John McCarthy (Eds.). *The Dynamics of Social Movements*. Cambridge, MA: Winthrop, pp. 94–125.

25. Bob, Clifford. 2005. *The Marketing of Rebellion: Insurgents, Media, and International Activism*. New York: Cambridge University Press.

26. For elaborate explorations of government infiltration into movements to destroy them, see Cunningham, David. 2005. *There's Something Happening Here: The New Left, the Klan, and FBI Counter Intelligence*. Berkeley and Los Angeles: University of California Press.

27. Bob, Clifford, and Sharon Erickson Nepstad. 2007. "Kill a Leader, Murder a Movement? Leadership and Assassination in Social Movements." *American Behavioral Scientist* 50(10): 1370–1394.

28. Binnendijk and Marovic, "Protest and Persuasion," p. 415.

29. Forest, Jim, and Nancy Forest. 1988. *Four Days in February: The Story of the Nonviolent Overthrow of the Marcos Regime*. London: Marshall Pickering, pp. 98–100.

30. Sharp, Gene. 1973. *The Politics of Nonviolent Action*. Boston: Porter-Sargent.

31. Martin, Brian. 2007. *Justice Ignited: The Dynamics of Backfire*. Lanham, MD: Rowman & Littlefield.

32. Dalton, Dennis. 1993. *Mahatma Gandhi: Nonviolent Power in Action*. New York: Columbia University Press; Weber, Thomas. 1993. "'The Marchers Simply Walked Forward Until They Were Struck Down': Nonviolent Suffering and Conversion." *Peace & Change* 18(3): 267–289.

33. Wheaton, Bernard, and Zdenek Kavan. 1992. *The Velvet Revolution: Czechoslovakia, 1988–1991*. Boulder, CO: Westview Press.

34. Vengroff, Richard. 1993. "Governance and the Transition to Democracy: Political Parties and the Party System in Mali." *Journal of Modern African Studies* 31(4): 541–562.

35. Hess, David, and Brian Martin. 2006. "Repression, Backfire, and the Theory of Transformative Events." *Mobilization* 11(1): 249–267.

36. This diagram is from Hess and Martin, "Repression, Backfire, and the Theory of Transformative Events."

37. Also see Francisco, Ronald A. 2004. "After the Massacre: Mobilization in the Wake of Harsh Repression." *Mobilization* 92(2): 107–126; Francisco, Ronald A. 2005. "The Dictator's Dilemma." In Christian Davenport, Carole Mueller, and Hank Johnston (Eds.). *Repression and Mobilization*. Minneapolis: University of Minnesota Press, pp. 58–84.

38. This account of the movement is drawn from Aspinall, Edward. 2005. *Opposing Suharto: Compromise, Resistance, and Regime Change in Indonesia*. Stanford, CA: Stanford University Press; Boudreau, Vincent. 2004. *Resisting Dictatorship: Repression and Protest in Southeast Asia*. New York: Cambridge University Press; and Martin, Brian, and Wendy Varney. 2003. *Nonviolence Speaks: Communicating Against Repression*. Cresskill, NJ: Hampton Press.

39. Cribb, Robert and Colin Brown. 1995. *Modern Indonesia: A History Since 1945*. London and New York: Longman Press.

40. Purdey, Jemma. 2006. *Anti-Chinese Violence in Indonesia: 1996–1999*. Honolulu: University of Hawaii Press.

41. Martin and Varney, "Nonviolence Against Indonesian Repression."

42. Berfield, Susan, and Dewi Loveard. 1998. "Ten Days That Shook Indonesia." *Asiaweek*. July 24: 30–41.

43. For more on the divisions within Indonesia's armed forces, see Lee, Terence. 2009. "The Armed Forces and Transitions from Authoritarian Rule: Explaining the Role of the Military in 1986 Philippines and 1998 Indonesia." *Comparative Political Studies* 42(5): 640–669.

44. Aspinall, Ed. 1995. "Students and the Military: Regime Friction and Civilian Dissent in the Late Suharto Period." *Indonesia* 59: 36.

45. Hafidz, Tatik. S. 2006. *Fading Away? The Political Role of the Military in Indonesia's Trasition to Democracy*. Singapore: Institute of Defence and Strategic Studies.

46. Berfield and Loveard, "Ten Days That Shook Indonesia."

47. Charlé, Suzanne. 1998. "Banning is Banned." *The Nation* 267(10) (October 5): 18.

48. Lee, "The Armed Forces and Transitions from Authoritarian Rule."

CHAPTER 6

1. Although recent research shows that numerous factors shape the outcomes of civil resistance struggles, a few people do propose that a sound strategy of non-violent resistance can lead to victory regardless of structural conditions and the political environment. For an example of this, see Ackerman, Peter. 2007. "Skills or Conditions? What Key Factors Shape the Success or Failure of Civil Resistance." Unpublished paper from the Conference on Civil Resistance and Power Politics, Oxford University, Oxford, Great Britain.

2. Chenoweth, Erica, and Maria Stephan. 2011. *Why Civil Resistance Works: The Strategic Logic of Nonviolent Conflict*. New York: Columbia University Press, pp. 7–10.

3. Maney, Gregory. 2012. "The Paradox of Reform: The Civil Rights Movement in Northern Ireland." *Research in Social Movements, Conflict, and Change* 34: 3–26; Santoro, Wayne, and Max Fitzpatrick. Forthcoming in 2015. "The Ballot or the Bullet: The Crisis of Victory and the Institutionalization and Radicalization of the Civil Rights Movement." *Mobilization*.

4. Schock, Kurt. 2005. *Unarmed Insurrections: People Power Movements in Nondemocracies*. Minneapolis, MN: University of Minnesota Press, p. 142.

5. Chenoweth and Stephan, *Why Civil Resistance Works*, p. 57.

6. Ackerman, Peter, and Christopher Kruegler. 1994. *Strategic Nonviolent Conflict: The Dynamics of People Power in the Twentieth Century*. Westport, CT: Praeger; Francisco, Ronald A. 2005. "The Dictator's Dilemma." In Christian Davenport, Carole Mueller, and Hank Johnston (Eds.). *Repression and Mobilization*. Minneapolis: University of Minnesota Press, pp. 58–84; Schock, *Unarmed Insurrections;* Chenoweth and Stephan, *Why Civil Resistance Works*.

7. Ackerman and Kruegler, *Strategic Nonviolent Conflict*, pp. 38–40.

8. McManus, Philip, and Gerald Schlabach. 1991. *Relentless Persistence: Nonviolent Action in Latin America*. Philadelphia: New Society Publishers; Navarro, Marysa. 2001 [1989]. "The Personal is the Political: Las Madres de Plaza de Mayo." In Susan Eckstein (Ed.). *Power and Popular Protest: Latin American Social Movements*. Berkeley and Los Angeles: University of California Press, pp. 241–258.

9. Ackerman and Kruegler, *Strategic Nonviolent Conflict*, pp. 39–40.

10. Ackerman and Kruegler, *Strategic Nonviolent Conflict*, p. 39.

11. There is a larger debate about the role of sabotage or demolition in nonviolent movements. In *The Politics of Nonviolent Action, Volume 2*, Gene Sharp lists eight reasons why sabotage should not be used in civil resistance. On the other hand, groups such as the Plowshares movement argue that destroying weaponry is nonviolent because it is protecting human life. Furthermore, they argue that some weapons, particularly weapons of mass destruction, are illegal and thus have no right to exist. For more on the Plowshares movement's view of sabotage, see Nepstad, Sharon Erickson. 2008. *Religion and War Resistance in the Plowshares Movement*. New York: Cambridge University Press, pp. 63–64.

12. Bergfeldt, Lennart. 1993. *Experiences of Civil Resistance: The Case of Denmark, 1940–1945*. Uppsala, Sweden: University of Uppsala; Duvall, Jack, and Peter Ackerman. *A Force More Powerful: A Century of Nonviolent Conflict*. New York: Palgrave.

13. Francisco, Ronald. 2004. "After the Massacre: Mobilization in the Wake of Harsh Repression." *Mobilization* 9(2): 107–126.

14. Coogan, Tim Pat. 1995. *The Troubles: Ireland's Ordeal and the Search for Peace*. New York: Palgrave; McKittrick, David, and David McVea. 2002. *Making Sense of the Troubles: The Story of the Conflict in Northern Ireland*. Chicago: New Amsterdam Books.

15. Malcolm X. 1994 [1965]. "The Ballot or the Bullet." In George Breitman (Ed.). *Malcolm X Speaks: Selected Speeches and Statements*. New York: Grove Press, pp. 23–44 (esp. p. 24).

16. Cone, James. 1991. *Martin, Malcolm and America: Dream or a Nightmare?* Maryknoll, NY: Orbis Books.

17. There are divergent views on radical flank effects, yet in many of these debates the evidence is anecdotal or the causal influence unclear. For further reading, see Boudreau, Vincent. 2004. *Resisting Dictatorship: Repression and Protest in Southeast Asia*. New York: Cambridge University Press; Goodwin, Jeff. 2001. *No*

Other Way Out: States and Revolutionary Movement, 1945–1991. New York: Cambridge University Press, p. 298; McAdam, Doug, Sidney Tarrow, and Charles Tilly. 2001. *Dynamics of Contention*. New York: Cambridge University Press.

18. Schock, Kurt, and Erica Chenoweth. Forthcoming in 2015. "The Impact of Violence on the Outcome of Nonviolent Resistance Campaigns: An Examination of Intermovement Radical Flank Effects." *Mobilization* 20(4).

19. Chenoweth, Erica. 2011. "Armed Wing in Syria: To What Effect?" Posted on *The Rational Insurgent* (http://rationalinsurgent.wordpress.com), October 10.

20. Chenoweth and Stephan, *Why Civil Resistance Works*, p. 39.

21. Wood, Elisabeth Jean. 2000. *Forging Democracy From Below: Insurgent Transitions in South Africa and El Salvador*. New York: Cambridge University Press.

22. For more on how internal conflicts can derail nonviolent movements, see the cases of China and Kenya in Nepstad, Sharon Erickson. 2011. *Nonviolent Revolutions: Civil Resistance in the Late 20th Century*. New York: Cambridge University Press.

23. For an extensive analysis and comparison of these two movements, see Cone, *Martin, Malcolm and America*.

24. Smith, Christian. 1996. *Resisting Reagan: The U.S. Central America Peace Movement*. Chicago: University of Chicago Press.

25. Bob, Clifford, and Sharon Erickson Nepstad. 2007. "Kill a Leader, Murder a Movement? Leadership and Assassination in Social Movements." *American Behavioral Scientists* 50(10): 1370–1394.

26. See Nepstad, *Religion and War Resistance in the Plowshares Movement*; Polletta, Francesca. 2002. *Freedom is an Endless Meeting: Democracy in American Social Movements*. Chicago: University of Chicago Press.

27. Pearlman, Wendy. 2011. *Violence, Nonviolence, and the Palestinian National Movement*. New York: Cambridge University Press.

28. Pearlman, *Violence, Nonviolence*, p. 2.

29. Forest, Jim, and Nancy Forest. 1988. *Four Days in February: The Story of the Nonviolent Overthrow of the Marcos Regime*. London: Marshall Pickering.

30. Bartee, Wayne C. 2000. *A Time to Speak Out: The Leipzig Citizens Protests and the Fall of East Germany*. Westport, CT: Praeger; Pierard, Richard V. 1990. "Religion and the East German Revolution." *Journal of Church and State* 32(3): 501–509.

31. Nepstad, *Nonviolent Revolutions*.

32. Stephan, Maria, and Erica Chenoweth. 2008. "Why Civil Resistance Works: The Strategic Logic of Nonviolent Conflict." *International Security* 33(1): 22.

33. Stephan and Chenoweth, "Why Civil Resistance Works," p. 22.

34. Stephan and Chenoweth, "Why Civil Resistance Works," p. 23.

35. Marinov, Nikolay. 2005. "Do Economic Sanctions Destabilize Country Leaders?" *American Journal of Political Science* 49(3): 564–576.

36. For a more thorough discussion of the issues surrounding sanctions, see Drezner, Daniel W. 1999. *The Sanctions Paradox: Economic Statecraft and International Relations*. New York: Cambridge University Press; Lopez, George, and David Cortright. 1997. "Economic Sanctions and Human Rights: Part of the Problem or Part of the Solution?" *International Journal of Human Rights* 1: 1–25; Pape, Robert. 1997. "Why Economic Sanctions Do Not Work." *International Security* 22: 90–136.

37. Cortright, David. 2001. "Powers of Persuasion: Sanctions and Incentives in the Shaping of International Society." *International Studies* 38(2): 113–125; Nepstad, *Nonviolent Revolutions*, p. 69.

38. Nepstad, *Nonviolent Revolutions.*
39. This, for instance, was a problem with the Serbian movement Otpor. The movement received financial assistance from the U.S. National Endowment for Democracy, which led to accusations that the movement to oust Milošević was actually engineered by the United States.
40. Chenoweth and Stephan, *Why Civil Resistance Works,* p. 54.
41. Cortright, David, and George Lopez (Eds.). 2002. *Smart Sanctions: Targeting Economic Statecraft.* Lanham, MD: Rowman & Littlefield.
42. Stephan and Chenoweth, "Why Civil Resistance Works," pp. 22–23.
43. Haynes, Jeff. 2001. *Democracy in the Developing World: Africa, Asia, Latin America and the Middle East.* Cambridge, UK: Polity Press, pp. 25–26.
44. Karatnycky, Adrian, and Peter Ackerman. 2005. *How Freedom is Won: From Civic Resistance to Durable Democracy.* New York: Freedom House.
45. Chenoweth and Stephan, *Why Civil Resistance Works,* pp. 213–215.
46. Johnstad, Petter Grahl. 2010. "Nonviolent Democratization: A Sensitivity Analysis of How Transition Mode and Violence Impact the Durability of Democracy." *Peace and Change* 35(3): 464–482.
47. Celestino, Mauricio Rivera, and Kristian Skrede Gleditsch. 2013. "Fresh Carnations or All Thorn, No Rose? Nonviolent Campaigns and Transitions in Autocracies." *Journal of Peace Research* 50(3): 385–400. Note that Celestino and Gleditsch emphasize that other factors are also involved in democratic consolidation. Specifically, they note that successful democratization is more likely in nations that are surrounded geographically by other democracies.
48. Johnstad, "Nonviolent Democratization," p. 475.
49. Chenoweth and Stephan, *Why Civil Resistance Works,* p. 208.
50. Chenoweth and Stephan, *Why Civil Resistance Works,* p. 217.
51. Johnstad, "Nonviolent Democratization," p. 475.
52. Collier, Paul, and Nicholas Sambanis 2002. "Understanding Civil War: A New Agenda." *Journal of Conflict Resolution* 46(3): 3–12; Walter, Barbara F. 2004. "Does Conflict Beget Conflict? Explaining Recurring Civil War." *Journal of Peace Research* 41(3): 371–388.
53. For more on how violent political struggle "begets" civil war, see Doyle, Michael W., and Nicholas Sambanis. 2000. "International Peacebuilding: A Theoretical and Quantitative Analysis." *American Political Science Review* 94(4): 779–801; Hartzell, Caroline, Matthew Hoddie, and Donald Rothchild. 2001. "Stabilizing the Peace After Civil War: An Investigation of Some Key Variables." *International Organization* 55(1): 183–208.
54. Johnstad, "Nonviolent Democratization," p. 476.
55. Collier, Paul. 1999. "On the Economic Consequences of Civil War." *Oxford Economic Papers* 51: 168–183.

CHAPTER 7

1. Forest, Jim, and Nancy Forest. 1988. *Four Days in February: The Untold Story of the Nonviolent Overthrow of the Marcos Regime.* London: Pickering Marshall, p. 103.
2. Ivan Marovic, quoted in Chenoweth, Erica. 2013. "Changing Sides Doesn't Always Make for Transformation—Just Look At Egypt." *Open Democracy,* July 31. Retrieved at http://www.opendemocracy.net
3. Pfaff, Steven. 2006. *Exit-Voice Dynamics and the Collapse of East Germany: The Crisis of Leninism and the Revolution of 1989.* Durham, NC: Duke University Press, p. 176.

4. Foos, Paul. 2002. *A Short, Offhand, Killing Affair: Soldiers and Social Conflict in the Mexican-American War.* Chapel Hill, NC: University of North Carolina Press.

5. This table and summary of the literature is drawn from Nepstad, Sharon Erickson. 2013. "Mutiny and Nonviolence in the Arab Spring: Exploring Military Defections and Loyalty in Egypt, Bahrain, and Syria." *Journal of Peace Research* 50(3): 337–349.

6. Valenzuela, Arturo. 1991. "The Military in Power: The Consolidation of One-Man Rule." In Paul W. Drake and Ivan Jaksik (Eds.). *The Struggle for Democracy in Chile, 1982–1990.* Lincoln: University of Nebraska Press, pp. 21–72.

7. Belkin, Aaron, and Evan Schofer. 2003. "Toward a Structural Understanding of Coup Risk." *Journal of Conflict Resolution* 47(5): 594–620; Quinlivan, James T. 1999. "Coup-Proofing: Its Practices and Consequences in the Middle East." *International Security* 24(2): 131–165.

8. Powell, Jonathan. 2012. "Determinants of the Attempting and Outcome of Coups d'etat." *Journal of Conflict Resolution* 56(6): 1017–1040. Silverman, Daniel. 2012. " The Arab Military in the Arab Spring: Agent of Continuity or Change? A Comparative Analysis of Tunisia, Egypt, Libya, and Syria." Unpublished paper, p. 16 .

9. Cook, Steven A. 2007. *Ruling But Not Governing: The Military and Political Development in Egypt, Algeria, and Turkey.* Baltimore, MD: Johns Hopkins University Press; Springborg, Robert. 2011. "Economic Involvements of Militaries." *International Journal of Middle East Studies* 43(3): 397–399.

10. Reno, William. 1998. *Warlord Politics and African States.* Boulder, CO: Lynne Reiner Publishers.

11. Quinlivan, "Coup-Proofing," p. 133.

12. Quinlivan, "Coup-Proofing."

13. Gould, John A., and Edward Moe. 2012. "Beyond Rational Choice: Ideational Assault and the Strategic Use of Frames in Nonviolent Civil Resistance." *Research in Social Movements, Conflict, and Change* 34: 123–151.

14. Han, Minzhu. 1990. *Cries for Democracy: Writings and Speeches from the 1989 Chinese Democracy Movement.* Princeton, NJ: Princeton University Press.

15. Kurzman, Charles. 2004. *The Unthinkable Revolution in Iran.* Cambridge, MA: Harvard University Press.

16. Geddes, Barbara. 1999. "What Do We Know About Democratization After Twenty Years?" *Annual Review of Political Science* 2: 115–144.

17. Ross, Michael. 2001. "Does Oil Hinder Democracy?" *World Politics* 53(3): 325–361; Ross, Michael. 1999. "The Political Economy of the Resource Curse." *World Politics* 51(2): 297–322.

18. McLauchlin, Theodore. 2010. "Loyalty Strategies and Military Defection in Rebellion." *Comparative Politics* 42(3): 333–350.

19. Kou, Chien-Wen. 2000. "Why The Military Obeys the Party's Orders to Repress Popular Uprisings: The Chinese Military Crackdown of 1989." *Issues and Studies* 36(6): 27–51.

20. See, for instance, David Cortright's study of U.S. soldiers in Vietnam: Cortright, David. 2005 [1975]. *Soldiers in Revolt: GI Resistance During the Vietnam War.* Chicago: Haymarket.

21. In the rational choice literature, this is known as the "assurance problem" in which each actor seeks assurance that others will join in.

22. This, according to Steven Pfaff (2006), occurred during the 1989 East German uprising.

23. Granovetter, Mark. 1978. "Threshold Models of Collective Behavior." *American Journal of Sociology* 83(6): 1420–1443.
24. Kuran, Timur. 1991. "Now or Never: The Element of Surprise in the East European Revolution of 1989." *World Politics* 44(1): 7–48.
25. Variations of this argument are supported by the following studies: Brooks, Risa. 2013. "Abandoned at the Palace: Why The Tunisian Military Defected From the Ben Ali Regime in January 2011." *Journal of Strategic Studies* 36(2): 205–220; Lee, 2009, "The Armed Forces and Transitions from Authoritarian Rule: Explaining the Role of the Military in 1986 Philippines and 1998 Indonesia." *Comparative Political Studies* 42: 640–669; Nepstad, 2013, " Mutiny and Nonviolence in the Arab Spring"; and McLauchlin, 2010, " Loyalty Strategies."
26. Goldstone, Jack A. 2011. "Understanding the Revolutions of 2011: Weakness and Resilience in Middle Eastern Autocracies." *Foreign Affairs* 90(3): 8–16.
27. Goldstone, "Understanding the Revolutions of 2011."
28. Goldstone, Jack. 2011. "Cross-class Coalitions and the Making of the Arab Revolts of 2011." *Swiss Political Science Review* 17(4): 457–462.
29. Brooks, Risa, "Abandoned at the Palace."
30. Randeree, Bilal. 2011. "Tunisia President Warns Protesters: President Warns that Rare Display of Public Defiance Over Unemployment Will Be Met With 'Firm' Punishment." *Al Jezeera English*, January 3.
31. British Broadcasting Company. 2011. "Tunisia Closes Schools and Universities Following Riots." January 10.
32. Randeree, Bilal. 2011. "Tunisian Leader Promises New Jobs." *Al Jazeera English*. January 14.
33. Dalacoura, Katerina. 2012. "The 2011 Uprising in the Arab Middle East: Political Change and Geopolitical Implications." *International Affairs* 88: 63–79.
34. Anderson, Lisa. 2011. "Demystifying the Arab Spring: Parsing Out Differences Between Tunisia, Egypt, and Libya." *Foreign Affairs* 90(3): 2–7.
35. Schneider, Cathy Lisa. 2011 "Violence and State Repression." *Swiss Political Science Review* 17(4): 480–484.
36. Nepstad, Sharon Erickson. 2011. "Nonviolence in the Arab Spring: The Critical Role of Military-Opposition Alliances." *Swiss Political Science Review* 17(4): 485–491.
37. Gelvin, James L. 2012. *The Arab Uprisings: What Everyone Needs to Know*. New York: Oxford University Press.
38. Brooks, "Abandoned at the Palace," pp. 210–212.
39. Cook, Steven A. 2011. "The Calculations of Tunisia's Military." *Foreign Policy*, January 20. (http://mideastafrica.foreignpolicy.com/posts/2011/01/20/the_calculations_of_tunisias_military)
40. Brooks, "Abandoned at the Palace," pp. 213–214.
41. Lutterbeck, Derek. 2013. "Arab Uprisings, Armed Forces, and Civil-Military Relations." *Armed Forces & Society* 39(1): 28–52.
42. Springborg, "Economic Involvement of Militaries," p. 397.
43. Nepstad, "Mutiny and Nonviolence in the Arab Spring," p. 342.
44. Kechichian, Joseph, and Jean Nazimek. 1997. "Challenges to the Military in Egypt." *Middle East Policy* 5(3): 125–139.
45. Hashim, Ahmed. 2011. "The Egyptian Military, Part II: From Mubarak Onward." *Middle East Policy* 18(4): 106–128 (esp. p. 118).
46. Lutterbeck, "Arab Uprisings," p. 37.
47. Bahry, Louay. 2000. "The Socioeconomic Foundations of Shiite Opposition in Bahrain." *Mediterranean Quarterly* 11(3): 129–143; Lawson, Fred H. 2004.

"Repertoires of Contention in Contemporary Bahrain." In Quintan Wiktorow-icz (Ed.). *Islamic Activism: A Social Movement Theory Approach.* Bloomington: Indiana University Press, pp. 89–111.

48. Al-Shehabi, Omar. 2011. "Demography and Bahrain's Unrest: Report for the Carnegie Endowment for International Peace." (http://carnegieendowment.org/2011/03/16/demography-and-bahrain-s-unrest/6b7y).
49. Lutterbeck, "Arab Uprisings," p. 43.
50. Gelvin, *The Arab Uprisings.*
51. Zunes, Stephen. 2011. "America Blows It on Bahrain: The Non-Violent Pro-democracy Struggle in Bahrain Has Failed to Gain Support from the Obama Administration." *Foreign Policy in Focus,* 2 March. (http://fpif.org/america_blows_it_on_bahrain/)
52. Zunes, "America Blows It on Bahrain."
53. Gelvin, *The Arab Uprisings.*
54. Chick, Kristen. 2011. "Bahrain's Calculated Campaign of Intimidation—Bahraini Activists and Locals Describe Midnight Arrests, Disappearances, Beatings at Checkpoints, and Denial of Medical Care—All Aimed at Deflated the Country's Pro-Democracy Protest Movement." *Christian Science Monitor,* 1 April. (http://csmonitor.com/World/Middle-East/2011/0401/Bahrain-s-ca;ci;ated-campaign-of-intimidation).
55. Nepstad, "Mutiny and Nonviolence in the Arab Spring."
56. McLauchlin, "Loyalty Strategies."
57. Silverman, Daniel. 2012. "The Arab Military in the Arab Spring: A Comparative Analysis of Tunisia, Egypt, Libya and Syria." Presented at the American Political Science Association annual meeting.
58. Kirkpatrick, David. 2011. "In a New Libya, Ex-Loyalists Race to Shed Ties to Qadaffi." *New York Times,* September 7, p. 2.
59. Fildis, Ayse Tekdal. 2012. "Roots of Alawite-Sunni Rivalry in Syria." *Middle East Policy* 19(2): 148–156.
60. Brooks, Risa. 1999. *Political-Military Relations and the Stability of Arab Regimes.* New York: Routledge Press.
61. Springborg, "Economic Involvement of Militaries."
62. Lesch, David W. 2012. *The Fall of the House of Assad.* New Haven: Yale University Press; Wieland, Carsten. 2012. *Syria—A Decade of Lost Chances: Repression and Revolution from Damascus Spring to the Arab Spring.* Seattle, WA: Cune Press.
63. Clanet, Christian. 2011. "Inside Syria's Slaughter: A Journalist Sneaks into Dara'a, the 'Ghetto of Death'." *Time,* June 10.
64. Nepstad, "Mutiny and Nonviolence in the Arab Spring," p. 344.
65. For further information, see McLauchlin, "Loyalty Strategies"; Pierret, Thomas. 2013. *Religion and State in Syria.* Cambridge and New York: Cambridge University Press; Van Dam, Nikolaos. 2011. *The Struggle for Power in Syria: Politics and Society Under Assad and the Ba'th Party.* London: IB Tauris.
66. McEvers, Kelly. 2012. " Defectors Offer Insider's View of Syrian Army." *National Public Radio,* April 9.
67. Chenoweth, Erica, and Maria Stephan. 2011. *Why Civil Resistance Works: The Strategic Logic of Nonviolent Conflict.* New York: Columbia University Press; Nep-stad, *Nonviolent Revolutions;* Stephan, Maria, and Chenoweth, Erica. 2008, "Why Civil Resistance Works: The Strategic Logic of Nonviolent Conflict." *International Security* 33(1): 22.
68. Chenoweth, "Changing Sides."
69. Chenoweth, "Changing Sides."

CHAPTER 8

1. Quoted in Jackson, John. 2011. "The Professors of Protest and the University of Revolution." *Hufffington Post*, March 30.
2. This term was coined by Charles Tilly in his 1986 book, *The Contentious French* (Cambridge, MA: Harvard University Press).
3. For more on this process, see Tarrow, Sidney. 2005. *The New Transnational Activism*. New York: Cambridge University Press.
4. An overview of this model is discussed in McAdam, Doug, and Dieter Rucht. 1993. "The Cross-National Diffusion of Movement Ideas." *Annals of the American Academy of Political and Social Science* 528: 56–74.
5. Gallo-Cruz, Selina. 2012. "Organizing Global Nonviolence: The Growth and Spread of Nonviolent INGOs, 1949–2003." *Research in Social Movements, Conflict, and Change* 34: 213–256.
6. Snow, David A., and Robert D. Benford. 1999. "Alternative Types of Cross-national Diffusion in the Social Movement Arena." In Donatella della Porta, Hanspeter Kriesi, and Dieter Rucht (Eds.). *Social Movements in a Globalizing World*. London: Macmillan.
7. For an illustration of this experimentation and reinvention in new contexts, see Nepstad, Sharon Erickson, and Stellan Vinthagen. 2008. "Strategic Changes and Cultural Adaptations: Explaining Differential Outcomes in the International Plowshares Movement." *International Journal of Peace Studies* 13(1): 15–42.
8. This model is also referred to as the "dialogical diffusion model." For more on this process, also see Sean Scalmer's 2011 book, *Gandhi in the West: The Mahatma and the Rise of Radical Protest*. New York: Cambridge University Press.
9. Chabot, Sean. 2011. *Transnational Roots of the Civil Rights Movement: African American Explorations of the Gandhian Repertoire*. Lanham, MD: Lexington Books, p. 4.
10. Chabot, Sean. 2010. "Dialogue Matters: Beyond the Transmission Model of Transnational Diffusion of Social Movements." In Rebecca Kolins Givans, Kenneth M. Roberts, and Sarah A. Soule (Eds.). *The Diffusion of Social Movements: Actors, Mechanisms, and Political Effects*. New York: Cambridge University Press, pp. 99–124.
11. Eddy, Matthew. 2012. "When Your Gandhi is not My Gandhi: Memory Templates and Limited Violence in the Palestinian Human Rights Movement." *Research in Social Movements, Conflict, and Change* 34: 185–214.
12. King, Jr., Martin Luther. 2010 [1958]. *Stride Toward Freedom: The Montgomery Story*. New York: Beacon Press.
13. For more on early news coverage of Gandhi in the United States, see Chatfield, Charles (Ed.). 1976. *The Americanization of Gandhi: Images of the Mahatma*. New York: Garland.
14. Chabot, *Transnational Roots*, p. 47.
15. Chabot, *Transnational Roots*, p. 58, footnote 2.
16. Cortright, David. 2008. *Peace: A History of Movements and Ideas*. New York: Cambridge University Press.
17. Kapur, Sudarshan. 1992. *Raising Up a Prophet: The African American Encounter with Gandhi*. Boston: Beacon Press.
18. Chabot, *Transnational Roots*, p. 50.
19. Chabot, Sean, and Jan Willem Duyvendak. 2002. "Globalization and Transnational Diffusion Between Social Movements: Reconceptualizing the Dissemination of the Gandhian Repertoire and the 'Coming Out' Routine." *Theory and Society* 31(6): 697–740.

20. Shridarani, Krishnalal. 1939. *War Without Violence: A Study of Gandhi's Method and Its Accomplishments*. New York: Harcourt and Brace.
21. Du Bois as quoted in Chabot, *Transnational Roots*, pp. 51–52.
22. Fox, Richard G. 1997. "Passage From India." In Richard G. Fox and Orin Starn (Eds.). *Between Resistance and Revolution: Cultural Politics and Social Protest*, New Brunswick: Rutgers University Press. pp. 65–82.
23. Chabot, *Transnational Roots*, p. 56.
24. Quoted in Kapur, *Raising Up a Prophet*, p. 58.
25. Chabot, *Transnational Roots*, p. 50.
26. Chabot, *Transnational Roots*, p. 7.
27. Reddy, E. S. (Ed.). 1998. *Mahatma Gandhi: Letters to Americans*. Mumbai: Bhavan's Book University.
28. Gregg, Richard G. 1959 [1935]. *The Power of Nonviolence*. Philadelphia: J.B. Lippincott.
29. Gregg, *The Power of Nonviolence*, pp. 10–11.
30. As quoted in Chabot, *Transnational Roots*, p. 76.
31. Thurman, Howard. 1949. *Jesus and the Disinherited*. Nashville, TN: Abingdon Press.
32. Chabot, *Transnational Roots*, p. 74.
33. Farmer, James. 1985. *Lay Bare the Heart*. Fort Worth: Texas Christian University Press.
34. Meier, August, and Elliot Rudwick. 1973. *CORE: A Study in the Civil Rights Movement, 1942–1968*. New York: Oxford University Press.
35. For more on these experiments, see Houser, George M. 1945. *Erasing the Color Line*. New York: Fellowship Publications.
36. Chabot, *Transnational Roots*.
37. For more on the specific conditions in Montgomery that made this a ripe opportunity, see Schulzinger, Doron. 2013. "The Social-Psychological Origins of the Montgomery Bus Boycott: Social Interaction and Humiliation in the Emergence of Social Movements." *Mobilization* 18(2): 117–142.
38. Robinson, Jo Ann Gibson, and David J. Garrow. 1987. *The Montgomery Bus Boycott and the Women Who Started It: The Memoir of Jo Ann Gibson Robinson*. Knoxville: University of Tennessee Press.
39. For a full account of the Montgomery bus boycott, see King, *Stride Toward Freedom*.
40. King, Jr. Martin Luther. 1964. *Why We Can't Wait*. New York: Harper and Row Publishers.
41. Isaac, Larry, Daniel B. Cornfield, Dennis C. Dickerson, James M. Lawson, and Jonathan S. Coley. 2012. "'Movement Schools' and the Dialogical Diffusion of Nonviolent Praxis: Nashville Workshops in the Southern Civil Rights Movement." *Research in Social Movements, Conflict, and Change* 34: 155–184.
42. Isaac et al., "'Movement Schools,'" p. 172.
43. Lewis, John. 1998. *Walking with the Wind: A Memoir of the Movement*. New York: A Harvest Book.
44. For detailed analysis of how this nonviolent tactic spread, see Andrews, Kenneth, and Michael Biggs. 2006. "The Dynamics of Protest Diffusion: Movement Organizations, Social Networks, and News Media in the 1960 Sit-ins." *American Sociological Review* 71(5): 752–777; Morris, Aldon. 1981. "The Black Southern Sit-In Movement: An Analysis of Internal Organization." *American Sociological Review* 46(6): 744–767; Polletta, Francesca. 1999. "'It Was

Like a Fever . . . ': Spontaneity and Collective Identity in Collective Action." *Social Problems* 45: 137–159.

45. Cortright, David. 2009. *Gandhi and Beyond: Nonviolence for a New Political Age.* Boulder, CO: Paradigm. For a parallel type of diffusion process in the United Kingdom, see Scalmer, Sean. 2002. "The Labor of Diffusion: The Peace Pledge Union and the Adaption of the Gandhian Repertoire." *Mobilization* 7(3): 269–286.

46. Bunce, Valerie, and Sharon Wolchik. 2006. "Favorable Conditions and Electoral Revolutions." *Journal of Democracy* 17(4): 5–18.

CHAPTER 9

1. For a summary of how the field has developed over time, see Carter, April. 2009. "People Power and Protest: The Literature on Civil Resistance in Historical Context." In Adam Roberts and Timothy Garton Ash (Eds.). *Civil Resistance and Power Politics: The Experience of Nonviolent Action from Gandhi to the Present.* Oxford: Oxford University Press, pp. 25–42; Nepstad, Sharon Erickson. 2013. "Nonviolent Civil Resistance and Social Movements." *Sociology Compass* 7: 590–598.

2. This would include the following studies: Chenoweth, Erica, and Maria Stephan. 2011. *Why Civil Resistance Works: The Strategic Logic of Nonviolent Conflict.* New York: Columbia University Press; Nepstad, Sharon Erickson. 2011. *Nonviolent Revolutions: Civil Resistance in the Late 20th Century.* New York: Oxford University Press; Schock, Kurt. 2005. *Unarmed Insurrections: People Power Movements in Non-democracies.* Minneapolis: University of Minnesota Press; Semelin, Jacques. 1993. *Unarmed Against Hitler.* Westport, CT: Praeger; Zunes, Stephen, Lester R. Kurtz, and Sarah Beth Asher (Eds.). 1999. *Nonviolent Social Movements: A Geographic Perspective.* Malden, MA: Blackwell Publishers.

3. Bartkowski, Maciej (Ed.). 2013. *Recovering Nonviolent History: Civil Resistance in Liberation Struggles.* Boulder, CO: Lynne Rienner.

4. Chernus, Ira. 2004. *American Nonviolence: The History of An Idea.* Maryknoll, NY: Orbis Books; Cooney, Robert, and Helen Michalowski. 1987. *The Power of the People: Active Nonviolence in the United States.* Philadelphia: New Society Publishers; Lynd, Staughton, and Alice Lynd. 1995. *Nonviolence in America: A Documentary History.* Maryknoll, NY: Orbis Books.

5. This includes studies of the so-called color revolutions, such as Bunce, Valerie J., and Sharon L. Wolchik. 2011. *Defeating Authoritarian Leaders in Post-Communist Countries.* Cambridge: Cambridge University Press; Nikolayenko, Olena. 2012. "Tactical Interaction Between Youth Movements and Incumbent Governments in Post-Communist States." *Research in Social Movements, Conflicts, and Change* 34: 95–121.

6. Kaplan, Oliver. 2013. "Protecting Civilians in Civil War: The Institution of the ATCC in Colombia." *Journal of Peace Research* 50(3): 351–367.

7. Chenoweth and Stephan, *Why Civil Resistance Works.*

8. Brian Martin has argued that we ought to look at how nonviolent action operates against a variety of targets, including capitalism, bureaucracies, interpersonal bullies, and sexual harassers, for example. For more, see Martin, Brian. 2001. "Nonviolent Futures." *Futures* 33: 625–635.

9. Gitlin, Todd. 2012. *Occupy Nation: The Roots, the Spirit, and the Promise of Occupy Wall Street.* New York: HarperCollins.

10. Nepstad, Sharon Erickson. 2008. *Religion and War Resistance in the Plowshares Movement.* New York: Cambridge University Press.

11. Beyerle, Shaazke. 2014. *Curtailing Corruption: People Power for Accountability and Justice.* Boulder, CO: Lynne Rienner.
12. Schock, Kurt. 2013. "The Practice and Study of Civil Resistance." *Journal of Peace Research* 50(3): 277–290.
13. Galtung, Johan. 1969. "Violence, Peace, and Peace Research." *Journal of Peace Research* 6: 167–191; Galtung, Johan. 1990. "Cultural Violence." *Journal of Peace Research* 27: 291–305.
14. McGuinness, Kate. 1993. "Gene Sharp's Theory of Power: A Feminist Critique of Consent." *Journal of Peace Research* 30(1): 101–115.
15. Martin, Brian. 1989. "Gene Sharp's Theory of Power." *Journal of Peace Research* 26(2): 213–222.
16. Dajani, Souad R. 1994. *Eyes Without Country: Searching for a Palestinian Strategy of Liberation.* Philadelphia: Temple University Press.
17. Vinthagen, Stellan. 2015. "Four Dimensions of Nonviolent Action: A Sociological Perspective." Chapter 10 in Kurt Schock (Ed.). *Comparative Perspectives on Civil Resistance.* Minneapolis: University of Minnesota Press.
18. Chabot, Sean. 2015. "Making Sense of Civil Resistance: From Theories and Techniques to Social Movement Phronesis." Chapter 11 in Schock, *Comparative Perspectives on Civil Resistance.*
19. Chabot, "Making Sense of Civil Resistance," p. 379.
20. See, for instance, Verta Taylor's work on movement abeyance: Taylor, Verta. 1989. "Social Movement Continuity: The Women's Movement in Abeyance." *American Sociological Review* 54: 761–775.
21. This, for example, is mostly the perspective that I offered in my book *Nonviolent Revolutions: Civil Resistance in the Late 20th Century* (New York: Oxford University Press). In short, I emphasize the importance of training and clear leadership to maintain nonviolent discipline. This is also consistent with Pearlman (2011), who notes that a shift toward violent strategies occurs when movements lack internal cohesion and leadership.
22. Goodwin, Jeff. 2001. *No Other Way Out: States and Revolutionary Movements.* New York: Cambridge University Press.
23. Maney, Gregory. 2012. "The Paradox of Reform: The Civil Rights Movement in Northern Ireland." *Research in Social Movements, Conflict, and Change* 34: 3–26.
24. Santoro, Wayne, and Max Fitzpatrick. Forthcoming in 2015. "The Ballot or the Bullet: The Crisis of Victory and the Institutionalization and Radicalization of the Civil Rights Movement." *Mobilization.*
25. Shellman, Stephen M., Brian P. Levey, and Joseph K. Young. 2013. "Shifting Sands: Explaining and Predicting Phase Shifts by Dissident Organizations." *Journal of Peace Research* 50(3): 319–336.
26. Dudouet, Veronique. 2013. "Dynamics and Factors of Transition from Armed Struggle to Nonviolent Resistance." *Journal of Peace Research* 50(3): 401–413.
27. For instance, see the contrasting views of the Philippine people power movement in Chenoweth and Stephan (2011) versus Boudreau (2004).
28. I thank John Markoff for this point, which he articulates in his 2013 review essay, "Opposing Authoritarian Rule with Nonviolent Civil Resistance." *Australian Journal of Political Science* 48(2): 233–245.
29. Smith, Christian. 1996. *Disruptive Religion: The Force of Faith in Social Movements.* New York: Routledge.
30. Nepstad, *Nonviolent Revolutions.*

31. Also see Nepstad, Sharon Erickson. 2004. *Convictions of the Soul: Religion, Culture, and Agency in the Central America Solidarity Movement.* New York: Oxford University Press.

32. Pagnucco, Ron. 1996. "A Comparison of the Political Behavior of Faith-Based and Secular Peace Groups." In Christian Smith (Ed.). *Disruptive Religion.* New York: Routledge, pp. 205–222.

33. Dudouet, Véronique. 2015. "Sources, Functions, and Dilemmas of External Assistance to Civil Resistance Movements." Chapter 7 in Schock, *Comparative Perspectives on Civil Resistance.*

34. Cortright, David, and George A. Lopez (Eds.). 2002. *Smart Sanctions: Targeting Economic Statecraft.* New York: Rowman & Littlefield.

35. Zunes, Stephen, and Saad Eddin Ibrahim. 2009. "External Actors and Nonviolent Struggles in the Middle East." In Maria J. Stephan (Ed.). *Civilian Jihad: Nonviolent Struggle, Democratization, and Governance in the Middle East.* New York: Palgrave Macmillan, pp. 91–104.

36. Ritter, Daniel. 2014. *The Iron Cage of Liberalism: International Politics and Unarmed Revolutions in the Middle East and North Africa.* Oxford: Oxford University Press.

37. Ritter, *Iron Cage of Liberalism,* pp. 17–18.

38. Nepstad, *Nonviolent Revolutions.*

39. Zunes and Ibrahim, "External Actors and Nonviolent Struggles."

40. Drezner, Daniel. 2003. "How Smart Are Smart Sanctions?" *International Studies Review* 5: 108.

41. Chenoweth and Stephan, *Why Civil Resistance Works.*

42. Cohen, Roger. 2000. "Who Really Brought Down Milosevic?" *New York Times,* November 26.

43. Westerners still make up the majority in the organizations Peace Brigades International and Christian Peacemaker Teams. However, in Nonviolent Peaceforce, more than half come from the Global South.

GLOSSARY OF TERMS

A

Absolute pacifism: A stance in which all killing of humans is seen as wrong, regardless of the circumstances.

Ahimsa: A Hindi term that literally translates as non-injury, non-harm to all living creatures, or the denunciation of the desire to harm. This is the basis for Gandhi's commitment to nonviolence.

Anti-coups: A nonviolent movement of citizens who mobilize to protect their democratic state and to block any attempts at military coups and internal usurpation of power.

B

Backfire: A dynamic that occurs when an attack on nonviolent resisters generates increased public support or sympathy for the resisters and their cause while simultaneously undermining public opinion toward the attackers.

Beloved community: A term used by Martin Luther King, Jr. to describe a society guided by the principles of social justice and the spirit of *agape* or a love for all humanity.

C

Citizen-based power: A theory of power that holds that no state or authority structure has inherent power. Rather, a state gains power when its citizens choose to cooperate and consent. Specifically, this theory holds that citizens have various forms of power, including the ability to grant or withhold authority, financial resources, cooperation, skills, and so forth. If citizens withhold these forms of power, the state will not be able to function. Primary power resides with the people, not elites. Also referred to as "pluralistic power" or "relational power."

Civil disobedience: A tactic that entails intentionally breaking a law as a means of challenging an injustice.

Constructive program: This refers to Gandhi's idea that it is not enough to remove an unjust political ruler or system; civil resisters must simultaneously engage in constructive work to transform a society's economic system, cultural practices, and political institutions. Specifically in the Indian case, Gandhi advocated for the development of economic independence by creating meaningful local work, implementing land reform, transforming prejudicial attitudes, and establishing quality health services and educational institutions.

Coup-proofing: A term that refers to various practices that a regime uses to ensure its officers loyally uphold the state and will not attempt to overthrow it.

Covert resistance: A form of resistance that is disguised or hidden in hopes of avoiding confrontation with authorities. However, unlike everyday resistance, this type of nonviolent action is planned and carried out in a coordinated fashion. Thus actors work to subvert oppressive structures and carry out a strategic plan of action but try to do so without being detected.

D

Defections: When elites—such as those with high-ranking military, political, or business positions—cut ties to the state and join the opposition. They not only withhold their support from authorities but also actively work to oppose them.

Desertions: Leaving one's military post without permission and without the intention of returning.

Duragraha: A Gandhian term that is often translated as coercive force or a hard force. Gandhi used the term to note actions that may be nonviolent in nature, such as boycotts or strikes, but are done in a coercive spirit that humiliates opponents or forces them into defeat.

E

Economic noncooperation: Acts of nonviolent resistance in which citizens withhold economic resources, thereby depleting their opponents' financial base. Examples are boycotts and refusal to pay taxes.

Electoral revolution: A nonviolent movement that seeks regime change by contesting unfair elections. This typically occurs in "hybrid regimes" where a semi-authoritarian leader works with an elected legislature that has been put in office through fraudulent means. Through a multistage strategic process, civil resisters use elections as an opportunity to mobilize the population, to expose the autocratic nature of the regime, and to build genuine democracy.

Elite-based theory of power: This view of political power assumes that power resides within elite individuals, who intrinsically possess the capacity to impose their will on others. This approach perceives the average citizen as having little to no power, making the general public dependent upon the good will of its leaders. If those leaders are corrupt, self-serving, or authoritarian, and no democratic means of change exist, this theory argues, citizens have little recourse or capacity to enact change short of violent rebellion. This theory is sometimes referred to as a "monolithic view of power."

Everyday resistance: Disguised acts of defiance that require little to no planning and avoid any direct confrontation with authorities. Typically executed in a covert manner.

F

Fallibility pacifism: This stance argues that while the use of physical force in war can be justified in principle, it cannot be justified in practice since there is always a strong possibility that the warring parties do not have full or accurate information about the conflict. If war is waged on the basis of false or partial information, there is a risk of promoting an unjust cause or harming innocent individuals. This position is also sometimes referred to as "epistemological pacifism."

Free spaces: Autonomous places that are relatively free of state control and influence. Such spaces permit resisters to develop counter-hegemonic views and an ideology of rebellion that encourages citizens to take action.

I

Interpositioning: A type of third-party intervention in which nonviolent interventionists physically get in the way of conflicting groups who are experiencing escalating tensions.

L

Leverage: Civil resisters' ability to undermine the opponents' strength by systematically withholding key sources of support and by mobilizing people to engage in noncooperation with authorities.

M

Mechanisms of change: The four processes through which nonviolent resisters can bring out social transformation: conversion, accommodation, coercion, and disintegration.

Monolithic theory of power: Theory of power that views the state like a pyramid in which power is concentrated in the hands of a small, elite group of individuals. The majority of the population, therefore, is dependent on these elites to look out for citizens' needs and interests since they have all the power; the average person has virtually no capacity to enact political change. This is generally the view of those who advocate armed struggle, believing that no change will come until the state is destroyed and then rebuilt.

Moral jiu-jitsu: Inspired by a martial arts technique of redirecting the force of an attack, this term refers to a psychological dynamic that occurs when civil resisters voluntarily suffer an attack without striking back. The belief is that when the attackers observe resisters' firm commitment to their cause, the attackers gain respect for the resisters while losing their own moral balance or credibility.

Movement midwives: Organizations or groups that provide assistance and resources to help form a new movement organization that will coordinate an emerging civil resistance struggle. Example are the black churches that helped to form the Southern Christian Leadership Conference in the U.S. civil rights struggle.

Mutiny: When security forces break ties with the state, cast their support with the opposition, and work to oust the incumbent government.

N

Negotiated revolutions: A grassroots movement that uses nonviolent pressure to implement democratic practices and a written constitution of rights and policies. In the post-revolutionary stage, this type of movement emphasizes restorative justice and reconciliation rather than punitive justice for those who committed atrocities under the old regime. Examples include the anti-apartheid movement in South Africa.

Nonviolent accommodation: One of the mechanisms of change whereby opponents make changes voluntarily, not because of a transformation of the heart but simply because it is in their best interest to do so. Examples are corporate concessions to laborers and the Montgomery bus company altering its policies in response to the 1955 bus boycott.

Nonviolent coercion: One of the mechanisms of change whereby opponents lose control and are involuntarily forced to make changes because civil resisters have so thoroughly disrupted a situation that authorities can no longer function. An example is the Philippine "people power" movement of 1986.

Nonviolent conversion: One of the mechanisms of change in which opponents come to see that the movement's cause and goals are just, and thus they voluntarily agree to civil resisters' demands.

Nonviolent disintegration: One of the mechanisms of change whereby nonviolent resistance is used until the entire social structure falls apart so that authorities are not even able to surrender.

P

Pacifism: The principled opposition to war and the use of violence for political purposes. Pacifism is an ideological or moral position, grounded in religious, humanitarian, or ideological principles.

Patronage: Benefits provided by a state or other authorities to encourage loyalty, particularly among security forces. Patronage can be regulated, such as expanded budgets and new equipment, or unregulated, which refers to personal benefits such as access to private-sector contracts.

People power revolutions: Citizen-based movements that use the weapons of nonviolence to force rulers out of office by making the country ungovernable. The transition occurs through nonviolent force, not negotiation. An example occurred in the Philippines in 1986.

Pluralistic theory of power: See "citizen-based power."

Political jiu-jitsu: Also known as "backfire"; the dynamic that occurs when attacks on nonviolent resisters increase public sympathy for the resisters while undermining public opinion of the attackers. The term was introduced by Gene Sharp, who wanted to emphasize the political effects of repression on third-party observers (in contrast to Gregg's concept of moral jiu-jitsu, which emphasizes the sense of shame that is evoked in the oppressors themselves).

Political noncooperation: Refusal to participate in political activities or to comply with political policies. Examples are election boycotts.

Power elite: This concept, developed by sociologist C. Wright Mills, refers to leaders in three powerful institutions: the state, corporations, and the military. Mills maintained that these individuals form a triangle of power that is self-reinforcing and excludes others from having influence on U.S. policies and practices.

Pragmatic nonviolence: An approach to conflict in which participants select nonviolence because they think it is the best and most viable method for achieving their goals, not because of any ethical commitment to nonviolent principles or philosophies. It sees nonviolent resistance as simply a set of techniques, not a way of life or moral commitment.

Prefigurative politics: The belief that practicing and implementing the goals of the movement in the present moment can help to achieve them in the future. The methods can advance the goal, even before the end goal is fully attained.

Principled nonviolence: An approach to conflict in which participants eschew the use of violence because they view violence as immoral or unethical. Those subscribing to principled nonviolence see it as a way of life, not just a political strategy, and aim to change the opponents' hearts and minds as well as their behavior.

Protective accompaniment: A form of third-party intervention where nonviolent activists travel to intense conflict zones. Relying on their outsider influence, they help create space for organizing and resistance by remaining in the constant company of local activists who are at risk for attack or repression. The premise behind this type of intervention is that an act of political violence against foreigners or those in their presence will exact high political costs. As a result, a state is less likely to repress the local resisters, enabling organizing to occur.

R

Realistic pacifism: The opposition to violence and killing to achieve political goals, tempered by a recognition that limited force may be needed in some circumstances to protect the innocent or in self-defense.

Reformist nonviolence: Nonviolent action aimed at making improvements in social institutions, not overthrowing those institutions. Examples include the United Farm Workers or the gay marriage movement.

Resilience: A movement's capacity to sustain resistance in the face of repression. Resilience is measured by a movement's ability to retain its members, recruit new ones, and launch additional campaigns.

S

Satyagraha: A Gandhian term for nonviolence that translates as "truth force," "soul force," "love force," or "holding firmly to the truth." It refers to a form of principled nonviolent action in which civil resisters try to transform their opponent rather than coerce or harm the opponent.

Selective compliance: Carrying out some orders while refusing others. For example, troops may issue warnings to protesters but refuse to attack them.

Shirking: When security force members or laborers intentionally do a poor job, pretending to misunderstand orders and executing them incorrectly. This is generally done as covert disobedience, typically to withhold cooperation without provoking punishment.

Social noncooperation: The refusal to participate in cultural practices or activities. An example would be refusing to salute the flag of an occupying force.

Strategic nonviolence: An approach to nonviolent conflict in which participants choose civil resistance techniques because they believe this course of action is more effective than violence or at least the best choice given the circumstances. The goal in strategic nonviolence is to win your objectives, not necessarily to evoke a change of heart in the opponent. Also referred to as "pragmatic nonviolence."

Structural violence: Structures of domination that systematically limit the life chances and opportunities of particular groups. It refers to any obstacle, imposition, or restraint that keeps humans from meeting basic needs or developing their full potential. Examples are racism and economic systems of exploitation.

Symbolic moral witness: A form of nonviolent action that uses symbols to highlight or expose the human and ethical costs of a social injustice and/or point the way to a solution.

T

Tactical diversity: Shifting between various types of campaigns and actions instead of relying on one or two primary forms of action. Movements that engage in tactical diversification are more likely to win because (1) opponents are unlikely to anticipate their moves; (2) civil resisters can shift tactics to avoid repression; and (3) civil resisters are more likely to withhold more sources of power from their opponent.

Tapasya: Gandhian term that refers to self-suffering or willingness to sacrifice for one's cause. The belief is that voluntary suffering will demonstrate civil resisters' commitment to the struggle and the sincerity of their commitment to not harm adversaries.

Technological pacifism: This position holds that war may have been justifiable in the past but modern weapons of mass destruction now make war immoral. In the contemporary era, warfare means that inevitably innocent lives will be lost and the amount of destruction that can occur is so excessive that war is not justifiable.

Third-party intervention: This refers to a set of nonviolent actions taken by outside groups in an effort to support social change work in intense conflict situations. Examples are accompaniment movements that seek to protect civil resisters from repression.

Trigger events: Events that evoke such moral outrage that citizens feel compelled to mobilize. Such actions, also referred to as "moral shocks," galvanize longstanding grievances and push people to protest and resistance. Examples are the self-immolation of the Tunisian produce vendor in the jasmine revolution and the assassination of Aquino in the Philippines.

REFERENCES

Abrahms, Max. 2006. "Why Terrorism Does Not Work." International Security 31(2): 42–78.

Abu-Nimer, Mohammed. 2003. *Nonviolence and Peace Building in Islam: Theory and Practice*. Gainsville: University of Florida Press.

Ackerman, Peter. 2007. "Skills or Conditions? What Key Factors Shape the Success or Failure of Civil Resistance." Unpublished paper from the Conference on Civil Resistance and Power Politics, Oxford University, Oxford, United Kingdom.

Ackerman, Peter, and Jack DuVall. 2000. *A Force More Powerful: A Century of Nonviolent Action*. New York: Palgrave.

Ackerman, Peter, and Christopher Kruegler. 1994. *Strategic Nonviolent Conflict: The Dynamics of People Power in the Twentieth Century*. Westport, CT: Praeger.

Afsaruddin, Asma. 2010. "Recovering the Early Semantic Purview of Jihad and Martyrdom: Challenging Statist-Military Perspectives." In Qamar-ul Huda (Ed.). *Crescent and Dove: Peace and Conflict Resolution in Islam*. Washington, DC: United States Institute of Peace Press, pp. 39–62.

Ahmad, Razi. 1993. "Islam, Nonviolence, and Global Transformation." In Glenn Paige, Chaiwat Satha-Anand, and Sarah Gilliatt (Eds.). *Islam and Nonviolence*. Honolulu: Center for Global Nonviolence Planning Project, Matsunaga Institute for Peace, University of Hawaii, pp. 27–53.

Akers, Keith. 2000. *The Lost Religion of Jesus: Simple Living and Nonviolence in Early Christianity*. New York: Lantern Books.

Alinsky, Saul. 1989 [1971]. *Rules for Radicals*. New York: Vintage Books.

Alonso, Harriet Hyman. 1993. *Peace as a Women's Issue: A History of the U.S. Movement for World Peace and Women's Rights*. Syracuse, NY: Syracuse University Press.

Al-Shehabi, Omar. 2011. "Demography and Bahrain's Unrest." Report for the Carnegie Endowment for International Peace, March 16.

Amore, Roy C., and Julia Ching. 2002. "The Buddhist Tradition." In Willard G. Oxtoby (Ed.). *World Religions: Eastern Traditions*. Don Mills, Ontario: Oxford University Press Canada, pp. 198–315.

Anderson, Lisa. 2011. "Demystifying the Arab Spring: Parsing Out Differences Between Tunisia, Egypt, and Libya." *Foreign Affairs* 90(3): 2–7.

Andrews, Kenneth, and Michael Biggs. 2006. "The Dynamics of Protest Diffusion: Movement Organizations, Social Networks, and News Media in the 1960 Sit-ins." *American Sociological Review* 71(5): 752–777.

Arditti, Rita. 1999. *Searching for Life: The Grandmothers of the Plaza del Mayo and the Disappeared Children of Argentina*. Los Angeles and Berkeley: University of California Press.

Ashworth, Scott, Joshua D. Clinton, Adam Meirowitz, and Kristopher W. Ramsey. 2008. "Design, Inference, and the Strategic Logic of Suicide Terrorism." *American Political Science Review* 102(2): 269–273.

Aslund, Anders, and Michael McFaul (Eds.). 2006. *Revolution in Orange: The Origins of Ukraine's Democratic Breakthrough*. Washington, DC: Carnegie Endowment for International Peace.

Aspinall, Edward. 1995. "Students and the Military: Regime Friction and Civilian Dissent in the Late Suharto Period." *Indonesia* 59: 36.

Aspinall, Edward. 2005. *Opposing Suharto: Compromise, Resistance, and Regime Change in Indonesia*. Stanford, CA: Stanford University Press.

Babb, Lawrence A. 1994. *Absent Lord: Ascetics and Kings in a Jain Ritual Culture*. Berkeley: University of California Press.

Bahry, Louay. 2000. "The Socioeconomic Foundations of Shiite Opposition in Bahrain." *Mediterranean Quarterly* 11(3): 129–143.

Bainton, Roland. 1960 [1923]. *Christian Attitudes Toward War and Peace: A Historical Survey and Critical Reevaluation*. New York: Abindon Press.

Bartee, Wayne C. 2000. *A Time to Speak Out: The Leipzig Citizens Protests and the Fall of East Germany*. Westport, CT: Praeger.

Bartkowski, Maciej (Ed.). 2013. *Recovering Nonviolent History: Civil Resistance in Liberation Struggles*. Boulder, CO: Lynne Rienner.

Bass, Gary J. 2004. "Jus Post Bellum." *Philosophy and Public* Affairs 32(4): 384–412.

Belkin, Aaron, and Evan Schofer. 2003. "Toward a Structural Understanding of Coup Risk." *Journal of Conflict Resolution* 47(5): 594–620.

Bennett, Scott H. 2001. "Radical Pacifism and the General Strike Against War: Jessie Wallace Hughan, the Founding of the War Resisters League, and the Socialist Origins of Secular Radical Pacifism in America." *Peace and Change* 26(3): 352–373.

Bennett, Scott H. 2004. *Radical Pacifism: The War Resisters League and Gandhian Nonviolence in America, 1915–1963*. Syracuse, NY: Syracuse University Press.

Berfield, Susan, and Dewi Loveard. 1998. "Ten Days That Shook Indonesia." *Asiaweek*. July 24, pp. 30–41.

Bergfeldt, Lennart. 1993. *Experiences of Civil Resistance: The Case of Denmark, 1940–1945*. Uppsala, Sweden: University of Uppsala.

Berrigan, Daniel. 1987. "Swords Into Plowshares." In *Swords Into Plowshares: Nonviolent Direct Action for Disarmament*. San Francisco: Harper & Row, pp. 54–65.

Beyerle, Shaazke. 2014. *Curtailing Corruption: People Power for Accountability and Justice*. Boulder, CO: Lynne Rienner.

Biddle, Stephen D. 2004. *Military Power: Explaining Victory and Defeat in Modern Battle*. Princeton, NJ: Princeton University Press.

Binnendijk, Anika Locke, and Ivan Marovic. 2006. "Power and Persuasion: Nonviolent Strategies to Influence State Security Forces in Serbia (2000) and Ukraine (2004)." *Communist and Post-Communist Studies* 39(3): 411–429.

Bleich, Rabbi J. David. 1991. "Nuclear War Through the Prism of Jewish Law: The Nature of Man and War." In Daniel Landes (Ed.). *Confronting Omnicide: Jewish Reflections on Weapons of Mass Destruction*. Northvale, NJ: Jason Aronson, pp. 209–223.

Boaz, Cynthia. 2012. "Must We Change Our Hearts Before Throwing Off Our Chains?" *Waging Nonviolence* (July 9, 2012). Accessed online at: www.wagingnonviolence.org/2012/07/must-we-change-our-hearts-before-throwing-off-our-chains/

Bob, Clifford. 2005. *The Marketing of Rebellion*. New York: Cambridge University Press.

Bob, Clifford, and Sharon Erickson Nepstad. 2007. "Kill a Leader, Murder a Movement?: Leadership and Assassination in Social Movements." *American Behavioral Scientist* 50(10): 1370–1394.

Boétie, Etienne. 1975 [1552–1553]. *The Politics of Obedience: The Discourse of Voluntary Servitude*. Translated by Harry Kurz. New York: Free Life Editions.

Bondurant, Joan. 1988 [1958]. *Conquest of Violence: The Gandhian Philosophy of Conflict*. Princeton, NJ: Princeton University Press.

Boothe, Ivan, and Lee A. Smithey. 2007. "Privilege, Empowerment and Nonviolent Intervention." *Peace and Change* 32(1): 39–61.

Boudreau, Vincent. 2004. *Resisting Dictatorship: Repression and Protest in Southeast Asia*. New York: Cambridge University Press.

Brock, Peter. 1999. *Varieties of Pacifism: A Survey From Antiquity to the Outset of the Twentieth Century*. Syracuse, NY: Syracuse University Press.

Brook, Timothy. 1992. *Quelling the People: The Military Suppression of the Beijing Democracy Movement*. New York: Oxford University Press.

Brooks, Risa. 2013. "Abandoned at the Palace: Why The Tunisian Military Defected from the Ben Ali Regime in January 2011." *Journal of Strategic Studies* 36(2): 205–220.

Brown, Judith M. 1972. *Gandhi's Rise to Power*. Cambridge: Cambridge University Press.

Brown, Judith M. 1989. *Gandhi: Prisoner of Hope*. New Haven: Yale University Press.

Brown, Judith M. 2008. *Gandhi and Civil Disobedience: The Mahatma in Indian Politics, 1928–1934*. Cambridge: Cambridge University Press.

Broyde, Michael J. 1996. "Fighting the War and the Peace: Battlefield Ethics, Peace Talks, Treaties, and Pacifism in the Jewish Tradition." In J. Patout Burns (Ed.). *War and Its Discontents: Pacifism and Quietism in the Abrahamic Traditions*. Washington, DC: Georgetown University Press, pp. 1–30.

Bruce, Tricia. 2011. *Faithful Revolution: How Voice of the Faithful is Changing the Church*. New York: Oxford University Press.

Brysk, Alison. 1994. *The Politics of Human Rights in Argentina: Protest, Change, and Democratization*. Stanford, CA: Stanford University Press.

Bunce, Valerie, and Sharon Wolchik. 2006. "Favorable Conditions and Electoral Revolutions." *Journal of Democracy* 17(4): 5–18.

Bunce, Valerie, and Sharon Wolchik. 2011. *Defeating Authoritarian Leaders in Post-Communist Societies*. New York: Cambridge University Press.

Burrowes, Robert J. 1996. *The Strategy of Nonviolent Defense: A Gandhian Approach*. Albany: SUNY Press.

Burton, Sandra. 1989. *Impossible Dream: The Marcoses, the Aquinos, and the Unfinished Revolution*. New York: Warner.

Cadoux, C. John. 1919. *The Early Christian Attitude Toward War*. London: Headley Bros.

Cady, Duane. 1989. *From Warism to Pacifism: A Moral Continuum*. Philadelphia: Temple University Press.

Camp, Stephanie. 2004. *Closer to Freedom: Enslaved Women and Everyday Resistance in the Plantation South*. Chapel Hill: University of North Carolina Press.

Carter, April. 2009. "People Power and Protest: The Literature on Civil Resistance in Historical Context." In Adam Roberts and Timothy Garton Ash (Eds.). *Civil Resistance and Power Politics: The Experience of Nonviolent Action from Gandhi to the Present*. Oxford: Oxford University Press, pp. 25–42.

Carter, April, Howard Clark, and Michael Randle. 2006. *People Power and Protest Since 1945: A Bibliography of Nonviolent Action*. London: Housmans Bookshop.

Case, Clarence Marsh. 1923. *Non-Violent Coercion: A Study in the Methods of Social Pressure*. New York: Century.

Celestino, Mauricio Rivera, and Kristian Skrede Gleditsch. 2013. "Fresh Carnations or All Thorn, No Rose? Nonviolent Campaigns and Transitions in Autocracies." *Journal of Peace Research* 50(3): 385–400.

Cevallos, Albert. 2001. *Whither the Bulldozer?: Nonviolent Revolution and the Transition to Democracy in Serbia*. Washington, DC: United States Institute of Peace Special Report.

Chabot, Sean. 2010. "Dialogue Matters: Beyond the Transmission Model of Transnational Diffusion of Social Movements." In Rebecca Kolins Givans, Kenneth M. Roberts, and Sarah A. Soule (Eds.). *The Diffusion of Social Movements: Actors, Mechanisms, and Political Effects*. New York: Cambridge University Press, pp. 99–124.

Chabot, Sean. 2011. *Transnational Roots of the Civil Rights Movement: African American Explorations of the Gandhian Repertoire*. Lanham, MD: Lexington Books.

Chabot, Sean. Forthcoming in 2015. "Making Sense of Civil Resistance: From Theories and Techniques to Social Movement Phronesis." Chapter 11 in Kurt Schock (Ed.). *Comparative Perspectives on Civil Resistance*. Minneapolis: University of Minnesota Press.

Chabot, Sean, and Jan Willem Duyvendak. 2002. "Globalization and Transnational Diffusion Between Social Movements: Reconceptualizing the Dissemination of the Gandhian Repertoire and the 'Coming Out' Routine." *Theory and Society* 31(6): 697–740.

Chabot, Sean, and Majid Sharifi. 2013. "The Violence of Nonviolence: Problematizing Nonviolent Resistance in Iran and Egypt." *Sociologists Without Borders* 8: 205–232.

Chabot, Sean, and Stellan Vinthagen. 2007. "Rethinking Nonviolent Action and Contentious Politics: Political Cultures of Nonviolent Opposition in the Indian Independence Movement and Brazil's Landless Workers Movement." *Research in Social Movements, Conflicts, and Change* 27: 91–121.

Chappel, Christopher Key. 2007. "Jainism and Nonviolence." In Daniel L. Smith-Christopher (Ed.). *Subverting Hatred: The Challenge of Nonviolence in Religious Traditions*. Maryknoll, NY: Orbis Books, pp. 1–13.

Chatfield, Charles (Ed.). 1976. *The Americanization of Gandhi: Images of the Mahatma*. New York: Garland.

Chenoweth, Erica. 2011. "Armed Wing in Syria: To What Effect?" Posted on *The Rational Insurgent* (http://rationalinsurgent.wordpress.com), October 10.

Chenoweth, Erica. 2013. "Changing Sides Doesn't Always Make for Transformation—Just Look At Egypt." *Open Democracy*, July 31.

Chenoweth, Erica, and Maria Stephan. 2011. *Why Civil Resistance Works: The Strategic Logic of Nonviolent Conflict*. New York: Columbia University Press.

Chernus, Ira. 2004. *American Nonviolence: The History of An Idea*. Maryknoll, NY: Orbis Books.

Chick, Kristen. 2011. "Bahrain's Calculated Campaign of Intimidation—Bahraini Activists and Locals Describe Midnight Arrests, Disappearances, Beatings at Checkpoints, and Denial of Medical Care—All Aimed at Deflated the Country's Pro-Democracy Protest Movement." *Christian Science Monitor*, April 1.

Chuman, Joseph. 206. "Does Religion Cause Violence?" In Karikottuchira K. Kuria-kose (Ed.). *Religion, Terrorism, and Globalization*. New York: Nova Science Publishers, pp. 15–30.

Churchill, Ward. 1998. *Pacifism as Pathology*. Winnipeg: Arbeiter Ring.

Clanet, Christian. 2011. "Inside Syria's Slaughter: A Journalist Sneaks into Dara'a, the 'Ghetto of Death'." *Time*, June 10. http://content.time.com/time/world/article/0,8599,2076778,00.html

Cohen, Roger. 2000. "Who Really Brought Down Milosevic?" *New York Times*, November 26. http://www.nytimes.com/2000/11/26/magazine/who-really-brought-down-milosevic.html.

Colaiaco, James A. 1993. *Martin Luther King, Jr.: Apostle of Militant Nonviolence*. New York: St. Martin's Press.

Collier, Paul. 1999. "On the Economic Consequences of Civil War." *Oxford Economic Papers* 51: 168–183.

Collier, Paul, and Nicholas Sambanis 2002. "Understanding Civil War: A New Agenda." *Journal of Conflict Resolution* 46(3): 3–12.

Cone, James. 1991. *Martin, Malcolm and America: Dream or a Nightmare?* Maryknoll, NY: Orbis Books.

Coogan, Tim Pat. 1995. *The Troubles: Ireland's Ordeal and the Search for Peace*. New York: Palgrave.

Cook, Steven A. 2007. *Ruling But Not Governing: The Military and Political Development in Egypt, Algeria, and Turkey*. Baltimore, MD: Johns Hopkins University Press.

Cook, Steven A. 2011. "The Calculations of Tunisia's Military." *Foreign Policy*, January 20. http://foreignpolicy.com/2011/01/20/the-calculations-of-tunisias-military/

Cooney, Robert, and Helen Michalowski. 1987. *The Power of the People: Active Nonviolence in the United States*. Philadelphia: New Society Publishers.

Corr, Anders. 1999. *No Trespassing: Squatting, Rent Strikes, and Land Struggle Worldwide*. Cambridge, MA: South End Press.

Cortright, David. 2001. "Powers of Persuasion: Sanctions and Incentives in the Shaping of International Society." *International Studies* 38(2): 113–125.

Cortright, David. 2005 [1975]. *Soldiers in Revolt: GI Resistance During the Vietnam War*. Chicago: Haymarket.

Cortright, David. 2006. *Gandhi and Beyond: Nonviolence in an Age of Terrorism*. Boulder, CO: Paradigm Publishers.

Cortright, David. 2008. *Peace: A History of Movements and Ideas*. New York: Cambridge University Press.

Cortright, David, and George Lopez (Eds.). 2002. *Smart Sanctions: Targeting Economic Statecraft*. Lanham, MD: Rowman & Littlefield.

Coy, Patrick. 1997. *Protecting Human Rights: The Dynamics of International Nonviolent Accompaniment by Peace Brigades International in Sri Lanka*. Dissertation, Syracuse University.

Coy, Patrick. 2001. "Shared Risks and Ethical Dilemmas on a Peace Brigades International Team in Sri Lanka." *Journal of Contemporary Ethnography* 30(5): 575–606.

Coy, Patrick. 2011. "The Privilege Problematic in International Nonviolent Accompaniment's Early Decades." *Journal of Religion, Conflict, and Peace* 4(2) [online].

Crossan, John Dominic. 1992. *The Historical Jesus: The Life of a Mediterranean Jewish Peasant*. San Francisco: Harper Collins.

Cunningham, David. 2005. *There's Something Happening Here: The New Left, the Klan, and FBI Counter Intelligence*. Berkeley and Los Angeles: University of California Press.

Dajani, Souad R. 1994. *Eyes Without Country: Searching for a Palestinian Strategy of Liberation*. Philadelphia: Temple University Press.

Dalacoura, Katerina. 2012. "The 2011 Uprising in the Arab Middle East: Political Change and Geopolitical Implications." *International Affairs* 88: 63–79.

Dalton, Dennis. 1993. *Mahatma Gandhi: Nonviolent Power in Action*. New York: Columbia University Press.

Deming, Barbara. 1971. *Revolution and Equilibrium*. New York: Grossman Publishers.

Deming, Barbara. 1982. *Two Essays/New Men New Women: Some Thoughts on Nonviolence*. Philadelphia: New Society Publishers.

Domhoff, G. William. 2013. *Who Rules America?* Englewood Cliffs, NJ: Prentice-Hall.

Donner, Fred, 1991. "The Sources of Islamic Conceptions of War." In John Kelsay and James Turner Johnson (Eds.). *Just War and Jihad: Historical and Theoretical Perspectives on War and Peace in Western and Islamic Traditions*. New York: Greenwood Press, pp. 31–69.

Doyle, Michael W., and Nicholas Sambanis. 2000. "International Peacebuilding: A Theoretical and Quantitative Analysis." *American Political Science Review* 94(4): 779–801.

Drezner, Daniel W. 1999. *The Sanctions Paradox: Economic Statecraft and International Relations*. New York: Cambridge University Press.

Drezner, Daniel W. 2003. "How Smart Are Smart Sanctions?" *International Studies Review* 5: 107–110.

Dudouet, Véronique. 2013. "Dynamics and Factors of Transition from Armed Struggle to Nonviolent Resistance." *Journal of Peace Research* 50(3): 401–413.

Dudouet, Véronique (Ed.). 2015. *Civil Resistance and Conflict Transformation: Transitions from Armed to Nonviolent Struggle*. New York: Routledge.

Dudouet, Véronique. Forthcoming in 2015. "Sources, Functions, and Dilemmas of External Assistance to Civil Resistance Movements." Chapter 7 in Kurt Schock (Ed.). *Comparative Perspectives on Civil Resistance*. Minneapolis: University of Minnesota Press.

Dundas, Paul. 1992. *The Jains*. London: Routledge.

Earl, Jennifer. 2003. "Tanks, Tear Gas and Taxes: Toward a Theory of Movement Repression." *Sociological Theory* 21: 44–68.

Eddy, Matthew. 2012. "When Your Gandhi is not My Gandhi: Memory Templates and Limited Violence in the Palestinian Human Rights Movement." *Research in Social Movements, Conflict, and Change* 34: 185–214.

Engineer, Ashgar. 1994. "Sources of Nonviolence in Islam." In Mahendra Kumar (Ed.). *Nonviolence: Contemporary Issues and Challenges*. New Delhi: Gandhi Peace Foundation, pp. 98–106.

Erikson, Erik. 1970. *Gandhi's Truth: On the Origins of Militant Nonviolence*. New York: W.W. Norton and Company.

Farmer, James. 1985. *Lay Bare the Heart*. Fort Worth: Texas Christian University Press.

Fildis, Ayse Tekdal. 2012. "Roots of Alawite-Sunni Rivalry in Syria." *Middle East Policy* 19(2): 148–156.

Foos, Paul. 2002. *A Short, Offhand, Killing Affair: Soldiers and Social Conflict in the Mexican-American War*. Chapel Hill, NC: University of North Carolina Press.

Foran, John, and Jean-Pierre Reed. 2002. "Political Cultures of Opposition: Exploring Idioms, Ideologies, and Revolutionary Agency in the Case of Nicaragua." *Critical Sociology* 28(3): 335–370.

Ford, John C. 1970. "The Morality of Obliteration Bombing." In Richard Wasserstrom (Ed.). *War and Morality*. Belmont, CA: Wadsworth.

Forest, Jim, and Nancy Forest. 1988. *Four Days in February: The Story of the Nonviolent Overthrow of the Marcos Regime*. London: Marshall Pickering.

Foster, Catherine. 1989. *Women for All Seasons: The Story of the Women's International League for Peace and Freedom*. Athens: University of Georgia Press.

Fox, Richard G. 1997. "Passage From India." In Richard G. Fox and Orin Starn (Eds.). *Between Resistance and Revolution: Cultural Politics and Social Protest*. New Brunswick: Rutgers University Press, pp. 65–82.

Francisco, Ronald A. 2004. "After the Massacre: Mobilization in the Wake of Harsh Repression." *Mobilization* 92(2): 107–126.

Francisco, Ronald A. 2005. "The Dictator's Dilemma." In Christian Davenport, Carole Mueller, and Hank Johnston (Eds.). *Repression and Mobilization*. Minneapolis: University of Minnesota Press, pp. 58–84.

Frankel, Philip H. 2001. *An Ordinary Atrocity: Sharpeville and Its Massacre*. New Haven, CT: Yale University Press.

Futrell, Robert, and Pete Simi. 2004. "Free Spaces, Collective Identity, and the Persistence of U.S. White Power Activism." *Social Problems* 51(1): 16–42.

Gallo-Cruz, Selina. 2012. "Organizing Global Nonviolence: The Growth and Spread of Nonviolent INGOs, 1949–2003." *Research in Social Movements, Conflict, and Change* 34: 213–256.

Galtung, Johan. 1969. "Violence, Peace, and Peace Research." *Journal of Peace Research* 6: 167–191.

Galtung, Johan. 1990. "Cultural Violence." *Journal of Peace Research* 27: 291–305.

Gandhi, Mohandas K. 1965. *Gita, My Mother*. Bombay, India: Bharatiya Vidya Bhavan.

Ganz, Marshall. 2010. *Why David Sometimes Wins: Leadership, Organization, and Strategy in the California Farm Worker Movement*. New York: Oxford University Press.

Garrow, David. 1981. *The FBI and Martin Luther King, Jr.: From Solo to Memphis*. New York: W.W. Norton & Company.

Geddes, Barbara. 1999. "What Do We Know About Democratization After Twenty Years?" *Annual Review of Political Science* 2: 115–144.

Gelderloos, Peter. 2007. *How Nonviolence Protects the State*. Cambridge, MA: South End Press.

Gelvin, James L. 2012. *The Arab Uprisings: What Everyone Needs to Know*. New York: Oxford University Press.

Gendler, Everett E. 1981. "Therefore Choose Life." In Allan Solomonow (Ed.). *Roots of Jewish Nonviolence*. Nyack, NY: Jewish Peace Fellowship, 7–16.

Gendler, Rabbi Everett. 1996. "The Pursuit of Peace: A Singular Commandment." In J. Patout Burns (Ed.). *War and Its Discontents: Pacifism and Quietism in the Abrahamic Traditions*. Washington, DC: Georgetown University Press, pp. 31–46.

Gethin, Rupert. 1998. *Foundations of Buddhism*. Oxford: Oxford University Press.

Gitlin, Todd. 2012. *Occupy Nation: The Roots, the Spirit, and the Promise of Occupy Wall Street*. New York: HarperCollins.

Goldstone, Jack. 2001. "Toward a Fourth Generation of Revolutionary Theory." *Annual Review of Political Science* 4: 139–187.

Goldstone, Jack. 2011. "Cross-class Coalitions and the Making of the Arab Revolts of 2011." *Swiss Political Science Review* 17(4): 457–462 [online].

Goldstone, Jack. 2011. "Understanding the Revolutions of 2011: Weakness and Resilience in Middle Eastern Autocracies." *Foreign Affairs* 90. http://www.foreignaffairs.com/articles/67694/jack-a-goldstone/understanding-the-revolutions-of-2011

Goodman, Naomi. 1996. "Pacifism and Nonviolence: Another Jewish View." In J. Patout Burns (Ed.). *War and Its Discontents: Pacifism and Quietism in the Abrahamic Traditions*. Washington, DC: Georgetown University Press, pp. 67–73.

Goodwin, Jeff. 2001. *No Other Way Out: States and Revolutionary Movement, 1945–1991*. New York: Cambridge University Press.

Gould, John, and Edward Moe. 2012. "Beyond Rational Choice: Ideational Assault and the Strategic Use of Frames in Nonviolent Civil Resistance." *Research in Social Movements, Conflict, and Change* 34: 123–151.

Granovetter, Mark. 1978. "Threshold Models of Collective Behavior." *American Journal of Sociology* 83(6): 1420–1443.

Greenberg, Moshe. 1978. "Rabbinic Reflections on Defying Illegal Orders: Amasa, Abner, and Joab." In Menachem Marc Kellner (Ed.). *Contemporary Jewish Ethics*. New York: Hebrew, pp. 211–220.

Gregg, Heather Selma. 2004. "The Causes of Religious Wars: Holy Nations, Sacred Spaces, and Religious Revolutions." PhD Dissertation, Department of Political Science, Massachusetts Institute of Technology.

Gregg, Richard. 1935. *The Power of Nonviolence*. London: George Routledge.

Griffin-Nolan, Ed. 1991. *Witness for Peace*. Louisville, KY: Westminster/John Knox.

Hafidz, Tatik. S. 2006. *Fading Away? The Political Role of the Military in Indonesia's Transition to Democracy*. Singapore: Institute of Defence and Strategic Studies.

Hallie, Philip P. 1994. *Lest Innocent Blood Be Shed: The Story of the Village of Le Chambon and How Goodness Happened There*. New York: Harper Perennial.

Halverson, Jeffrey R. 2012. *Searching for a King: Muslim Nonviolence and the Future of Islam*. Washington, DC: Potomac Books.

Han, Minzhu. 1990. *Cries for Democracy: Writings and Speeches from the 1989 Chinese Democracy Movement*. Princeton, NJ: Princeton University Press.

Hanh, Thich Nhat. 1987. *Being Peace*. Berkeley: Parallax Press.

Hanh, Thich Nhat. 1987. *Interbeing: 14 Guidelines for Engaged Buddhism*. Berkeley: Parallax Press.

Hartzell, Caroline, Matthew Hoddie, and Donald Rothchild. 2001. "Stabilizing the Peace After Civil War: An Investigation of Some Key Variables." *International Organization* 55(1): 183–208.

Harvey, Peter. 1990. *Introduction to Buddhism: Teachings, History and Practices*. Cambridge: Cambridge University Press.

Harwell, Mark A. 1984. *Nuclear Winter: The Human and Environmental Consequences of Nuclear War*. New York: Springer-Verlag.

Hashim, Ahmed. 2011. "The Egyptian Military, Part II: From Mubarak Onward." *Middle East Policy* 18(4): 106–128.

Hashmi, Sohail. 1996. "Interpreting the Islamic Ethics of War and Peace." In Terry Nardin (Ed.). *The Ethics of War and Peace: Religious and Secular Perspectives*. Princeton, NJ: Princeton University Press, pp. 146–166.

Haynes, Jeff. 2001. *Democracy in the Developing World: Africa, Asia, Latin America and the Middle East*. Cambridge: Polity Press.

Hendrick, George. 1956. "The Influence of Thoreau's 'Civil Disobedience' on Gandhi's *Satyagraha.*" *New England Quarterly* 29(4): 462–471.

Hershberger, Guy F. 1944. *War, Peace, and Nonresistance.* Scottdale, PA: Herald Press.

Hess, David, and Brian Martin. 2006. "Repression, Backfire, and the Theory of Transformative Events." *Mobilization* 11(1): 249–267.

Hornus, Jean Michel. 1980. *It is Not Lawful for Me to Fight: Early Christian Attitudes toward War, Violence, and the State.* Scottdale, PA: Herald Press.

Horsely, Richard A. 1987. *Jesus and the Spiral of Violence: Popular Jewish Resistance in Roman Palestine.* San Francisco: Harper & Row.

Houser, George M. 1945. *Erasing the Color Line.* New York: Fellowship Publications.

Howes, Dustin Ells. 2009. *Toward a Credible Pacifism: Violence and the Possibilities of Politics.* Albany: SUNY Press.

Howes, Dustin Ells. 2013. "The Failure of Pacifism and the Success of Nonviolence." *Perspectives on Politics* 11(2): 427–446.

Hunter, Doris. 1990. "On the Baghavad-Gita." In Robert L. Holmes (Ed.). *Nonviolence in Theory and Practice.* Belmont, CA: Wadsworth Publishing Company, pp. 16–19.

Hutchins, Francis G. 1973. *India's Revolution: Gandhi and the Quit India Movement.* Cambridge, MA: Harvard University Press.

Isaac, Larry, Daniel B. Cornfield, Dennis C. Dickerson, James M. Lawson, and Jonathan S. Coley. 2012. "'Movement Schools' and the Dialogical Diffusion of Nonviolent Praxis: Nashville Workshops in the Southern Civil Rights Movement." *Research in Social Movements, Conflict, and Change* 34: 155–184.

Jackson, John. 2011. "The Professors of Protest and the University of Revolution." *Hufffington Post*, March 30.

Jahanbegloo, Ramin. 2014. *Introduction to Nonviolence.* New York: Palgrave Macmillan.

Jasper, James. 1997. *The Art of Moral Protest.* Chicago: University of Chicago Press.

Jerryson, Michael, and Mark Juergensmeyer (Eds.). 2010. *Buddhist Warfare.* New York: Oxford University Press.

Johansen, Robert C. 1997. "Radical Islam and Nonviolence: A Case Study of Religious Empowerment and Constraint among Pashtuns." *Journal of Peace Research* 34(1): 53–71.

Johnstad, Petter Grahl. 2010. "Nonviolent Democratization: A Sensitivity Analysis of How Transition Mode and Violence Impact the Durability of Democracy." *Peace and Change* 35(3): 464–482.

Juergensmeyer, Mark. 2001. *Terror in the Mind of God: The Global Rise of Religious Violence.* Berkeley: University of California Press.

Kalin, Ibrahim. 2010. "Islam and Peace: A Survey of the Sources of Peace in the Islamic Tradition." In Qamar-ul Huda (Ed.). *Crescent and Dove: Peace and Conflict Resolution in Islam.* Washington, DC: United States Institute of Peace Press, pp. 3–37.

Kaplan, Oliver. 2013. "Protecting Civilians in Civil War: The Institution of the ATCC in Colombia." *Journal of Peace Research* 50(3): 351–367.

Kapur, Sudarshan. 1992. *Raising Up a Prophet: The African American Encounter with Gandhi.* Boston: Beacon Press.

Karatnycky, Adrian. 2005. "Ukraine's Orange Revolution." *Foreign Affairs* 84(2): 35–42 March/April.

Karatnycky, Adrian, and Peter Ackerman. 2005. "How Freedom is Won: From Civil Resistance to Durable Democracy." Washington, DC: Freedom House Report.

Kechichian, Joseph, and Jean Nazimek. 1997. "Challenges to the Military in Egypt." *Middle East Policy* 5(3): 125–139.

Kelsay, John. 1993. *Islam and War: A Study in Comparative Ethics*. Louisville, KY: Westminster/John Knox Press.

Kempe, Frederick. 1990. *Divorcing the Dictator: America's Bungled Affair with Noriega*. New York: G.P. Putnam's Sons.

Kimelman, Reuven. 1990. "Nonviolence in the Talmud." In Robert L. Holmes (Ed.). *Nonviolence in Theory and Practice*. Belmont, CA: Wadsworth Publishing, pp. 20–27.

King, Martin Luther, Jr. 2000.[1964]. *Why We Can't Wait*. Boston: Beacon Press.

King, Sallie B. 2005. *Being Benevolence: The Social Ethics of Engaged Buddhism*. Honolulu: University of Hawaii Press.

King, Sallie B. 2010 [1958]. *Stride Toward Freedom: The Montgomery Story*. New York: Beacon Press.

Kirkpatrick, David. 2011. "In a New Libya, Ex-Loyalists Race to Shed Ties to Qadaffi." *New York Times*, September 7, p. 2.

Konvitz, Milton R. 1994. "Conscience and Civil Disobedience in the Jewish Tradition." In Murray Polner and Naomi Goodman (Eds.). *The Challenge of Shalom: The Jewish Tradition of Peace and Justice*. Philadelphia: New Society Publishers, pp. 174–185.

Koontz, Theodore J. 2008. "Christian Nonviolence: An Interpretation." In *Christian Political Ethics*, edited by John Aloysius Coleman. Princeton, NJ: Princeton University Press.

Kou, Chien-Wen. 2000. "Why The Military Obeys the Party's Orders to Repress Popular Uprisings: The Chinese Military Crackdown of 1989." *Issues and Studies* 36(6): 27–51.

Kraft, Kenneth (Ed.). 1992. *Inner Peace, World Peace: Essays on Buddhism and Nonviolence*. Albany: SUNY Press.

Kuran, Timur. 1991. "Now or Never: The Element of Surprise in the East European Revolution of 1989." *World Politics* 44(1): 7–48.

Kurzman, Charles. 2004. *The Unthinkable Revolution in Iran*. Cambridge, MA: Harvard University Press.

Lackey, Douglas P. 1988. *The Ethics of War and Peace*. Upper Saddle River, NJ: Prentice Hall.

Lawson, Fred H. 2004. "Repertoires of Contention in Contemporary Bahrain." In Quintan Wiktorowicz (Ed.). *Islamic Activist: A Social Movements Approach*. Bloomington, IN: Indiana University Press, pp. 89–111.

Lawson, George. 2005. "Negotiated Revolutions: The Prospect of Radical Change in Contemporary World Politics." *Review of International Studies* 31(3): 473–493.

Lee, Terence. 2009. "The Armed Forces and Transitions from Authoritarian Rule: Explaining the Role of the Military in 1986 Philippines and 1998 Indonesia." *Comparative Political Studies* 42: 640–669.

Lesch, David W. 2012. *The Fall of the House of Assad*. New Haven, CT: Yale University Press.

Lewis, John. 1998. *Walking with the Wind: A Memoir of the Movement*. New York: A Harvest Book.

Lodge, Tom. 1988. "State of Exile: The African National Congress of South Africa, 1976–1986." In Philip Frankel, Noam Pines, and Mark Swilling (Eds.). *State, Resistance, and Change in South Africa*. London: Croom Helm, pp. 229–258.

Lopez, George, and David Cortright. 1997. "Economic Sanctions and Human Rights: Part of the Problem or Part of the Solution?" *International Journal of Human Rights* 1: 1–25.

Loy, David. 2004. "What's Buddhist about Socially-Engaged Buddhism?" *Zen Occidental* (February/March). Retrieved on January 11, 2013, at http://www.zenoccidental.net/articles1/loy12-english.html.

Loy, David. 2008. *Money, Sex, War, Karma: Notes on a Buddhist Revolution.* Somerville, MA: Wisdom Publications.

Lutterbeck, Derek. 2013. "Arab Uprisings, Armed Forces, and Civil-Military Relations." *Armed Forces & Society* 39(1): 28–52.

Lynd, Staughton, and Alice Lynd. 1995. *Nonviolence in America: A Documentary History.* Maryknoll, NY: Orbis Books.

Majmudar, Uma. 2005. *Gandhi's Pilgrimage of Faith: From Darkness to Light.* Albany, NY: SUNY Press.

Malcolm X. 1994 [1965]. "The Ballot or the Bullet." In George Breitman (Ed.). *Malcolm X Speaks: Selected Speeches and Statements.* New York: Grove Press, pp. 23–44.

Maney, Gregory. 2012. "The Paradox of Reform: The Civil Rights Movement in Northern Ireland." *Research in Social Movements, Conflict, and Change* 34: 3–26.

Margalit, Avishai. 2002. *The Ethics of Memory.* Cambridge, MA: Harvard University Press.

Marinov, Nikolay. 2005. "Do Economic Sanctions Destabilize Country Leaders?" *American Journal of Political Science* 49(3): 564–576.

Markoff, John. 2013. "Opposing Authoritarian Rule with Nonviolent Civil Resistance." *Australian Journal of Political Science* 48(2): 233–245.

Martin, Brian. 1989. "Gene Sharp's Theory of Power." *Journal of Peace Research* 26(2): 213–222.

Martin, Brian. 2001. "Nonviolent Futures." *Futures* 33: 625–635.

Martin, Brian. 2007. *Justice Ignited: The Dynamics of Backfire.* Lanham, MD: Rowman & Littlefield.

Martin, Brian. 2008. "How Nonviolence is Misrepresented." *Gandhi Marg* 30(2): 235–257.

Martin, Brian. 2009. "Dilemmas in Promoting Nonviolence." *Gandhi Marg* 31(3): 429–453

Martin, Brian, and Wendy Varney. 2003. *Nonviolence Speaks: Communicating Against Repression.* Cresskill, NJ: Hampton Press.

Marx, Gary T. 1979. "External Efforts to Damage or Facilitate Social Movements: Some Patterns, Explanations, Outcomes, and Complications." In Mayer Zald and John McCarthy (Eds.). *The Dynamics of Social Movements.* Cambridge, MA: Winthrop, pp. 94–125.

McAdam, Doug. 1983. "Tactical Innovation and the Pace of Insurgency." *American Sociological Review* 48: 735–754.

McAdam, Doug, and Dieter Rucht. 1993. "The Cross-National Diffusion of Movement Ideas." *Annals of the American Academy of Political and Social Science* 528: 56–74.

McAdam, Doug, Sidney Tarrow, and Charles Tilly. 2001. *Dynamics of Contention.* New York: Cambridge University Press.

McAllister, Pam. 1982. *Reweaving the Web of Life: Feminism and Nonviolence.* Philadelphia: New Society Publishers.

McCarthy, Ronald, and Christopher Kruegler. 1993. *Toward Research and Theory Building in the Study of Nonviolent Action*. Boston: Albert Einstein Institution.

McCarthy, Ronald M., and Gene Sharp. 1997. *Nonviolent Action: A Research Guide*. New York: Garland.

McEvers, Kelly. 2012. "Defectors Offer Insider's View of Syrian Army." *National Public Radio*, April 9.

McGuinness, Kate. 1993. "Gene Sharp's Theory of Power: A Feminist Critique of Consent." *Journal of Peace Research* 30(1): 101–115.

McKittrick, David, and David McVea. 2002. *Making Sense of the Troubles: The Story of the Conflict in Northern Ireland*. Chicago: New Amsterdam Books.

McLauchlin, Theodore. 2010. "Loyalty Strategies and Military Defection in Rebellion." *Comparative Politics* 42(3): 333–350.

McManus, Philip, and Gerald Schlabach. 1991. *Relentless Persistence: Nonviolent Action in Latin America*. Philadelphia: New Society Publishers.

McNeal, Patricia. 1992. *Harder Than War: Catholic Peacemaking in Twentieth Century America*. New Brunswick, NJ: Rutgers University Press.

Meconis, Charles A. 1979. *With Clumsy Grace: The American Catholic Left, 1961–1975*. New York: Seabury Press.

Meier, August, and Elliot Rudwick. 1973. *CORE: A Study in the Civil Rights Movement, 1942–1968*. New York: Oxford University Press.

Merriman, Hardy. 2005. "California Grape Workers' Strike and Boycott, 1965–1970." In Gene Sharp (Eds.). *Waging Nonviolent Struggle: 20th Century Practice and 21st Century Potential*. Boston: Extending Horizons Books, pp. 173–188.

Merton, Thomas (Ed.). 1965. *Gandhi on Nonviolence: A Selection from the Writings of Mahatma Gandhi*. New York: A New Directions Book.

Mills, C. Wright. 2000 [1956]. *The Power Elite*. New York and Oxford: Oxford University Press.

Mirsky, Yehuda. 1998. "The Political Morality of Pacifism and Nonviolence: One Jewish View." In J. Patout Burns (Ed.). *War and Its Discontents: Pacifism and Quietism in the Abrahamic Traditions*. Washington, DC: Georgetown University Press, pp. 47–66.

Montgomery, Anne. 1987. "Divine Obedience." In Arthur Laffin and Anne Montgomery (Eds.). *Swords into Plowshares: Nonviolent Direct Action for Disarmament*. San Francisco: Harper & Row, pp. 25–31.

Morris, Aldon. 1981. "The Black Southern Sit-In Movement: An Analysis of Internal Organization." *American Sociological Review* 46(6): 744–767.

Moskos, Charles, and John W. Chambers II. 1993. *The New Conscientious Objection: From Sacred to Secular*. New York: Oxford University Press.

Myers, Ched. 1988. *Binding the Strong Man: A Political Reading of Mark's Story of Jesus*. Maryknoll, NY: Orbis.

Naess, Arne. 1958. "A Systemization of Gandhian Ethics of Conflict Resolution." *Journal of Conflict Resolution* 2(4): 140–155.

Nagler, Michael. 2004. *The Search for a Nonviolent Future: A Promise of Peace for Ourselves, Our Families, and Our World*. Novato, CA: New World Library.

Narayahan, Vasudha. 2002. "The Hindu Tradition." In Willard G. Oxtoby (Ed.). *World Religions: Eastern Traditions*. Don Mills, Ontario: Oxford University Press Canada, pp. 13–125.

Navarro, Marysa. 2001 [1989]. "The Personal is the Political: Las Madres de Plaza de Mayo." In Susan Eckstein (Ed.). *Power and Popular Protest: Latin American*

Social Movements. Berkeley and Los Angeles: University of California Press, pp. 241–258.

Ndura, Elavie. 2013. "Fostering a Culture of Nonviolence through Multicultural Education." In Randall Amster and Elavie Ndura (Ed.). *Exploring the Power of Nonviolence: Peace, Politics, and Practice*. Syracuse, NY: Syracuse University Press, pp. 206–222.

Nepstad, Sharon Erickson. 2004. *Convictions of the Soul: Religion, Culture, and Agency in the Central America Solidarity Movement*. New York: Oxford University Press.

Nepstad, Sharon Erickson. 2008. *Religion and War Resistance in the Plowshares Movement*. New York: Cambridge University Press.

Nepstad, Sharon Erickson. 2011a. "Nonviolence in the Arab Spring: The Critical Role of Military-Opposition Alliances." *Swiss Political Science Review* 17(4): 485–491.

Nepstad, Sharon Erickson. 2011b. *Nonviolent Revolutions: Civil Resistance in the Late 20th Century*. New York: Oxford University Press.

Nepstad, Sharon Erickson. 2013a. "Mutiny and Nonviolence in the Arab Spring: Exploring Military Defections and Loyalty in Egypt, Bahrain, and Syria." *Journal of Peace Research* 50(3): 337–349.

Nepstad, Sharon Erickson. 2013b. "Nonviolent Civil Resistance and Social Movements." *Sociology Compass* 7: 590–598.

Nepstad, Sharon Erickson, and Stellan Vinthagen. 2008. "Strategic Changes and Cultural Adaptations: Explaining Differential Outcomes in the International Plowshares Movement." *International Journal of Peace Studies* 13(1): 15–42.

Nikolayenko, Olena. 2011. *Citizens in the Making in Post-Soviet States*. New York: Routledge.

Nikolayenko, Olena. 2012. "Tactical Interactions Between Youth Movements and Incumbent Governments in Post-Communist States." *Research in Social Movements, Conflict, and Change* 34: 27–61.

Nuttall, Geoffrey. 1971. *Christian Pacifism in History*. Berkeley, CA, World Without War Council, Oxford: Blackwell.

O'Donovan, Oliver. 2003. *The Just War Revisited*. Cambridge: Cambridge University Press.

Orend, Brian. 2007. "*Jus Post Bellum*: The Perspective of a Just War Theorist." *Leiden Journal of International Law* 20: 571–591.

Oxtoby, Willard. 2002. *World Religions: Eastern Traditions*. New York: Oxford University Press.

Pagnucco, Ron. 1996. "A Comparison of the Political Behavior of Faith-Based and Secular Peace Groups." In Christian Smith (Ed.). *Disruptive Religion*. New York: Routledge, pp. 205–222.

Pape, Robert A. 1997. "Why Economic Sanctions Do Not Work." *International Security* 22:90–136.

Pape, Robert A. 2003. "The Strategic Logic of Suicide Terrorism." *American Political Science Review* 102(2): 343–361.

Parkman, Patricia. 1988. *Nonviolent Insurrection in El Salvador: The Fall of Maximiliano Hernández Martínez*. Tucson: University of Arizona Press.

Peace, Roger. 2012. *Call to Conscience: The Anti-Contra War Campaign*. Amherst and Boston: University of Massachusetts Press.

Pearlman, Wendy. 2011. *Violence, Nonviolence, and the Palestinian National Movement*. New York: Cambridge University Press.

Pfaff, Steven. 2006. *Exit-Voice Dynamics and the Collapse of East Germany: The Crisis of Leninism and the Revolution of 1989*. Durham, NC: Duke University Press.

Pierard, Richard V. 1990. "Religion and the East German Revolution." *Journal of Church and State* 32(3): 501–509.

Pierret, Thomas. 2013. *Religion and State in Syria*. Cambridge and New York: Cambridge University Press.

Polletta, Francesca. 1999. "'Free Spaces' in Collective Action." *Theory and Society* 28: 1–38.

Polletta, Francesca. 1999. "'It Was Like a Fever . . .': Spontaneity and Collective Identity in Collective Action." *Social Problems* 45: 137–159.

Polletta, Francesca. 2002. *Freedom is an Endless Meeting: Democracy in American Social Movements*. Chicago: University of Chicago Press.

Polner, Murray, and Jim O'Grady. 1997. *Disarmed and Dangerous: The Radical Lives and Times of Daniel and Philip and Berrigan*. New York: Basic Books.

Popovic, Srdja, Slobodan Djinovic, Andrej Milivojevic, Hardy Merriman, and Ivan Marovic. 2007. *CANVAS Core Curriculum: A Guide to Effective Nonviolent Struggle*. Serbia: Canvas Publications.

Powell, Jonathan. 2012. "Determinants of the Attempting and Outcome of Coups d'etat." *Journal of Conflict Resolution* 56(6): 1017–1040.

Powers, Roger S., William B. Vogele, Douglas Bond, and Christopher Kruegler (Eds.). 1997. *Protest, Power, and Change: An Encyclopedia of Nonviolent Action from ACT-UP to Women's Suffrage*. New York: Garland.

Price, Robert M. 1991. *The Apartheid State in Crisis: Political Transformation in South Africa, 1975–1990*. Oxford: Oxford University Press.

Purdey, Jemma. 2006. *Anti-Chinese Violence in Indonesia: 1996–1999*. Honolulu: University of Hawaii Press.

Queen, Christopher S. 2007. "The Peace Wheel: Nonviolent Action in the Buddhist Tradition." In Daniel L. Smith-Christopher (Ed.). *Subverting Hatred: The Challenge of Nonviolence in Religious Traditions*. Maryknoll, NY: Orbis, pp. 14–37.

Quinlivan, James T. 1999. "Coup-Proofing: Its Practices and Consequences in the Middle East." *International Security* 24(2): 131–165.

Randeree, Bilal. 2011. "Tunisia President Warns Protesters: President Warns that Rare Display of Public Defiance Over Unemployment Will Be Met With 'Firm' Punishment." *Al Jazeera English*, January 3.

Randeree, Bilal. 2011. "Tunisian Leader Promises New Jobs." *Al Jazeera English*. January 14.

Raqib, Mohammad. 2009. "The Muslim Pashtun Movement of the North-West Frontier of India, 1930–1934." In *Civilian Jihad: Nonviolent Struggle, Democratization, and Governance in the Middle East*. New York: Palgrave Macmillan, pp. 107–118.

Read, Anthony, and David Fisher. 1998. *The Proudest Day: India's Long Road to Independence*. New York: W.W. Norton.

Reddy, E. S. (Ed.). 1998. *Mahatma Gandhi: Letters to Americans*. Mumbai: Bhavan's Book University.

Reno, William. 1998. *Warlord Politics and African States*. Boulder, CO: Lynne Reiner Publishers.

Richards, Jerald. 1991. "Gene Sharp's Pragmatic Defense of Nonviolence." *International Journal of Applied Philosophy* 6(1): 59–63.

Rigby, Andrew. 2001. *Justice and Reconciliation: After the Violence*. Boulder, CO: Lynne Reinner Publishers.

Ritter, Daniel. 2012. "Inside the Iron Cage of Liberalism: International Contexts and Nonviolent Success in the Iranian Revolution." *Research in Social Movements, Conflict, and Change* 34: 95–121.

Ritter, Daniel. 2015. *The Iron Cage of Liberalism: International Politics and Unarmed Revolutions in the Middle East and North Africa.* Oxford: Oxford University Press.

Roberts, Adam, and Timothy Garton Ash (Eds.). 2009. *Civil Resistance and Power Politics: Non-Violent Action from Gandhi to the Present.* Oxford: Oxford University Press.

Robinson, Jo Ann Gibson, and David J. Garrow. 1987. *The Montgomery Bus Boycott and the Women Who Started It: The Memoir of Jo Ann Gibson Robinson.* Knoxville: University of Tennessee Press.

Romulo, Beth Day. 1987. *Inside the Palace: The Rise and Fall of Ferdinand and Imelda Marcos.* New York: G.P. Putnam's Sons.

Ross, Michael. 1999. "The Political Economy of the Resource Curse." *World Politics* 51(2): 297–322.

Ross, Michael. 2001. "Does Oil Hinder Democracy?" *World Politics* 53(3): 325–361.

Sachedina, Abdul Aziz. 2001. *The Islamic Roots of Democratic Pluralism.* New York: Oxford University Press.

Santoro, Wayne, and Max Fitzpatrick. Forthcoming in 2015. "The Ballot or the Bullet: The Crisis of Victory and the Institutionalization and Radicalization of the Civil Rights Movement." *Mobilization.*

Scalmer, Sean. 2002. "The Labor of Diffusion: The Peace Pledge Union and the Adaptation Adaption of the Gandhian Repertoire." *Mobilization* 7(3): 269–286.

Scalmer, Sean. 2011. *Gandhi in the West: The Mahatma and the Rise of Radical Protest.* Cambridge and New York: Cambridge University Press.

Schneider, Cathy Lisa. 2011 "Violence and State Repression." *Swiss Political Science Review* 17(4): 480–484.

Schock, Kurt. 2003. "Nonviolence and Its Misconceptions: Insights for Social Scientists." *PS: Political Science and Politics* 36:705–712.

Schock, Kurt. 2005. *Unarmed Insurrections: People Power Movements in Nondemocracies.* Minneapolis: University of Minnesota Press.

Schock, Kurt. 2012. "Land Struggles in the Global South: Strategic Innovations in Brazil and India." In Gregory Maney, Rachel Kutz-Flamenbaum, Deana Rohlinger, and Jeff Goodwin (Eds.). *Strategies for Social Change.* Minneapolis: University of Minnesota Press, pp. 221–244.

Schock, Kurt. 2013. "The Practice and Study of Civil Resistance." *Journal of Peace Research* 50(3): 277–290.

Schock, Kurt. Forthcoming in 2015. "Civil Resistance in the Twenty-First Century." Chapter 12 in Kurt Schock (Ed.). *Comparative Perspectives on Civil Resistance.* Minneapolis: University of Minnesota Press.

Schock, Kurt, and Erica Chenoweth. 2010. "The Impact of Violence on the Outcome of Nonviolent Resistance Campaigns: An Examination of Intermovement Radical Flank Effects." Unpublished paper presented at the annual meeting of the International Peace Research Association, Sydney, Australia.

Schulzinger, Doron. 2013. "The Social-Psychological Origins of the Montgomery Bus Boycott: Social Interaction and Humiliation in the Emergence of Social Movements." *Mobilization* 18(2): 117–142.

Schwarzschild, Steven S. 1981. "Shalom." In Murray Polner and Naomi Goodman (Eds.). *The Challenge of Shalom: The Jewish Tradition of Peace and Justice.* Philadelphia: New Society Publishers, pp. 16–25.

Scott, James C. 1985. *Weapons of the Weak: Everyday Forms of Peasant Resistance.* New Haven, CT: Yale University Press.

Semelin, Jacques. 1993. *Unarmed Against Hitler: Civilian Resistance in Europe, 1939–1943.* Westport, CT: Praeger.

Sharp, Gene. 1973. *The Politics of Nonviolent Action, Volume I: Power and Struggle.* Boston: Porter-Sargent.

Sharp, Gene. 1973. *The Politics of Nonviolent Action, Volume II: The Methods of Nonviolent Action.* Boston: Porter-Sargent.

Sharp, Gene. 1973. *The Politics of Nonviolent Action, Volume III: The Dynamics of Nonviolent Action.* Boston: Porter-Sargent.

Sharp, Gene. 1979. "Nonviolence: Moral Principle or Political Technique? Clues From Gandhi's Thought and Experience." In Gene Sharp (Ed.). *Gandhi as a Political Strategist: With Essays on Ethics and Politics.* Boston: Porter Sargent, pp. 273–209.

Sharp, Gene. 1980. *Social Power and Political Freedom.* Boston: Porter Sargent.

Sharp, Gene. 1990. *Civilian-Based Defense: A Post-Military Weapons System.* Princeton, NJ: Princeton University Press.

Sharp, Gene. 1990. *The Role of Power in Nonviolent Struggle.* Cambridge, MA: Albert Einstein Institute.

Sharp, Gene. 2002. *From Dictatorship to Democracy: Conceptual Framework for Liberation.* Cambridge, MA: Albert Einstein Institute.

Sharp, Gene. 2005. *Waging Nonviolent Struggle: 20th Century Practice and 21st Century Potential.* Boston: Porter Sargent.

Sharp, Gene, and Bruce Jenkins. 2003. *The Anti-Coup.* Boston: Albert Einstein Institution.

Shastri, Sunanda Y., and Yajneshwar S. Shastri. 2007. "Ahimsa and the Unity of All Things: A Hindu View of Nonviolence." In Daniel L. Smith-Christopher (Ed.). *Subverting Hatred: The Challenge of Nonviolence in Religious Traditions.* Maryknoll, NY: Orbis, pp. 57–75.

Shaw, Randy. 2008. *Beyond the Fields: Cesar Chavez, the UFW, and the Struggle for Justice in the 21st Century.* Berkeley and Los Angeles: University of California Press.

Shellman, Stephen M., Brian P. Levey, and Joseph K. Young. 2013. "Shifting Sands: Explaining and Predicting Phase Shifts by Dissident Organizations." *Journal of Peace Research* 50(3): 319–336.

Shepherd, Mark. 2001. *Mahatma Gandhi and His Myths.* Los Angeles: Simple Productions.

Shridarani, Krishnalal. 1939. *War Without Violence: A Study of Gandhi's Method and Its Accomplishments.* New York: Harcourt and Brace.

Silverman, Daniel. 2012. " The Arab Military in the Arab Spring: Agent of Continuity or Change? A Comparative Analysis of Tunisia, Egypt, Libya, and Syria." Unpublished manuscript.

Simmen, Edward R., and Richard F. Bauerle. 1969. "Chicano: Origin and Meaning." *American Speech* 44(3): 225–230.

Smith, Christian. 1996. *Disruptive Religion: The Force of Faith in Social Movements.* New York: Routledge.

Smith, Christian. 1996. *Resisting Reagan: The U.S.-Central America Peace Movement.* Chicago: University of Chicago Press.

Snow, David, and Robert Benford. 1999. "Alternative Types of Cross-National Diffusion in the Social Movement Arena." In Donatella della Porta, Hanspeter Kriesi, and Dieter Rucht (Eds.). *Social Movements in a Globalizing World.* London: Macmillan, pp. 23–39.

Sombutpoonsiri, Janjira. 2012. *The Use of Humour as a Vehicle for Nonviolent Struggle: Serbia's 1996–7 Protests and the OTPOR (Resistance) Movement*. PhD dissertation, School of Politics and International Relations, La Trobe University.

Sørensen, Majken Jul. 2008. "Humor as a Serious Strategy of Nonviolent Resistance to Oppression." *Peace & Change* 33(2): 167–190.

Sparks, Allistair. 1995. *Tomorrow is Another Country: The Inside Story of South Africa's Road to Change*. Chicago: University of Chicago Press.

Springborg, Robert. 2011. "Economic Involvements of Militaries." *International Journal of Middle East Studies* 43(3): 397–399.

Springer, Kimberly. 2006. "Black Feminists Respond to Black Power Masculinism." In Peniel E. Joseph (Ed.). *The Black Power Movement: Rethinking the Civil Rights-Black Power Era*. New York: Routledge, pp. 105–118.

Steffen, Lloyd. 2007. *Holy War, Just War: Exploring the Moral Meaning of Religious Violence*. Lanham, MD: Rowman & Littlefield.

Steinhoff, Uwe. 2007. *On the Ethics of War and Terrorism*. Oxford: Oxford University Press.

Stephan, Maria, and Erica Chenoweth. 2008. "Why Civil Resistance Works: The Strategic Logic of Nonviolent Conflict." *International Security* 33(1): 7–44.

Stiehm, Judith. 1968. "Nonviolence Is Two." *Sociological Inquiry* 38: 23–30.

Summy, Ralph. 1994. "Nonviolence and the Case of the Extremely Ruthless Opponent." *Pacifica Review* 6(1): 1–29.

Tarrow, Sidney. 2005. *The New Transnational Activism*. New York: Cambridge University Press.

Taylor, Diana. 1997. *Disappearing Acts: Spectacles of Gender and Nationalism in Argentina's Dirty War*. Durham, NC: Duke University Press.

Taylor, Verta. 1989. "Social Movement Continuity: The Women's Movement in Abeyance." *American Sociological Review* 54: 761–775.

Teichman, Jenny. 1986. *Pacifism and the Just War: A Study in Applied Philosophy*. Oxford: Basil Blackwell.

Thompson, Mark R. 1995. *The Anti-Marcos Struggle: Personalistic Rule and Democratic Transition in the Philippines*. New Haven, CT: Yale University Press.

Thoreau, Henry David. 2008 [1849]. *On The Duty of Civil Disobedience*. Radford, VA: Wilder.

Thurman, Howard. 1949. *Jesus and the Disinherited*. Nashville: Abingdon Press.

Tibi, Bassam. 1995. "War and Peace in Islam." In Terry Nardin (Ed.). *The Ethics of War and Peace: Religious and Secular Perspectives*. Princeton, NJ: Princeton University Press, pp. 128–145.

Tilly, Charles. 1986. *The Contentious French*. Cambridge, MA: Harvard University Press.

Tutu, Desmond. 2000. *No Future Without Forgiveness*. New York: Doubleday.

Unsworth, Richard P. 2012. *A Portrait of Pacifists: Chambon, the Holocaust, and the Lives of Andre and Magda Trocme*. Syracuse, NY: Syracuse University Press.

Valenzuela, Arturo. 1991. "The Military in Power: The Consolidation of One-Man Rule." In Paul W. Drake and Ivan Jaksik (Eds.). *The Struggle for Democracy in Chile, 1982–1990*. Lincoln: University of Nebraska Press, pp. 21–72.

Van Dam, Nikolaos. 2011. *The Struggle for Power in Syria: Politics and Society Under Assad and the Ba'th Party*. London: IB Tauris.

Van Hook, Stephanie. 2012. "How to Sustain a Revolution." Posted on January 4. Retrieved September 28, 2012, at http://truthout.org/index.php?option=com_k2&view=item&id=5895:how-to-sustain-a-revolution.

Vejvoda, Ivan. 2009. "Civil Society versus Slobodan Milosevic: Serbia, 1991–2000." In Adam Robers and Timothy Garton Ash (Eds.). *Civil Resistance and Power Politics: The Experience of Nonviolent Action from Gandhi to the Present.* Oxford: Oxford University Press, pp. 295–316.

Vengroff, Richard. 1993. "Governance and the Transition to Democracy: Political Parties and the Party System in Mali," *Journal of Modern African Studies* 31(4): 541–562.

Victoria, Brian A. 2007. "Holy War: Toward a Holistic Understanding." *Journal of Religion, Conflict, and Peace* 1(1) [online].

View, Jenice L. 2013. "I Was and Am: Historical Counternarrative as Nonviolent Resistance in the United States." In Randall Amster and Elavie Ndura (Eds.). *Exploring the Power of Nonviolence: Peace, Politics, and Practice.* Syracuse, NY: Syracuse University Press, pp. 57–77.

Vinthagen, Stellan. Forthcoming in 2015. "Four Dimensions of Nonviolent Action: A Sociological Perspective." Chapter 10 in Kurt Schock (Ed.). *Comparative Perspectives on Civil Resistance.* Minneapolis: University of Minnesota Press.

Walpola, Rahula. 1974 [1959]. *What the Buddha Taught.* New York: Grove Press.

Walter, Barbara F. 2004. "Does Conflict Beget Conflict? Explaining Recurring Civil War." *Journal of Peace Research* 41(3): 371–388.

Walzer, Michael. 1977. *Just and Unjust Wars: A Moral Argument with Historical Illustrations.* New York: Basic Books.

Weber, Thomas. 1993. "The Marchers Simply Walked Forward Until Struck Down: Nonviolent Suffering and Conversion." *Peace and Change* 18(3): 267–289.

Weber, Thomas. 2001. "Gandhian Philosophy, Conflict Resolution Theory and the Practical Approaches to Negotiation." *Journal of Peace Research* 38(4): 493–513.

Weber, Thomas. 2003. "Nonviolence Is Who? Gene Sharp and Gandhi." *Peace & Change* 28(2): 250–270.

Wehr, Paul. 1979. *Conflict Regulation.* Boulder, CO: Westview Press.

Wheaton, Bernard, and Zdenek Kavan. 1992. *The Velvet Revolution: Czechoslovakia, 1988–1991.* Boulder, CO: Westview Press.

White, Deborah Gray. 2000. "Let My People Go: 1804–1860." In Robin D. G. Kelley and Earl Lewis (Eds.). *To Make Our World Anew: A History of African Americans.* New York: Oxford University Press, pp. 169–226.

Wieland, Carsten. 2012. *Syria—A Decade of Lost Chances: Repression and Revolution from Damascus Spring to the Arab Spring.* Seattle, WA: Cune Press.

Wilson, Andrew. 2005. *Ukraine's Orange Revolution.* New Haven, CT: Yale University Press.

Wink, Walter. 1987. *Violence and Nonviolence in South Africa: Jesus' Third Way.* Philadelphia: New Society Publishers.

Wink, Walter. 1996. "Beyond Just War and Pacifism." Chapter 7 in J. Patout Burns (Ed.). *War and Its Discontents: Pacifism and Quietism in the Abrahamic Traditions.* Washington, DC: Georgetown University Press, pp. 102–121.

Winter, Jay. 2007. "The Moral Witness and the Two World Wars." *Ethnologie française* 37(3): 467–474.

Wolchik, Sharon L. 2012. "Putinism Under Siege: Can There Be a Color Revolution?" *Journal of Democracy* 23(3): 63–70.

Wolpert, Stanley. 2006. *A Shameful Flight: The Last Years of the British Empire in India.* Oxford: Oxford University Press.

Wood, Elisabeth Jean. 2000. *Forging Democracy From Below: Insurgent Transitions in South Africa and El Salvador*. New York: Cambridge University Press.

Yoder, John Howard. 1992 [1971]. *Nevertheless: Varieties of Religious Pacifism*. Scottdale, PA: Herald Press.

Zunes, Stephen. 1994. "Unarmed Insurrections Against Authoritarian Governments in the Third World: A New Kind of Revolution?" *Third World Quarterly* 15: 403–426.

Zunes, Stephen. 2008. "Nonviolent Action and Pro-Democracy Struggles." *Foreign Policy in Focus*, January 24. http://fpif.org/nonviolent_action_and_pro-democracy_struggles/

Zunes, Stephen. 2011. "America Blows It on Bahrain: The Non-Violent Pro-democracy Struggle in Bahrain Has Failed to Gain Support from the Obama Administration." *Foreign Policy in Focus*, March 2. http://fpif.org/america_blows_it_on_bahrain/

Zunes, Stephen. 2015. "South Africa: The Townships Rise Up." In Véronique Duduoet (Ed.). *Civil Resistance and Conflict Transformation: Transitions from Armed to Nonviolent Struggle*. New York: Routledge, pp. 100–125.

Zunes, Stephen, and Saad Eddin Ibrahim. 2009. "External Actors and Nonviolent Struggles in the Middle East." In Maria J. Stephan (Ed.). *Civilian Jihad: Nonviolent Struggle, Democratization, and Governance in the Middle East*. New York: Palgrave Macmillan, pp. 91–104.

Zunes, Stephen, Lester R. Kurtz, and Sarah Beth Asher (Eds.). 1999. *Nonviolent Social Movements: A Geographical Perspective*. Malden, MA: Blackwell Publishing.

INDEX

Note: Locators followed by the letter 'n' refer to notes.